❖
MIKE LEVINE

BILLBOARD BOOKS
an imprint of Watson-Guptill Publications/New York

I'd like to thank my wife Laura and my two sons, Zack and Nick, for all their support. I'd also like to thank Ken Schlager for introducing me to the folks at Billboard Books. Speaking of Billboard Books, thanks also to senior editor Bob Nirkind, for his patience and superb editing skills, and to editor Joy Aquilino, for her tireless contribution to fine-tuning the manuscript. In addition, I owe a debt of gratitude to Lia Royle and David Baer for legal help, and to Les Morsillo for taking the author photograph.

Thanks to Al Vescovo for sitting through two interviews, and for providing me with the names of so many people on the L.A. music scene. I also wish to thank all the other people who graciously gave their free time to allow me to interview them for this book. They are (in alphabetical order): Luce Amen, Tim Berens, Jim Berry, Stu Blumberg, Leland Bond, Bonnie Boss, Larry Campbell, Perry Cavari, Buddy Collette, Richard Crooks, Bill Dennison, John England, Dave Foster, Richard Frank, Gary Grant, Marshall Grantham, Bob Haligan, Doug Hall, Gene Hicks, Bill Hughes, Chip Jenkins, Mike Kenny, Karl Kawahara, Mark McCarron, Gordon Messick, John Miller, Jeff Mironov, Cory Morgenstern, Andre Pluess, Ray Potenza, Michael Rice, Chip Riedeburg, Dave Rimelis, Jan Rosenberg, Lou Ross, George "The Fat Man" Sanger, Laura Seaton, Carol Sharar, Kathy Sommer, Dale Stuckenbruck, Ben Sussman, Eric Suttman, Brian Swanson, Rob Taube, Bill Troiani, Patrick Vernon, Frank Vilardi, Neil Wetzel, Ethyl Will, and Steve Wood.

Library of Congress Cataloging-in-Publication Data
Levine, Mike.
    How to be a working musician: a practical guide to earning
  money in the music business/Mike Levine.
        p. cm
    Includes bibliographical references and index.
    ISBN 0-8230-8329-2
    1. Music trade—Vocational guidance. 2. Music—Economic aspects.
  I. Title.
  ML3790.L5 1997
  780'.23'73—dc21   97-19904
                                                        CIP
                                                        MN

Manufactured in the United States of America

First printing, 1997

1 2 3 4 5 6 7 8 9 / 05 04 03 02 01 00 99 98 97

CONTENTS

❖

INTRODUCTION

For many musicians, the music business is a "can't live with it, can't live without it" proposition. People working in it find it simultaneously wondrous and maddening, nasty and nice, but always hard to comprehend. For players and singers looking to get seriously involved for the first time, it can appear especially daunting and intimidating.

The purpose of this book is to help you navigate through the various pitfalls and hazards that constitute the landscape of the music business. First and foremost, you'll get useful, down-to-earth advice on how to obtain paying work, both as a performer and as a composer. You'll also get "insider" information and common-sense tips that will help you avoid some of the hard knocks and wild goose chases that many of your fellow musicians have had to endure. I hope it will help make your journey through the music world a more profitable, palatable, and enjoyable experience.

Unlike so many other books about "the biz," this one doesn't claim to be able to help you become a star. The only thing it promises is that after reading it you'll be more knowledgeable about getting work in a variety of areas within the industry.

How To Be a Working Musician is divided into three main sections. The first section provides an overview of what it takes to break into the music business, the second section pertains to playing live, while the third covers various aspects of the studio experience, including both playing and composing. Although it would serve you well to read the entire book, you should feel free to zero in on the areas that are most appropriate to your career plans.

In addition, each section contains profiles and interviews of working musicians who've achieved success in various areas of the business. You'll learn how they started, how their careers progressed, and how they've reached their current professional level. These accounts illustrate the point that, for a talented musician, becoming successful is not a magical process, but rather the result of hard work and persistence.

Also included are interviews with industry insiders, as well as "survival guides" that provide invaluable tips on how to get through various types of gigs and musical situations.

Finally, there's a listing at the end of the book that provides you with the names of books, articles, Web sites, and other sources of information regarding the subjects that are covered.

If you read the entire book, you'll notice that there's a common thread that runs throughout. It applies to all the different sectors of the business, from clubs to Broadway to jingles. This recurring theme is that most musical employment is attained as a result of recommendations from other musicians, and in order to get them you need to put yourself out into the scene and do whatever it takes to get your name known. Conversely, if you're not aggressive, and you wait for success to come to you, the odds are you'll be in another line of business before too long.

PART ONE

❖

LEARNING THE ROPES

❖

CHAPTER 1 | BREAKING INTO THE MUSIC BUSINESS

"Music is spiritual.
The music business is not."
—Van Morrison

❖

Like other sectors of the entertainment industry, the music business is an extremely competitive place to work. There are many more people who want to get in than people who are actually working. Unless you're unbelievably talented, the odds are that you'll have to scuffle and struggle from time to time during your career. You need to be both confident in your abilities and aggressive in your actions in order to succeed. The work will not come to you; you need to go get the work.

To help you get through the hard times, there's always that Holy Grail of "making it" that gives musicians something to dream about and strive for. But there are also many smaller thrills, like playing a killer solo, singing a perfect harmony, or receiving an enthusiastic encore, that are hard to duplicate in any other part of your life. It's moments like these that enable you to put up with the insecurities of being a musician.

Whether you're part-time or full-time, there's one important fact you need to keep in mind about the music industry: Underneath all the glamour it's still a business, and it exists for the purpose of making money. You may be in it for the art (or, then again, you might not), but the people who'll be hiring you are in it for the dough. Always remember that and be on your guard.

THE CHALLENGES FACING TODAY'S MUSICIAN

Earning money in the music field has never been easy, but today it's become even more challenging. The last decade-and-a-half has seen enormous technological and social changes that have had strong reverberations on the way musicians make a living. The biggest wave of change for the music business has been brought about by computers. The technological revolution we're experiencing is so profound that it's been compared in scope to the industrial revolution. In the last ten years we've seen the impact of the microchip on all facets of our lives, including the entertainment industry.

The most profound agent of change in the music field has been the development of computer music technology such as MIDI (Musical Instrument Digital Interface) and digital sampling. These developments have fundamentally altered the way music is produced and, to a lesser extent, performed. The replacement of live players with MIDI sequences has greatly diminished musical employment. In the past, all record and jingle sessions would employ live rhythm sections and often live strings and horns. Due to MIDI, this is now the exception rather than the rule. There are also many occasions in theater music and other types of performances where live players have been replaced by sequences, or parts played on a synthesizer or sampler by a keyboard player. In an alarming number of cases, tapes have been substituted for live orchestras.

One of the positive impacts of new music technology has been the "democratization" of the recording process. Today, almost anyone with a small amount of capital can buy equipment good enough to produce CD-quality audio. This rise of the home studio has turned the recording industry upside down and caused many full-service studios to go out of business. With so many singers and groups putting out their own home-recorded CDs, new methods of distribution have evolved, with the Internet playing a large role. The Web has made it a lot easier for these acts to disseminate their music, a trend that is likely to accelerate in the future. For those on the commercial side of the business, however, the problem with so many people having studios is that it spreads the work into a much larger number of hands, therefore making it more difficult for any one composer or session player to have enough work.

Other ways in which technology has affected the music business include the following:

- Entertainment options like cable and satellite TV, pay-per-view, videotapes, laser disks, and home video games have resulted in many more people staying home. In the past, some of these folks would have gone out to hear live entertainment. This factor alone has diminished musical employment.

- The popularity of house, techno, hip-hop, and other similar styles of music that do not rely primarily on live musicianship have contributed to the decline as well.

- The karaoke fad, another technologically based form of entertainment, has caused many musicians to lose work when clubs switched away from live music.

Music, like other industries caught up in this technological upheaval, has changed greatly. Gone are the days when a successful session player could do three or four sessions a day, five days a week. Gone, too, are the house band gigs at large hotels and theaters where a full orchestra could work steadily all year long. In addition, the American Federation of Musicians (commonly referred to as the *musicians union*) has had to wage a constant battle with producers who would like to replace live theater orchestras with recordings and sequencers. In most places, the union has been able to hold its ground. In Las Vegas, however, the local chapter was broken, resulting in a huge loss of show-related orchestra jobs. Overnight Las Vegas went from being a great musician's town to a lousy one.

Another factor that has had an enormous impact on the live music scene is the nationwide change in attitude toward drinking and driving. The combination of the drinking age being raised to twenty-one and the strict enforcement of DWI laws has resulted in a lot less people going out to bars to hear live music. Since the eighteen- to twenty-year-olds were a large part of the live music audience, their absence has been felt in a big way in the clubs. It's also had a measurable effect on the amount of live music played at colleges, because most college students are under twenty-one. In addition, the fear of DWI arrest has limited the range of clubgoers, who in the past might have traveled long distances to hear their favorite bands. The changes in drinking and driving laws and habits have been very beneficial from a public safety standpoint, but they've exacted a toll on the live music scene.

The aging of the baby boomer generation has also contributed to the downturn in club gigs. According to Peter Spellman, music business career advisor and author of *Music Biz Know-How: Do-It-Yourself Strategies for Independent Music Success* (see Appendix), there are 30 million fewer people between the ages of twenty and thirty than there were ten years ago. This demographic shift has had a major impact on the nightclub business because people in their twenties are most likely to go out and listen to music.

One of the side effects of the decline in bar business is that there has been little if any increase in pay for nightclub musicians over the last ten years. This flatness in wages is exacerbated by the fact that so many bands are now willing to accept substandard pay in an effort to achieve wider exposure.

In spite of these negatives, there are some positive signs for musicians, including an increase in the number of Broadway shows sending out touring companies. These companies hire both traveling and local pick-up musicians and pay quite well (see "Playing with Broadway Touring Companies" in Chapter 5). There are new (albeit not too high-paying) opportunities as well for studio musicians playing on independently produced and released CD projects.

Despite all the changes in the business, there are still musicians out there making a living, and for the most part they're the ones who've adjusted to the new climate by diversifying. These individuals aren't just instrumentalists or singers anymore; they're composers, producers, engineers, and arrangers. They don't just play one type of music, either. They play a wide variety of styles and all manner of gigs. Many are entrepreneurial and technologically savvy. They're positioning themselves to ride out the wave of change that's engulfing the business and end up on their feet.

In this difficult environment, the best way to help your career progress is to realize that things are in a state of flux and that you need to keep up with the changing times, not fight them. You don't have to become a computer whiz, but you can't be a technophobe either, or you'll soon be obsolete.

It's important, too, to widen your knowledge within the music field as much as possible. If you have access to recording equipment, learn as much as you can about it. If you've been playing only one style of music, start learning to play others. It's been my observation, as well as that of many of the musicians interviewed for this book, that the best way to keep busy is to have your hands in as many different pies as possible. Be flexible, open-minded, and versatile, and you'll increase your chances of lasting success by a large margin.

PLANNING YOUR MUSIC CAREER

It's not possible to plan your music career in the way that medical or law students might plan theirs. With the exception of some segments of the classical field, there's no set career path upon which a musician must travel. Each musician has his or her own unique combination of circumstances, skill, personality, and luck that have resulted in his or her success or lack of it. Nonetheless, you can engage in some career-planning and goal-setting that will keep you pointed in the right direction and help you avoid falling into too deep a rut.

For those of you who are contemplating getting seriously involved in the music business for the first time, the safest route in is to start playing part-time. There are some real advantages to being a part-time musician. You can continue with your other career and still enjoy a lot of the pleasures of music, such as recording, songwriting, and performing. You can test the waters without making the financial sacrifices that many full-time musicians must make. You can build your career slowly, and—if things begin to pick up—there's always the option of going full-time at a later date. Being a part-timer won't always be easy, especially when you have to get up to go to work three hours after arriving home from a gig, but it is doable. Starting off part-time is a good way to get going in the business without burning all of your bridges to the "real" world.

There's a particular breed of part-timers out there known as "Weekend Warriors." These are musicians who have nine-to-five jobs and only want to gig on the weekends. They generally don't have the ambition to make music their career, but enjoy playing their gigs and making some extra cash. There's a certain amount of resentment toward these players among full-time musicians, who feel that they take away jobs rightfully meant for them. A more valid criticism might be that because they have other income, these individuals sometimes accept gigs for low pay and therefore put downward pressure on the pay scales of all their fellow musicians. Because the musicians union is not a factor in the vast majority of gigs on the club circuit, there are often no predetermined pay scales and club owners can get away with paying very little. There's nothing inherently wrong with the "Weekend Warrior" approach, as long as you don't accept cheap-labor gigs.

A much bigger culprit when it comes to the lowering of band wages is the groups that play their own material and whose primary motivation is to get signed to a record deal. There are bands in cities all over the country who regularly accept gigs for virtually no pay. There are even some bands who pay for the "privilege" of playing. They may feel that it's in their best interest to do so, but their actions have caused many clubs that formerly paid bands to no longer do so.

There are also many part-timers who do have aspirations to be full-time players but who are financially unable to do so. For instance, they may have families or other obligations that do not allow them to live the "bohemian" existence that usually goes along with the early part of a music career. Many musicians have found that a good compromise is to secure a full-time job that's related to the music industry, like teaching music or working in a music store. These jobs allow them to stay involved in the business while earning a steady living.

If you're financially able to be a full-time musician, you'll be able to devote a lot more time to your career development than a part-timer can. You can practice for a couple of hours every day and still have time to pursue getting gigs and doing publicity. You can hang out at clubs and make contacts without having to worry about getting up the next morning. There's little doubt that, in most cases, you can make things happen more quickly if you devote yourself to them full-time.

PROFILE | **CAROL SHARAR**

Teaching by Day, Playing by Night

Many musicians view having a day job as a constraint that forces them to cut back on their gigging and scale back their goals. With the right job and the right attitude, however, it doesn't have to be that way. In violinist Carol Sharar's case, being a music teacher by day has given her the financial freedom to pursue her performing and recording career without having the pressure to take any gig that's offered in order to make money.

Over the course of her career, Sharar has performed with a wide variety of artists, including Stephane Grappelli, Waylon Jennings, Tony Bennett, and Smokey Robinson. As an indication of her versatility, she also toured Japan with the New York Symphonic Ensemble, a high-level classical group consisting mainly of members of the Metropolitan Opera Orchestra and the New York Philharmonic. In addition, she played and acted in the road company of the Off-Broadway show *Oil City Symphony*. Sharar has also recorded and performed extensively with an acoustic swing band called The Amazing Incredibles, whose first album was produced by Neil Dorfsman, who previously produced Sting, Dire Straits, and Paul McCartney.

Carol started gigging seriously in the early 1980s after she began to develop her contacts at college.

> Through somebody at college I heard that there was a country band in New York looking for a fiddle player; that's how I met Three Penny Opera, with whom I worked for three years. They were a six-piece, all-female country-and-western band. And that was a happenin' band. We worked a lot; there was a lot going on. We did all the "Battle of the Bands" and the clubs. . . . After I began playing with them, I saw all the other bands that were in that circuit, and once I started getting known I began subbing for people in the other bands. There were tons of bands after that.

Between her studies and her gigs, Sharar had quite a heavy workload during her college years.

> I got a double degree in music: one in education and one in performance . . . and I was gigging at night. The roughest part of

my life was when I was student-teaching during the day, all day, for no money, taking college classes in the afternoon, and then gigging at night. . . . I thought about leaving school after my second year of college because I was so exhausted from gigging all the time and trying to play Mozart the next morning.

After graduating in 1984 and getting her teaching job, Sharar continued playing out and doing sessions, and her career subsequently progressed to the point where she's now able to pick and choose the projects she works on.

Now I'm focused more on work that I want to do. I can be selective. And that's where my teaching job has come in handy. I started farming out and weeding out stuff where I wasn't growing musically. . . . I've seen friends stay totally locked in to, say, a wedding band because that's "their gig," like my teaching gig is my gig. For me, if my bread and butter had to come from playing a steady gig, then I wouldn't be free to do the other stuff, like doing a showcase for half an hour somewhere on a Saturday.

Carol's advice to new players is to get out there and be heard. "Just search out the places where you want to be playing and start networking with the people. That's how it all happens. It's just who you know. You have to start putting out the word about what you do." She advises that you should always put out your best effort no matter what the gig, because there might be someone watching who has the potential to give you work. "You never know. You always have to be professional on jobs, and be the way that you would want to be if you were auditioning for a great band, because you never know who's there, and everybody's going to remember you in terms of your playing and how professional you are."

As a woman on the music scene, Sharar has had to overcome a great deal of skepticism and even prejudice, but she feels the situation for is improving.

I've found that it's getting easier for women as side people on the circuit. There is definitely a lot of male-dominated stuff, especially in the country scene. I was the only woman in the band most of the time, for years and years and years. Now I'm feeling that, overall, not just specifically on the country circuit, it's getting a little bit easier. It's just that there are more women involved. More women are putting themselves out there. . . . It's very cool and it's very slow-going too, but it's starting to happen.

Setting Goals

No matter how much of your time you're able to devote to your music career, you can help yourself out a lot by setting progressive, achievable goals (see "Sample Goals," below). Not only will this give you something to shoot for, but it will allow you to monitor your progress and avoid getting sidetracked.

One way to maintain your focus is to put your goals on paper and check and revise them regularly. This process will only work, however, if you set realistic goals for yourself. If you put down "Record a hit record by the end of the first year," you're just setting yourself up for a disappointment. If, on the other hand, you put down something that's within reach, such as "Increase freelance gigs so that I'm working every weekend," you have a good shot at attaining it in a year or sooner. The realization that you haven't achieved a goal by the specified time will give you pause to reassess what you're doing and to make some tactical changes.

In addition to overall career goals, you also might want come up with some goals for improving your musical skills. For example, you could put down "Significantly improve sight-reading skills in the next six months," or "Take all tutorials and become proficient with notation software by the end of the year." Having clearly defined goals will help increase your motivation and perhaps even lessen the possibility that you'll spend your free time watching TV instead of practicing.

The point of all this is to keep yourself focused and in control of your career. It's like a rudder that helps keep you on course: If you don't use it, your work life will flow wherever the currents take it, and that might not be in a direction you want to go. Obviously, you can't plan for everything and it's often beneficial to go in an unexpected direction, but at least you'll be aware of what's going on and whether it's right for you.

SAMPLE GOALS

1. Join a working band and make contacts on the rock club circuit.

2. Practice for at least 30 minutes a day, five times a week, every week.

3. Save enough money to buy a home recording setup.

4. Improve my background vocal skills so that I can sing harmony at gigs.

Choosing a Market

Except for the most desolate of places, there's music work of some sort to be had just about anywhere in the United States. Naturally, you'll have more potential opportunities in the three major music markets—New York, Los Angeles, and Nashville—but you'll face a lot more competition. Other big cities are considered to be secondary markets to the big three. Some of the busier ones from a music production standpoint include Chicago, Dallas/Fort Worth, and Boston. In Canada, Toronto is the main music center.

There are some areas that have particular reputations for being good places for musicians to live. Austin, Texas, has been characterized by many as a very happening place for rock and roll as well as country. Seattle has also become an attractive city for musicians. In addition to being considered the capital of alternative music, Seattle has a robust club scene and a very receptive audience base for many styles of music. Another city that's considered a good player's town is Minneapolis, which has developed a first-rate indie rock scene.

Chicago has many advertising agencies, so it's one of the best places outside of New York and Los Angeles to get involved in the commercial music industry (also known as the "jingle business"). Other areas are equally good for various types of music, but you're likely to have the most options in New York, L.A., and, to a lesser degree, Nashville.

On the flip side, you'll face much more competition in the major markets, and, depending on your personality, you'll either find that challenging or oppressive. Because of all the musicians flocking there, Los Angeles, Nashville, and (to a smaller extent) New York have all developed club scenes that pay next to nothing in many cases. In some instances, bands even have to pay to play. The promise of fame and fortune tends to promote the exploitation of musicians, as has happened big-time in those three cities. It can often be easier to get paying work in medium-sized markets. There is definitely some value to being a big fish in small pond, rather than the other way around.

If you're considering relocating for your music career, you should keep a few things in mind. First, be sure you've exhausted all avenues of achieving your goals where you are. You probably have more contacts than you realize in your home area among friends, family, teachers, and work associates. Think long and hard before uprooting yourself and take stock of all of your possible contacts. You may find that you have a better chance to get gigs by staying put.

Secondly, if you are going to move, try to visit your target area before making your final decision. Consider it a scouting expedition and don't forget that your expenses may be tax-deductible, depending on how you file your musical income. Visit for a few days, check out the clubs, and talk to as many musicians there as you can. Try to get a handle on the particular scene you're interested in. See if you can find a local paper that includes music listings. Who knows, you might even make some contacts that you can utilize later. Scout out the housing market as well. Determine whether you can afford to live there.

If you can't afford to go on a scouting trip, call the people you know (preferably musicians) who live in the target area. See if you can get any information out of them. At the very least they can send you a copy of the local paper, which you can use for telephone research. If you don't know anyone who lives there, maybe a friend or family member can recommend someone.

Relocating is a big step, so the more information you have the more informed a decision you'll make. When I was in my early twenties, I had just moved back home to New York after being in a touring band for a year-and-a-half. At the time I was playing mostly country music and I soon discovered that New York didn't seem like a good place for me to work. I had heard through another musician that Washington, D.C., had a happening country music bar circuit, and I seriously considered moving there. Luckily it wasn't too far to go for a scouting trip, so I headed down for the weekend to see what I could find out. I discovered that the information I'd gotten was a couple of years out of date and that the D.C. scene was actually not very happening at all. By doing a little first-hand research, I was able to avoid making a big mistake. Sometimes the excitement of the idea of moving to a new area can blind you to the reality of the situation, so get as much information as you can before you make the big move.

If you're going to move to one of the three big cities, here's a little information about the music scenes in each area.

New York Some might refer to New York as the mother of all music markets. With the exception of country, just about every type of popular music is recorded and performed there. With all of the Broadway and Off-Broadway shows, it's a mecca for theater musicians. The New York tri-state area (New York, New Jersey, and Connecticut) also has the largest concentration of wedding and party work, known locally as *club dates.* Though it has diminished somewhat in recent years, the club-date scene is still a vital part of the New York music industry. In fact, with the decline in recording work, many formerly busy studio musicians who once ridiculed wedding work are now scrambling to get involved.

If the jingle business (a misnomer these days; see Chapter 8) is what you're into, New York is the capital. There's also a lot of film music recorded there, although not as much as in Los Angeles.

New York is one of the largest production centers for interactive media, so if you're into writing music for CD-ROMs, it's a good place to be. The city also boasts a large number of jazz clubs, cabaret, and nightclubs of all varieties. The rock scene in particular is extremely active and quite diverse. Guitarist Dave Foster, who fronts a band called Bubble, describes it this way: "There are all of these different subgenre-type clubs that handle a specific kind of clientele and music. There's a number of clubs that handle really heavy music, and then there's a folk circuit, and then there's the blues and roots rock circuit. And then there's this whole new crop of things that they're calling 'lounge,' which are kind of low-fi lounge acts." Unfortunately, most of the clubs that book original bands pay the musicians very little, if anything.

Despite everything that's going on there, New York is not an easy place for a musician to exist. The competition is incredibly stiff, and the sheer number of musicians is staggering. In addition, the cost of living is quite high, so you may feel a lot more economic pressure in New York than you would in other cities.

Los Angeles As a recording center, L.A. is at least as busy, if not busier than, New York. In addition to CDs, there's a great deal of music for advertising produced there and, of course, there's film music. The film music session scene is a very difficult nut to crack. Most of the work is controlled by a handful of contractors, and if you're not on their lists you're simply not going to work.

Though the recording scene is extremely busy, changes in technology have severely diminished the prospects for L.A. studio musicians. By some estimates there are only about a third as many musicians making substantial studio incomes as there were twenty years ago. Al Vescovo, a veteran session player, observes that there are significantly fewer live players used on record dates than there were in the days before MIDI: "Back then we used to go to a record session and they'd have five guitars on the date. Now they don't even have record sessions . . . they do it with samplers and synthesizers. . . . They'll call you in to do an overdub for something that's already done, [but] there's no live recordings, per se, anymore." More often than not, this is also the case in many other parts of the country, with the exception of Nashville, where the live rhythm section still rules.

Los Angeles has a good amount of *casual work* (the L.A. equivalent of New York's "club dates") playing weddings and parties, but (as in New York) a lot of it has become non-union. At the time of this writing, the scale for union "casuals" is in the neighborhood of $120 per night, plus pension and benefits. On non-union gigs you're paid as an independent contractor and have to pay your own taxes.

There are Top 40 and other cover band gigs in the L.A. area that pay decently, but a lot of the clubs now book original rock bands for virtually no pay. Los Angeles is notorious among musicians for it's "pay-to-play" clubs. One step up from these are clubs that pay original bands next to nothing to do one set on a bill with three or four other bands. Such venues have unfortunately become the norm in Los Angeles. Patrick Vernon, an L.A.-based guitarist who now works mostly outside of town, describes it this way: "It's not based on merit or how good your band is or how long you've been around or anything like that. If you can bring twenty-five of your friends in, you'll make them [the bar owners] happy."

Nashville Although it's a major recording center like New York and Los Angeles, Nashville has its own set of rules and customs that make it quite different from anywhere else. The biggest segment of the music industry there is, of course, country. But before you pack your Telecaster or your fiddle and head on down, there are a few things you should keep in mind.

First of all, Nashville does not have a good live music scene. The few clubs that hire local bands don't pay more than $30 or $40 a night per musician. There are so many musicians in Nashville that the law of supply and demand makes it easy for club owners to get away with paying the musicians next to nothing. The town is chock-full of great players who have to take jobs outside of music in order to survive.

There are also showcase clubs in Nashville that are similar to the ones in New York and Los Angeles. In these clubs, the band only makes money if it can bring in a good-sized audience.

Although there is an incredible amount of recording going on in Nashville, the best studio work is concentrated in the hands of a very small, elite group of musicians. To break into this circle, you need to be immensely talented and be willing to starve for a long time while attempting to get into the loop. Even with years of trying there's no guarantee you'll ever do it.

If you're very good and you spend a lot of time networking, you do stand a reasonable shot of getting yourself hooked up with a touring country act. According to Bob Haligan, a successful rock, pop, and country songwriter in Nashville: "The good news down here is that there are a lot of country artists, and during the summer they tour a lot. If you're a good picker, there are gigs. You might not get rich from them, but guys find ways to stay alive; also, there are demos to play on."

The "demos" Haligan refers to are *songwriter's demos,* which are the only part of the Nashville recording scene that newcomers are likely to find any work playing on. There are somewhere in the neighborhood of 30,000 songwriters in Nashville, and they're constantly recording their songs in an attempt to sell them. If you get to know some of these songwriters, you might be able to get a shot playing on their demos. This won't be great-paying work, but it can help you get on the track for bigger and better things. There's also work to be had playing in back-up bands for artists doing showcases.

There's a lot of Christian music that's produced in Nashville as well, but the same sort of hurdles you face trying to get country studio work apply here as well. The producers on this scene tend to hire the tried-and-true players, so it's difficult, though not impossible, to break in.

Because Nashville is a very insular town, if you're not from the South you can expect to run up against some anti-Northern prejudice. It's also a much more conservative city than L.A. or New York, so you may have to tone down your act a bit to fit in there.

Although the Nashville music scene is incredibly competitive and difficult, it's not impossible. According to Bob Haligan, "I would say that if you're great at anything you do and you have the personality and the attitude, you can find a way to get something going. The perseverance, the 'stick-to-it-iveness,' is always the ultimate ingredient that anyone has to have."

BUILDING A NETWORK OF CONTACTS

Despite the recent upheaval in the music industry, there are some things that never change. One of them is that the best way to get a lot of work is by developing contacts. The more people in the business you get to know, the more potential opportunities you'll have for the future.

When I was first starting out as a commercial music composer, I found myself running into one brick wall after another. I sent out my demo tape, followed up with phone calls, and got nowhere. Around that time, I started playing in a band with another composer who happened to be very well connected in the jingle business. He introduced me to some friends at a music production house, and within a week or so I was given my first composing assignment. The moral of this story is that personal contacts are by far the best way to get ahead. This is not to say that you shouldn't try to get work if you have no connections; it can and does happen. Your main focus, however, should be on networking.

Some people are very outgoing and find networking easy, while more introverted people find it extremely difficult. You may have to push yourself sometimes, but the results are worth any temporary embarrassment you may experience.

When I was first thinking about writing music for commercials, I heard about a seminar being given by a music producer from an ad agency. Being naturally shy I was somewhat hesitant to go, but at the last minute I decided to attend. While I was there I noticed someone in the audience who looked somewhat like a guitar play-er I'd known at college. I had a gut feeling that he could be a good contact, but I almost didn't introduce myself because I wasn't sure it was really him. Fearing a missed opportunity, I forced myself to speak with him and it was a good thing I did. It turned out that he owned a music production company, and he eventually hired me part-time. I learned a lot about the business and discovered that he was friends with the speaker from the seminar, who also taught a class in jingle-writing. I took his class and, as a result, made a lot of contacts, some of whom are hiring me for composing and ses-sion jobs almost ten years later.

The lessons to be learned from this story are many. First, involve yourself in every situation where you might be able to schmooze with people who are working in the business. Second, when you have a chance to make a contact, don't let shyness stop you. Third, one contact can lead to another, which can lead to another, and so on.

Networking by Working

There's more to networking than just walking around a party intro-ducing yourself. Most of the best contacts are made in working sit-uations. A fellow band member who's struggling on the same level as you might someday become a bigwig who could really help your career. By getting out there and working in any way that you can in the music business, you may be sowing the seeds for future suc-cess. It's a progressive process that builds on itself, but it can't get started unless you get out there. Every musician interviewed for this book agreed with the notion that the more you work, the more work you'll get.

In other words, what you want to strive for in your networking is to develop a momentum. Eventually, you'll have made enough contacts and developed your reputation to the point where you'll be getting work calls constantly.

Naturally, you have to come through in the work situations or you'll never get past the first level of contacts. To use a worn-out cliché, you not only have to talk the talk, you've got to walk the walk. In all your musical situations you should not only strive to perform at your highest level, but to meet all your responsibilities

PROFILE | **FRANK VILARDI**

New York
Session Drummer

Frank Vilardi is a drummer and percussionist who has toured and/or recorded with such artists as Jewel, Curtis Stigers, Suzanne Vega, Roseanne Cash, and Judy Collins, and played on numerous jingles, TV shows, and movie soundtracks. Like many other successful musicians, he built his career on talent and hard work and now enjoys a stellar reputation in the upper echelons of the New York music business. His story is a good example of how contacts made from working in the business can lead to bigger and better things.

Frank studied classical percussion at Hart College of Music in Hartford, Connecticut, and while there started gigging professionally. "I got into a blues band that was the hot band in Hartford. We would do all the opening concert slots . . . and a lot of college gigs, and we even traveled around the East coast a bit, opening for everybody from Taj Mahal to the Mahavishnu Orchestra."

The contacts Vilardi made from the college band eventually paid off when the lead singer got signed to a record deal. Frank was called in to play drums, and though the record never went anywhere it got him into the New York music scene.

Vilardi got his first major road gig playing with disco singer Evelyn "Champagne" King in Florida in 1979. He got the job through the guitar player of the band he was in.

> I was doing fusion with this guy Russ DeSalvo, who's now a successful writer. . . . He's also a great guitar player, and so we auditioned and got the gig. We went on the road and it was like two sets, one at twelve midnight and one at two A.M., when people were out in the discos till five in the morning. . . . I came back into [New York] after that and started meeting people, doing gigs. I got a gig subbing for Doane Perry, who's now the drummer for Jethro Tull, . . . playing for a singer named Zora Rasmussen. Marc Shaiman, who's a big film composer now, was the MD [musical director], Tony Cunnif was the bass player, and Larry Saltzman was the guitar player. So all of a

sudden I was meeting a whole bunch of the guys my age who were sort of the up-and-coming, in-town guys. . . . And basically, for a lot of years . . . there were a zillion gigs like that. All those singer-songwriter gigs and demos.

He got hooked into the jingle business, which in the early 1980s was flourishing. "I'd do ten jingles a week, maybe fifteen." By the time the jingle business slowed down in 1988, he had developed enough connections to start getting calls to tour and record with major artists.

When I asked him to describe the current state of his work, Frank replied

> It varies; when I'm touring I work all the time. The rest of the time I bounce back and forth between a couple of good original projects and record dates. Lately there's been a lot of film work. . . . Whenever the producers I work for work, I get called. [My workload] can go anywhere from not having a break for thirty days to working a couple of times a week to doing club dates (wedding gigs) on the weekend. Jingles are usually a couple of times a month.

Although he's gotten a lot of his gigs based solely on his reputation, Frank has also had to audition for a lot of his jobs: "As a sideman, you're always up against the record company's pick, the artist's pick, the producer's pick, the manager's pick. Everybody's always vying for someone [else] to get in there. I think I've done pretty well considering all that. And I've always done well when I had to audition. I've almost always gotten the gig."

Vilardi attributes his auditioning success to hard work: "I prepare a lot, I learn the tunes the best I can, and, if I'm friends with somebody in the band, we'll get together. You get an edge, you have to have an edge."

Frank's advice for musicians who are new to an area or scene is to work as much as they can but also to challenge themselves. "I think the best thing to do is to try to get work that's a little bit above your level. Try to aspire to working with the better people. Don't bring yourself down to where you're working with marginal people. . . . Do whatever you can and prepare well. Learn what you have to do and don't f--- up. You don't have too many shots at it."

and commitments. In this super-competitive environment, you can give yourself a big edge by being a reliable player who's easy to work with and can be counted on to show up on time, sober, and prepared. This is especially true because music attracts many people who have a lot of creative energy but aren't necessarily very dependable. In music, just as in any other field, those who work the hardest and are the most dedicated stand the best chance of succeeding.

Networking While You Learn

Another good place to network is in the classroom. While studying music, you'll meet many people, both teachers and students, who may be able to help your career at some time in the future. Even if you don't make any meaningful contacts you'll be increasing your musical knowledge, which can only help you.

In most urban and some suburban areas there are music courses that you can take without getting into a degree program. You can find, among other things, ensemble workshops to work on your reading, theory, and recording-engineering classes. If you put your mind to it, you can also get a musical education outside of the regular college environment. Of course, if you can swing going back to school to study full-time, that's even better.

Some players, rockers especially, sneer at the idea of getting a music education. While it may not be tremendously cool to be able to read and write music, I can just about guarantee that it will come in very handy if you plan on making a career in this business. Most of the successful musicians I've come across are musically literate, and almost all of the prime gigs that are out there, such as TV shows, commercials, Broadway shows, and record dates, require some reading chops.

HOW THE MUSICIANS UNION CAN HELP YOU

Over the course of my career I've talked to many players who ridicule the musicians union and say that it's useless. This assessment couldn't be further from the truth. While it's true that the union doesn't have jurisdiction over most of the nightclub work in the United States and Canada, it's very prominent in TV and film work, records, musical theater, and the field of "casual" gigs (weddings, private parties, and so on). In other words, if you're involved in any of the higher-paying musical fields, chances are that the union will represent you.

There will certainly be times in your career when you have to do non-union work. No one expects that all musicians will be able to restrict themselves to jobs covered by the union. It's in your best interest, however, to take as much union work as you can. Not only will your pay scale be better, but you'll receive pension benefits and, depending on how much work you do, health benefits as well. In addition, being a member of the American Federation of Musicians (AFM) gives you access to low-cost instrument insurance, disability benefits, reduced-rate credit cards, personal loans, and even reduced-rate mortgages.

The union even has a plan whereby, if you incorporate, you can pay yourself health and pension payments on non-union gigs. All this talk about pension may not seem important to you if you're young and starting out, but the older you get the more you'll appreciate it. Many non-union musicians end up with nothing to show for from a pension standpoint after years of gigs. That's not a situation that you want to get yourself into.

The union can also be useful in helping you find work. Most locals have a referral list you can get yourself on that can lead to getting called for gigs. In addition, the union is a good source for the names and numbers of other working musicians with whom you can network. For information about the musicians union local in your area, call the AFM at (800) 762-3444.

PART TWO

❖

GETTING PAID TO PLAY LIVE

❖

CHAPTER 2 | **PREPARING YOURSELF FOR THE CHALLENGE AHEAD**

❖

Playing gigs, or "playing out," can be exciting, scary, exhausting, and sometimes exhilarating. There are, however, a number of issues to consider before taking the plunge into the nightclub world. This chapter will help you assess these issues and aid you in determining your readiness.

KNOWING YOURSELF

It's assumed that most people reading this book have played at least some gigs somewhere. Most musicians start playing in bands during their high school years and usually have at least occasional opportunities to play in front of people. If you're looking to make the leap into playing for a living (or at least a part-time living), you need to cast a critical eye on yourself and honestly assess your skills.

• How do you stack up compared with your peers who play the same instrument? Are you one of the better players within the musical circles in which you travel?

• Are you able to hold your own and contribute when you play with other musicians?

• Do you have enough musical training to learn parts off tapes or CDs?

If you can answer affirmatively to these questions, then you're probably ready to start seriously gigging. You don't have to be the Jimi Hendrix of your instrument, just a solid player with a good attitude.

Remember, chops are only one of the ingredients that go into making a good musician. There's also creativity, discipline, and the ability to interact artistically with other players. These are all things you can work on to improve. Granted, there's a certain amount of God-given talent that gives some players an advantage over others, but you can make up for a lot of that with good practice habits, a good attitude, and, most of all, hard work.

POLISHING YOUR SKILLS

There are many ways you can go about improving your musical abilities. Here are a few suggestions that should help you on your way.

Taking Lessons

No matter what your skill level, you should be taking lessons if you can afford them. There are always more techniques to learn and more styles to explore. Studying will help you expand your mind musically and play better. One way you can really help yourself is by trying to find a teacher who's working in the same segment of the music business that you're aiming for. Not only will you be learning, but you'll also be making a contact who can potentially help you get work in the future. You might even want to approach a "name" player who you see playing at a club and ask if he or she teaches.

Other ways to find a teacher are to get a recommendation from someone you know, look in the classifieds, or contact a music school. If you're considering teachers for whom you don't have references, interview them carefully. Ask what methods they'll be using and try to get a sense of whether you can get along with them. Taking lessons isn't cheap, so don't waste your money and your time on a bad instructor.

Developing Good Practice Habits

Whether you're taking lessons or not, you need to develop good, disciplined practice habits. Try to practice daily, even if you can only do it for a short time. It's better to have brief daily practice sessions than long ones that occur only sporadically. Map out what you want to accomplish in your practicing and try to stick to that plan. It's very easy to get sidetracked and go off on a tangent, so always keep yourself focused.

It's a good idea to do as much of your practicing as you can with a metronome. Whether you're doing scales or playing a new piece, a metronome will not only sharpen your sense of rhythm, but it will also give you a benchmark against which to measure your future practice sessions. For example, if you have a certain exercise that helps develop speed in your playing, write down the maximum setting at which you can play it cleanly each day. In a couple of weeks you should notice some improvement. Having a way to actually see your progress can help you feel a lot more motivated about practicing. You can even make it into a game by trying to try to break your previous "record" on a given exercise.

Another trick to working with a metronome is to not always think of it as beating on every quarter note. It can really help your understanding of rhythm to think of the metronome as sounding only on the second and fourth beat (two and four) or the first and third beat (one and three) of each measure. The rest of the quarter notes in the measure you have to count in your head. You'll probably find at first that it's more difficult to keep your place, but the results will be worth it.

Learning from the Greats
A good method for improving your playing is to learn some parts, note for note, from a CD of an artist whose style you admire. Learning how an accomplished player approaches a given musical situation can be a mind-opening experience and can benefit you in a number of ways. The initial result will be that you'll add licks to your arsenal, but, more importantly, it will also help increase your understanding of your instrument. By doing so, you'll be another step closer to developing your own style, which is something all musicians should ultimately strive for.

Find a short passage, maybe a two- or four-bar phrase, and put it on a cassette. Then slowly learn it (a couple of notes at a time if necessary) until you've mastered the entire lick or section. If you're unable to figure out how to play it, you may have to slow it down using a tape player with a variable speed control. There are specially designed analog and digital decks that will slow anything down to half speed (on an analog deck the phrase sounds in the same key, only an octave lower). If you have a computer that records digital audio, there are programs you can get that will slow down audio without changing the key or the octave. You can also use an old reel-to-reel that allows you to set the record speed (15 ips, 7 1/2 ips, 3 3/4 ips).

Improving Your Reading

If you don't already read music, now is the time to start. You can be sure that this skill will come in handy down the line. As mentioned previously, many of the best-paying gigs in the industry require a musician who can read. The earlier you start, the better off you'll be.

The best way to improve your reading skills is to use them in real musical situations. Practicing at home is helpful, but it won't have nearly as big an impact on your reading chops as, for example, playing in a local theater production for which you have to read everything. The more real-life reading you do, the better. If you're in school, there'll be plenty of opportunities to read in stage bands, orchestras, and ensembles. If you're not in school, find out if there are any jazz workshops or other types of classes in your area in which you could gain sight-reading experience.

You can also get together with other musicians you know and read down some music. There's plenty of written music out there that you can use, from classical duets to Top 40 sheet music.

Remember that when you are in a pressured situation, such as a show or a session, it becomes much more difficult to read. Nervousness is a big impediment to good reading, so you've got to try and build your confidence. Here are some tips to help you get through a situation where you need to read and the pressure is on.

Try To Get a Copy of the Music in Advance If you can you're way ahead of the game, because you can learn your parts at home prior to the show or session. While this tactic is fairly common practice in theater and orchestras, it's almost unheard of in session work. For one thing, you're expected to be able to sight-read the music at a session. Asking for it in advance is a tacit admission that you're not that confident a reader, and that may make you look less than qualified in some people's eyes. Another problem is that, in many cases, the composer or arranger is just finishing up the chart as you walk in the session. My advice is to arrive ten or fifteen minutes early for the session. (Don't arrive too much earlier than that unless you have a lot of stuff to set up, or you'll appear too eager.) By arriving early, you'll probably have a few minutes to look over the chart while the engineer is working on sounds, or while you're waiting for the rest of the band to arrive. Those few minutes are precious, so use them to your advantage.

First, take a look at the chart and go through the "road map" of the song or piece. Look for repeat signs, codas, and other symbols that tell you how to navigate through it. Make sure you understand how to get through the chart from beginning to end. It's critical to get this right, otherwise you could end up getting lost in the middle. Next, look for passages that are particularly difficult, either rhythmically or melodically, that you need to work out. If you find any, try to figure out how you're going to play them, and run through them a few times while you have time. Pencil in any fingerings or other notations on your chart that will help you remember what you need to do. After that, if you still have time, try running down the whole piece.

When the piece starts, listen to the count-off and count along in your head. You should always be counting in your head or you're likely to get lost. This is especially true if you have a lot of multiple bar rests in your part. There is nothing more embarrassing than not coming in when you're supposed to, except maybe coming in where you're *not* supposed to.

As you may have already surmised, it's always a good idea to bring pencils with you when you're going to be in a reading situation. If you make a habit of carrying a couple in your instrument case, you'll always be prepared.

Practicing at Home Although at-home practice can't substitute for real-life reading situations, it can certainly help you improve. The most important thing to remember is that once you start reading a piece of music, you should *read it down completely without* *stopping.* The worst habit to get into as a sight-reader is to stop and read a section over every time you make a mistake. You can't do it in a real-life situation; everyone else will keep going and you'll lose your place. You can't raise your hand in the middle of a Broadway musical and say "Excuse me, I made a mistake and lost my place. Can we start again?" Therefore, the key is to get in the habit of continuing, even when you've made a major error. That way you'll be programming yourself to always keep your place.

UNDERSTANDING YOUR ROLE IN A BAND

One of the things that separates the contenders from the pretenders when it comes to musicianship is the ability to be a true ensemble player. Just as on a basketball team, each player has a role and must work with the others to make for a winning situation: If one player hogs the ball and doesn't pass, their team will probably lose. Similarly, musicians who think only of their own glory will end up being detriments to their band. Great musicianship is more than just chops; it's the ability to help make those around you sound better. Jazz and classical musicians have an advantage because they're more likely to learn ensemble playing as part of their education. Rock players, on the other hand, generally learn about ensemble playing by trial and error while playing in bands. Not surprisingly, many of them go into working situations without having a clue as to how to interact musically with their fellow players.

For those of you who are unsure of the role your instrument plays in the ensemble context, the following are capsule descriptions that help define the various elements in a typical band.

Bass The "glue" of the band, the bassist lays down a groove that, along with the bass drum, fills out the bottom end of the sound while reinforcing (usually) the root note of the chord. This individual must know the material well enough to be able to make all the chord changes without hesitation. He or she must also work closely with the drummer to lock in the groove. Especially important is that the bass and the bass drum are in sync with each other. In most cases (fusion notwithstanding), the bassist should refrain from too much filling or soloing.

Drums The drummer is also responsible for the groove of a song. Successful drummers are rock solid in their feel for time and tempo. They may be flashy at times, but their main role is to provide metronomic support of the beat, and to emphasize and ornament the accents.

Lead Guitar (and Other Lead Instruments) A good lead player will play concise, well-thought-out solos and fills that conform to the structure of the song and do not go on ad nauseam. There's nothing more annoying than an out-of-control soloist. Keep in mind that tasteful eighth notes are always preferable to obnoxious thirty-second notes.

Rhythm Guitar The responsibility of a rhythm guitarist is to lock in his or her part with the bass and drums so that they're all working together to create a cohesive groove. If there's another rhythm guitarist or a keyboardist playing chords, the two should try to avoid playing in the same register to keep the arrangement from becoming too muddy. For a great example of rhythm guitar–playing that grooves seamlessly with the rest of the band, listen to the work of Steve Cropper on the Stax recordings of the late 1960s.

Keyboards Besides traditional piano and organ sounds, keyboards are used to add various other instrument textures (whether from synths or samplers) to the band. Your sounds should be well organized so that you can switch to the appropriate ones quickly. As mentioned above, try to work out parts with the rhythm guitar so that you don't take up the same sonic real estate.

Lead Singer The lead singer is the focal point for the audience. He or she needs to relate to and engage the crowd, and should attempt to project an image befitting the band. What's more, the lead singer should try to resist the temptation to have the monitors turned up so high that the rest of the band has to crank themselves up to compensate. With a little practice, a singer can get used to hearing his or her voice at a lower level.

EVALUATING YOUR EQUIPMENT

It's very important to have professional-level equipment when you start to play gigs. Cheap gear will not hold up to the stresses and strains of constantly being transported, bumped, banged, and exposed to smoke and the elements.

Furthermore, if you expect to get hired by a band, your equipment must not appear sub-par or you might not get the job. I'm not saying that you need to buy top-of-the-line gear, but you should at least have decent-quality, brand-name stuff that's in good condition. The following are some equipment tips and suggestions for various instruments.

Electric Guitar You'll need a decent electric that plays in tune and doesn't break a lot of strings. When in doubt, consider a "Strat"-style guitar. They're incredibly versatile and appropriate for most types of music. If you can afford it, it's a great luxury to bring two electrics to your gigs so that you can easily switch during a song if you break a string.

You'll also need an amp that's at least 60 watts RMS (preferably 100 watts). Do yourself a favor and don't get too large an amp. They may look great on stage, but they're hell to lug around.

Unless you play without any effects, consider investing in a programmable multi-effects box with a foot switch. This will allow you to have preset *patches* (settings) that you can custom-tailor to the songs you're playing. If you prefer to carry individual stomp boxes, buy or make a pedal board that allows you to keep the boxes and their cables organized. If you can swing it, get the external power supplies that go with the effects. It's annoying to have to worry about batteries running out all the time.

One more hint regarding effects: When you first start using a programmable effects box, make sure to test out your settings at rehearsal or at the club during a sound check. Those great settings that you programmed in your living room with headphones on may sound totally different when played at stage volume with the band.

Another accessory to seriously consider is a volume pedal. It's superior to the guitar's volume knob in that it allows you to change level without substantially altering the tone. Even more important, it allows you to keep your hands free to play.

One thing all guitarists need is a good tuner. If properly connected, it will allow you to tune accurately and silently at any point during a gig. This can be a godsend, as even expensive, well-made guitars tend to slip out of tune fairly often. Using a tuner will eliminate the need to tune out loud between songs while the audience watches and waits (a major bummer).

It's important to have good-quality cables and spares, and you should get a small but sturdy guitar stand that you bring to all gigs. If you rely on the old "lean it against the amp trick," the odds are that you'll be visiting the guitar repair shop before long.

Acoustic Guitar Ideally, you should use an acoustic designed specifically for live situations. There are plenty of models on the market, including some thin-bodied guitars that are essentially useless acoustically but great through a sound system. You can put a pickup in a standard acoustic, but you probably won't get as good a tone and there'll be a much greater likelihood of feedback. To help reduce feedback in an electrified acoustic, put a towel or other cloth inside the sound hole. If you're still having problems, there are commercially available products for controlling acoustic guitar feedback, which you can find at good-quality music stores.

Remember that if you really want your guitar to sound like an acoustic rather than an acoustic/electric, you'll have more luck plugging it into the PA than through a standard guitar amp. This is because a PA is better suited to accurately reproduce the tonal range of your acoustic. The down side is that you'll have less individual control over volume and your guitar will have to be quite loud in the monitors, which your bandmates might not be too thrilled with. One solution is to use an amp as a monitor for yourself onstage, and take a line out of your guitar into the PA for the sound going to the audience. If you do choose to go through an amp exclusively, try to use one specifically designed for acoustic guitar, or at least a keyboard amp, which also reproduces the highs necessary for a good sound.

Electric Bass Although there are plenty of other good designs around, the "Precision"-style bass is a universally accepted standard and you certainly can't go wrong if you head in that direction. Make sure that whatever bass you get plays in tune (if not, bring it in for an adjustment) and is in good shape electronically. If your bass has active electronics, always try to carry a spare battery and any tools you may need so that you can change it quickly in case it dies on you during a gig.

In a perfect world, you'd have a full-size, powerful bass amp for the larger venues and a small combo amp for everywhere else. However, since the world is far from perfect, you'll have to base (no pun intended) your decision on what size clubs and halls you'll be playing. If you can get away with a smaller amp, your back will be eternally grateful. There are some excellent-quality combo bass amps that pack a lot of punch in a small package.

Like a guitarist, a bassist should have a tuner, a stand, and high-quality cables and spares.

Drums Unless you're playing at Madison Square Garden, you should try to resist the temptation to bring a huge drum kit to a gig. Stage space is usually at a premium, so compact is best. I can remember playing gigs where we had to set up on a tiny stage, and the drummer insisted on using a set that featured four rack toms, two floor toms, and a gong. In the vast majority of cases it's not necessary to have such a big kit. You shouldn't need more than a kick, a snare, two rack toms, one floor tom, and your cymbals and hardware.

It's always a plus if a drummer brings some small percussion instruments like an egg shaker and a tambourine. And, of course, don't forget to bring lots of extra sticks and spare drumheads.

Keyboards Be happy you weren't starting your career twenty-five years ago. Then you would have had to drag around a Fender Rhodes and maybe a Hammond B-3 and a Leslie. Everyone in the band would have had to help you schlep your gear and they'd all resent you for it. These days you can have access to thousands of sounds in one relatively small keyboard that you can carry yourself. If you play a lot of piano, the best route might be to get an eighty-eight key, weighted-action controller with its own sounds or hooked up via MIDI to a *sound module* (a keyboardless synth). You could use a smaller keyboard with synth-type action, but you probably won't be totally satisfied with it.

A note of caution: Try to keep your rig relatively uncomplicated. If you have too many modules MIDIed together, and all are dependent upon program changes to get to the right patch, you're brewing a recipe for disaster. You don't want to have to troubleshoot a stuck MIDI note in the middle of a song, or be forced to turn your whole rig on and off to fix it. You also don't want to have the wrong patches coming up with the volumes askew. There are too many variables involved in a complex MIDI setup to justify its use in all but the highest-level gigs, when you have technicians and roadies to assist you.

Make sure to get a space-efficient keyboard stand that's easy to set up and take down. In addition, you'll need an amp that's powerful enough to project distortion-free sound across the club. There are many such keyboard amps on the market. You also have the option of putting your keyboard through the PA in lieu of an amp, but for the same reasons as I mentioned regarding the acoustic guitar, it can be somewhat problematic.

INSURING YOUR GEAR

One commonsense precaution that all musicians would be wise to take is to purchase musical instrument insurance. If you leave your equipment uninsured, you're opening yourself up to a disaster. Most musicians would find it hard to replace all their instruments and equipment out of pocket, all at once; for that reason alone it's definitely worth the expense of getting insurance. If you're in the union, you'll find that your local has information on companies that offer relatively low-priced policies for union members. If you're not a union member, you'll have to call around to find an insurance carrier who'll cover your instruments and equipment. If you have a homeowner's policy, you might be able to get your gear covered under that.

A good policy will cover all of your equipment and instruments no matter where they are: at home, in the car, or at a club. Try to find one that covers replacement value for your gear, rather than current market value. Otherwise, due to the fact that some musical equipment depreciates so quickly, the insurance company might pay you a lot less than you need to replace a piece of gear if it gets stolen or is destroyed. Find out specifically how the insurance company determines the value of a given instrument or piece of gear. They might ask for appraisals, especially on acoustic instruments. They may also base your premium on figures you supply them for the value of each piece, but then pay any claims based on their own figures for the market value of your equipment. I've seen union-affiliated policies with annual premiums in the neighborhood of 1.25 percent of the value of the equipment on an annual basis. At that rate, if you had $20,000 worth of gear you'd only be paying $250 a year to cover it all. Not a bad deal, when you consider the piece of mind it will give you.

ASSESSING YOUR TRANSPORTATION

Another essential ingredient to becoming a gigging musician is to have good transportation. To put it simply, you can't do a gig that you can't get to. Your wheels are as important as your musical equipment when it comes to being a successful working musician. *You absolutely must have a reliable car.* It doesn't need to be fancy, just reliable. If you drive a heap of junk that breaks down constantly, bands will not want to work with you because they won't be able to depend on you to show up on time, or at all.

A decent car is important for your own sake as well. The last thing you want to do is break down in the middle of nowhere (or worse yet, a crime-ridden neighborhood) at 2:30 A.M. with all your gear in the backseat. As tempting as it may be to pour all your money into equipment, make sure to put enough of it into your wheels; you won't regret it.

If you're considering getting a van, here are some things to think about. Strongly consider buying one that seats more than just two people. I've had to ride to far-away gigs while sitting on the floor of a van or on top of an amplifier, and believe me it's not pleasant. Even if you're contemplating driving only yourself and your own equipment around, it's almost inevitable that there will be occasions when the whole band rides in your van, so be prepared.

It's also nice to have a carpet on the back floor of the van so that the equipment doesn't get scratched up as much when taking it in and out. In addition, make sure to keep the cargo area clean so that grease, ketchup, and various other nasty substances don't get on your equipment cases as well as your clothing.

Theft is always a problem when you have a van full of equipment. Thieves look in and see your gear and are tempted to steal it. One solution is to get a cargo van that has no side windows. The problem with this approach is that, in many places, a cargo van is considered a commercial vehicle and may be restricted from certain roadways. Another way to protect your equipment is to get mirrored windows that make it impossible to look in from the outside. I would also suggest that you refrain from putting any "Bassists Do It Lower" or similar bumper stickers on your vehicle. You don't want to give any would-be thieves a clue that your van might contain musical gear.

Whether you're driving a van or a car, try to avoid parking and leaving your instruments and equipment in the vehicle. This is especially true if the gear is visible through the window. In any type of urban or suburban setting, you're asking for trouble if you leave your valuable equipment unattended. If you absolutely must stop at the diner for that post-gig, three-in-the-morning omelet, park your vehicle where you can see it from your table. If you play guitar, bass, or any other relatively small instrument, bring it with you when you leave the car.

PROJECTING THE RIGHT IMAGE

The first thing that anyone notices about you is how you look. Image, especially that first impression, is extremely important in how others perceive you. For instance, if you're auditioning for an alternative rock band and you walk in after work wearing a suit and tie, you'll most likely be projecting an image contradictory to that of the other band members. You'll then have a strike against you before you even start to play. If you walk in wearing workboots and a plaid shirt, you'll be letting them know that you're into the alternative culture and they'll probably assume that you're more in touch with the music.

There is, of course, a fine line between being fashionable and being pretentious, and you must be careful not to cross it or you'll risk looking foolish. Furthermore, I'm certainly not advocating that you march in lockstep with the fashion trends of the music you play, just that you make an effort to appear somewhat hip. You'll find that it helps you gain acceptance.

There are certain kinds of gigs where you won't have to worry about looking hip because there'll be mandatory clothing requirements. For instance, on a wedding gig you're usually required to wear a tuxedo. You may also have the misfortune of working with a bandleader who insists that the band members all dress alike (this seems to happen a lot in country bands). In many of these situations, the bandleader will wear nice clothes while the rest of the players have to wear dorky (often polyester) "band shirts." Wearing them makes you feel like you're in the army or working in a gas station rather than playing in a band. In the greater scheme of indignities that a musician has to face, this is not one of the big ones, so I guess the operative phrase should be "shut up and play."

PROTECTING YOUR HEARING

If you were to take a decibel meter to a gig and put it in front of a typical band, you'd discover noise levels that can approach those of a jet plane taking off. When you factor in that most hearing damage is the result of *prolonged* exposure to excessive noise levels, you realize the danger inherent in an extended career playing live music.

Hearing loss is obviously a catastrophic occurrence for a musician. What's especially insidious about it is that it can sneak up on you without your realizing it. Imagine this scenario: Three days after a particularly loud gig you discover that the ringing in your ears, which usually goes away after a day or so, is still there. You go to a doctor who examines you, gives you an extensive hearing test, and then tells you that the ringing is a condition called tinnitus and will probably never go away. Tinnitus, explains the doctor, is a symptom of damage to your auditory system, in your case caused by excessive exposure to noise. You're then told that this exposure has induced hearing loss at frequencies that are critical for speech recognition.

Although this scenario sounds like a nightmare, it's actually fairly common among musicians who spend a lot of time performing. What's worse is that it's not just limited to those who play large concert halls or arenas; all gigging musicians are at risk. Pete Townshend is probably the most famous musician to admit to having noise-induced hearing problems, but there are undoubtedly many others as well.

The only way to be sure that you'll avoid long-term hearing damage is to wear hearing protection all of the time. Although at first it feels akin to taking a shower while wearing a raincoat, wearing earplugs becomes bearable once you get used to it, and the benefits are enormous.

If you can afford it, ask your audiologist about getting fitted for earplugs that are custom-designed for musicians. Unlike standard plugs, which cut heavily into the high frequencies, musicians' earplugs are more natural-sounding because they attenuate more evenly over the audio spectrum. I can't emphasize how important it is to protect your hearing. Beethoven notwithstanding, the career opportunities are not too bright for deaf musicians. For more information on this subject, contact the Hearing Education and Awareness for Rockers (H.E.A.R.) at (415) 773-9590. (See Appendix for their mailing and Web site addresses.)

You can help control the noise problem by making a concerted effort to keep the volume lower when you're playing. During a typical gig there are frequently instances in which one musician turns up the volume in response to a perceived increase by another band member. Over the course of a set, these little escalations can cause a cumulative increase in volume that's quite dramatic. The result of this is a band playing way too loud not only for the audience but for themselves as well.

Since there's a natural tendency to turn oneself up in these situations, the question becomes: How can these "noise wars" be avoided? The answer is that everyone needs to be aware of their impact on the band's loudness, and instead of turning up, encourage each other to turn down. Although this will not always work, making everyone in the band conscious of the problem can help a great deal.

A good tip for keeping volume under control is to avoid turning the stage monitors up too much. This will help deter everyone from turning their instruments up too high, because otherwise they'll drown out the vocals on stage. If you start out with the monitors real loud, everyone will adjust their levels up and the result will be cacophonous.

Another way to keep the noise level down is to make sure the drummer doesn't play unnecessarily loud. Other band members tend to set their individual volumes relative to the drums, so a loud drummer can make for a loud band. You must encourage your drummer to play under control for the sake of the band and the gig.

PREPARING FOR UNCLE SAM

Whether you're full- or part-time, you should see an accountant if you start to make any musical income, because there's a good chance that many of the expenses you incur in pursuit of your work will be tax-deductible.

The following is a breakdown of some of the more common deductions that a musician may be eligible to take. They may not apply in every case, so check with your tax advisor.

Travel You are allowed to deduct your automobile expenses for the business use of your vehicle. This means that you need to keep receipts for just about everything regarding your car. At the end of the year you'll have to separate what was business use and what was personal use. If you don't want to go through all that record-keeping, you can simply take a deduction of 31 cents per mile of business use. The easiest way to handle that is to keep a mileage log in which you note odometer settings before and after each time you use the car for business. You can also deduct the cost of out-of-town trips made for business purposes. Your travel, hotel, and meal expenses are deductible at varying percentages.

Other Expenses Keep records and receipts of all purchases made in pursuit of your music. Equipment, office supplies, musical supplies, and instruments all may be deductible. You can also deduct union dues, instrument insurance and repairs, purchase and cleaning of uniforms or stage clothes, and any expenses incurred publicizing yourself or your business, such as your phone calls.

To reiterate, I highly recommend that anyone reporting musical income get themselves a good accountant. You'll be surprised how many deductions he or she will know about that you might not have considered. Besides, it's very comforting when dealing with the IRS to have a professional on your side. As dull as it might sound, if you get in the habit of keeping meticulous records, you'll always be prepared in case you're ever audited.

PROFILE | **BILL TROIANI**

Hard-Working Bass Player

Bill Troiani is a veteran bass player who, until his recent move to pursue the music scene in Europe, was extremely busy with both gigs and session work in the New York area. Bill's story is an interesting case study because after spending years on the road, he came back to New York with very few contacts and had to basically reinvent his career. He ended up becoming very busy by using a strategy of taking almost any gig he could get, and using the contacts that he made from those gigs to get more.

After doing this for a few years he got to the point where he was working almost all of the time. According to Bill, "I work every night of the week, sometimes twice a day. . . . I'm working every day this week, except tonight, and hope springs eternal that someone will call me. And I've got a club date [wedding gig] on Friday, another on Saturday, and one on Sunday. And Sunday morning I got a gig."

Troiani began his career playing bar gigs in a college town in upstate New York. "It was a whole different era," he says. "If you had an instrument and an amplifier, you were in." From local gigs, he progressed to road work.

> In the early seventies there was a guy upstate who had a blues label called Trix Records. . . . He was going around the South finding these old blues guys, and he put together this "Blues Comes to Chapel Hill" thing. We went down there, me and a drummer, and we backed up about ten or twelve different blues guys. . . . Then from that I got hooked up with this guy named Eddie Kirkland, and I spent almost twelve years driving around the world with him.

Although it wasn't exactly a first-class touring situation, it was quite memorable.

> Eddie used to watch TV in the car while he was driving. He had a little portable TV hooked up to a battery. . . . The first time

we drove into Canada, in the middle of a blizzard, we're driving along from Montreal to Quebec City, where we had our first gig. He turns on the TV and they're all speaking French. It tickled him to death. He wakes me up and goes, "Hey, check this out, Bill." . . . He was laughing so hard that we drove right off the road. Into a ditch, in the middle of a blizzard.

In addition to the road work, Bill played bass on three of Kirkland's albums. He then went on to join up with indie singer/songwriter Tom Russell, with whom he spent ten years touring and recording albums. He finally gave up the road life and moved back to New York. "I think the reason I'm working so much is, like every one else in the nineties, I've diversified. I have a blues gig every Monday night, I have a country gig every Tuesday night. The last couple of years I've been learning how to do the club date [wedding] material. I've been doing those on the weekends."

Years of gigging and recording have given him some strong opinions on the role of a bass player.

Bass-playing is a supportive thing. A lot of bass players don't play like that. I get a lot of work from people who are just waking up to what the bass and drums are supposed to do. You'd be surprised by how many leaders have no idea what a rhythm section is supposed to do. They hire a bass player and a drummer and they go to work, and whether the guys are working together or not, they have no idea. . . . I get a lot of work, I think, because I try to play as simply as possible when they're singing. You know, keep to the root so they can hear the tone center of the chord and stuff like that.

Bill also has some general advice for gigging musicians:

Especially when you're on a gig for the first time, stay out of the way. . . . It's the old sideman joke—you don't walk into a club date and say, "Where's my table and when do I eat?" . . . You go in there and do what you're asked to do. If the guy asks you to learn a song, you learn the song, do your homework. And if the guy asks you to turn down, you turn down. What is this—art or money?

CHAPTER 3 | PLAYING THE CLUB CIRCUIT

❖

Throughout the United States, there are thousands of nightclubs and bars that hire musicians to play live music. Despite the downturn the nightclub business has taken over the last decade (see "The Challenges Facing Today's Musician" in Chapter 1), you can still find clubs that feature just about any popular musical style, ranging from alternative to zydeco.

THE GIGS THAT ARE OUT THERE

There's great diversity among the types of clubs that hire live music. At the top end are large concert clubs seating a thousand or more with state-of-the-art sound and lighting systems and featuring nationally known recording acts. On the bottom are divey gin joints where you have to set up your equipment on top of the bar and alternate sets with a stripper. In between those two extremes (but leaning toward the latter) are where most of the gigs are. You'll find the largest concentration of clubs in and around cities and college towns. More rural areas generally feature fewer clubs and less musical variety.

The typical club gig is about four hours long, broken up into three or four sets. Occasionally, you find a gig where you have to play for five hours. Needless to say, these can be a real marathon. You'll also encounter a lot of nightspots where you only have to play one set, and you share the bill with three or four other bands (see below).

Rock Gigs

For rock and pop bands, the club scene has changed quite a bit over the past fifteen years or so. It used to be that most clubs featured cover bands of some sort, and original music was something generally frowned upon by club owners. Extremely popular local bands with large followings could get away with playing their own music, but an average band had to base its show on popular cover material. With the exception of *showcase clubs* in big cities (venues where bands play for the express purpose of being heard by record or management people), bands generally got paid for a night's work. The pay scales were lousy, but in many cases musicians who worked four or five nights a week could still eke out a living, albeit bohemian.

Nowadays, the landscape is quite different. You can find a large number of clubs that feature multiple bands on one bill; these groups get paid very little, if anything. The origins of this phenomenon can probably be traced back to the emergence of the punk rock scene in the mid- to late 1970s. Punk's rebellion against the slickness of the music establishment at the time carried with it the assumption that anyone could be part of a band and that musical virtuosity was not an asset. As a result of this "do-it-yourself" attitude, numerous bands sprung up that consisted of musicians who were playing mainly to make a social statement or for the fun of it, rather than to make a living. The club owners were in the enviable position of having a virtually endless supply of bands willing to play for little or nothing. Although the glory of the punk movement has since faded, the idea of having multiple bands on a single bill for extremely low money has become accepted practice in vast areas of the urban rock club scene. It's a fact of life in the New York club scene, according to guitarist/singer Dave Foster. "There are so many different ways *not* to make money in Manhattan," he says, "that I could probably go on for hours."

One of the other major factors propelling this movement away from the one-band, multiple-set, play-for-pay night has been the rise of the indie-rock scene. Because the independent labels have become an accepted alternative to the majors, bands now have a lot more potential outlets for their own music. Consequently, many acts are focusing their energy on pushing their original material rather than trying to make a living playing gigs. This has resulted in even more clubs switching over to a multiple-band format, and a loss of even more paying gigs. This trend is worse in New York and Los Angeles, where it's fueled by the fantasy of being discovered by a major-label A & R (Artist and Repertoire) person who's out trolling the rock clubs looking for the next "big thing." This does happen occasionally, but the odds are extremely slim. What's worse, the sheer numbers make it harder for a good band to get noticed. Patrick Vernon from the Los Angeles band The Zookeepers (see "An Inside Look at a Working Band on the Road," later in this chapter) had this to say about the L.A. club scene:

> It's very easy to get gigs in L.A.; that's the positive side. The bad side is: The band before you will suck, and the band after you will suck. Your fan base will be paying a lot of money for a 45-minute show, something ridiculous like six bucks on a Thursday night. Your people learn to come right when you start and leave right when you're done. And you don't pick up any extra fans because the people who came before you are the buddies of the people who were in that band.

The biggest losers in all of this have been the full-time musicians who've already had to deal with a major reduction in the club scene due to changes in drinking age laws, demographics, and entertainment habits (see "The Challenges Facing Today's Musician" in Chapter 1). These same individuals now find their shrinking universe of clubs further eroded by legions of *original bands* (bands who play predominantly original music) that are willing to play for little more than the promise of "exposure." Because they're not making much money from these gigs, the members of original bands generally have to work day jobs to pay their bills. The upshot of it all is that a whole sector of gigs that was once available to full-time musicians has been replaced, in large part, by low- or non-paying engagements played by part-time players.

On the other hand, from a musical rather than economic standpoint, it's a good thing to have so much original material being featured. In addition, it's only fair to point out that there are areas, especially college towns, where you can find clubs that pay groups playing original music on a scale that's close to what cover bands make. The real problem lies in the fact that so much paying work has been lost.

Despite all the negative trends, there is still a good number of clubs out there that pay bands to play. Generally speaking, clubs that feature bands doing cover material tend to pay a decent wage (relatively speaking) for a night's work. Top 40 clubs are one of the best examples of this. Often located in hotel lounges, these gigs feature bands playing close renditions of hit songs. Though their numbers have diminished somewhat over the last fifteen years, you can still find work playing in this type of venue. Many players find it to be musically unfulfilling, but each band member typically walks out at the end of the night with somewhere around $75 to $100 in their pocket. It's not great pay, but it's a veritable king's ransom compared to what bands on the "original" circuit make.

In addition to Top 40, there are also paying gigs for cover bands that cater to the hard rock/metal audience. These clubs are usually located in suburban areas. You'll also find some clubs that hire specialty acts that can range from "clone" bands who imitate famous artists, to groups specializing in so-called "classic rock."

One area of the club scene that's experienced a real boom in recent years is casino gigs. The explosion of gambling venues across the United States has created a large demand for bands to play in casino lounges. Because many of the new casinos are in the Midwest, a sizable chunk of the casino work is for country bands, but there's rock work as well. These kinds of gigs are almost always booked through agents (see "Touring with a Band," later in this chapter).

Country Gigs

Although their numbers are down somewhat from the peak of a few years ago, there are still plenty of country nightclubs throughout North America. These venues vary a lot in size as well as in pay scale, but typically a musician can earn somewhere between $50 and $100 per night.

Despite the image portrayed in the now classic "chicken wire" scene in the movie *The Blues Brothers,* most country bars are not populated by rednecks who throw beer bottles at the band. Country has broadened its appeal and its clubs are patronized by a wide cross section of fans. I did once play at a club in Wyoming that had a sign out front that read, "Please check your guns at the door," but the patrons were polite, friendly, and looking only to have a good time. Country nightclubs run the gamut from this type of authentic, rural honky-tonk to trendy urban nightspots that were discos before country became stylish. There are also quite a few country nightclubs in suburban areas.

One thing that many of these clubs now have in common is that they're oriented toward line dancing. Although this may be fun for the dancers and good for the club owners, it's rotten for the bands. As a matter of survival, the bands have been forced to cater their repertoires to dancers who are less interested in the quality of the music than whether the band is playing the correct beat for their dance. This has led to a severing of the connection between band and audience that was one of the special things about playing in a country band. I know many country musicians who feel as if their groups have been turned into glorified jukeboxes. At this writing, there are some signs that this trend is abating. From a musician's standpoint, one can only hope so.

Blues Gigs

Clubs specializing in blues have become quite popular in recent years and have sprung up in many urban and suburban locations. Ironically, blues clubs tend to be located in areas where the potential audience is upscale and better educated. While there are some very big clubs featuring name acts, the average blues club is a small- to medium-sized Bar. The pay scales are not great, generally in the $50 to $100 per-player per-night range.

Jazz Gigs

Despite its status as one of America's most revered musical forms, jazz does not have the mass appeal of more popular genres such as rock and country. As a consequence, it has evolved as a music that's performed primarily in clubs. In fact, unlike other musical styles, many of the top-name jazz players still work the clubs. With so many high-quality musicians as their competition, new players face an uphill battle when trying to get gigs.

Jazz musicians have an unfortunate history of being exploited by club owners, and, with the exception of the big-name players, that legacy lives on to this day, manifested in low pay scales and long hours. It's not uncommon for highly skilled jazz musicians who've spent years developing their craft to make $60 or less per night playing at a club. Obviously it's tough to live on that kind of money, so many accomplished players have to teach, work a day job, or branch out into other areas of the business such as theater music, in order to make ends meet.

Jazz clubs are more likely to be found in urban areas and college towns, although there are some suburban locations as well.

Folk Gigs

Gigs for folk musicians differ from those of other musical genres in that many of the clubs are coffeehouses rather than bars and consequently don't serve liquor. As a result, the whole vibe is different, and the working conditions tend to be somewhat more pleasant because you don't have to deal with drunken patrons. Furthermore, many coffeehouses don't allow smoking, and this eliminates one of the other major bugaboos for club-playing musicians: second-hand smoke.

Despite these advantages, folk gigs have many negatives associated with them, and most of these are in regard to pay scale. Perhaps because many folk musicians are out to change the world rather than just trying to make money (a worthy attitude for sure), folk club owners have discovered that they don't need to pay very much to attract good talent. Probably more to the point is that there are a great deal more capable folk singers than there are gigs available, and this creates a supply-and-demand situation that's weighted heavily in favor of the club owners. As a result, wages tend to be low. It's not unheard of for the club to pay performers as little as $20 or $30 a night. It's often based on some sort of percentage of the cover charge, and you're at the mercy of the club to give you an honest accounting of what you're due. To make up for these minuscule wages, performers often engage in the humiliating practice of passing around a tip jar. There is some irony in the fact that the folk scene, which is heavily populated by people fighting injustice, is so exploitative of its musicians.

PROS AND CONS OF BAR BAND GIGS

Despite all the problems, playing on the bar circuit has many advantages for a musician. It provides you with a place to hone your chops, establish contacts, and (one would hope) get paid at the same time.

There's nothing better for improving your playing and performing abilities than doing lots of gigs. Just as a baseball player can spend years in the minor leagues developing his skills, a musician can do the same on the bar circuit. The largest growth of my skills as a guitarist came as a result of a year-and-a-half of playing six nights a week with a touring bar band. I know of very few successful musicians who did not spend some years playing the bars.

Although you may have studied music in school, playing gigs gives you practical experience that you usually can't get in a classroom. You'll learn how to handle audiences and overcome stage fright. You'll become more able to adapt to situations where the sound system and room acoustics are sub-par, and you'll discover how to maximize your equipment so that it functions well in all circumstances. In short, you'll become a professional. This will stand you in good stead for any level of the music business that you might eventually reach.

Playing bars can also help you along the path to those higher levels by greatly expanding your network of contacts. After a number of years playing in clubs, you'll have met many people who in the future may be able to help with your career. For example, the keyboard player in your band could end up being a producer a few years down the line and you'll have a great "in" with him or her. If you excel at what you do and develop a great reputation on the club circuit, you may very well get offers to join better bands with better gigs. The reputation that you develop can also help you get studio work (see "Getting the Work," in Chapter 7).

As we've discussed, playing the bars is not an entirely positive experience. To the layman, being a musician and performing in nightclubs looks like a glamorous, fun way to make a living without having to work very hard. If you've done any bar gigs at all you know that's a myth. What the audience doesn't see is all the behind-the-scenes work that leads up to relatively brief time you spend on stage.

First and foremost, you've got to rehearse. Over the course of a four-hour night, a band or singer usually plays upwards of forty songs. That requires quite a lot of time spent rehearsing and learning material.

A typical band also spends close to an hour before and after each gig (unless it's a multiple-night engagement) setting up and breaking down equipment. If you add in the time spent driving to and from the gig, your workday is in the neighborhood of seven or eight hours. When you look at the financial compensation you get for such work, it no longer seems as glamorous.

One of the biggest potential bummers of bar gigs is that your employment is at the whim of the club owner and is rarely secured with a contract. If the owner decides not to pay you for some reason, you often don't have much recourse. You could take him to small-claims court if he reneges on an agreement, but in most cases it won't be worth the time and trouble. I've been involved in a number of situations where an owner decided that because of a very low turnout he would lower our pay for the night. It's frustrating and maddening to be in that position, because you know damn well that if the club has an especially good night you'll never be paid *more* than what was agreed upon. You can't do much to defend against this injustice other than to be such a good band that club owners are afraid to alienate you and lose the business that you bring in.

Another downside to clubs is the working conditions. Almost every bar I've ever played in is extremely smoky. Despite the increase in anti-smoking regulations, the smoke level in nightclubs seems to be as high as ever. After playing a Friday-Saturday night engagement, not only do your clothes smell of smoke but your equipment does, too. With all the recent evidence linking second-hand smoke to heart disease, it's clear that too much playing in bars can be risky to your health.

Yet another hazard facing musicians in the nightclub environment is the drunks they must deal with on a regular basis. If you're working in a bar it's almost inescapable that you'll have some sort of dealings with inebriated patrons. Most of the time this interaction consists merely of having to listen to obnoxiously shouted requests, but it can occasionally get ugly if someone becomes confrontational. In the worst-case scenario, musicians can find themselves in the middle of a full-fledged bar fight. In my experience, such fights are relatively rare, but when they do occur, look out. Punches, chairs, and bodies fly, and the band is at risk of personal injury and damage to their equipment. If you're on a high stage you're often out of harm's way, but many clubs situate the band on or close to the floor, which is ground zero if a fight starts.

Perhaps the greatest occupational hazard that musicians face is the excessive noise levels they get exposed to at gigs (see "Protecting Your Hearing" in Chapter 2).

As long as we're talking negatives, remember that a musician playing bars will not have most of the rights and benefits that a normal employee does. A case in point: When office workers get the flu, they can call in sick. When nightclub musicians get the flu, they usually have to show up for work because more often than not there's no one to take their place and the band is depending on them. If you're lucky you'll know someone who can sub for you when you're under the weather. In many band situations, however, it's simply not practical to have a sub because it would be too hard for someone to justify learning a whole night's worth of material and only getting a few gigs a year out of it. Even if you do have a sub, or if the band can get by without you, the biggest drag about being sick is that you lose your night's pay if you can't make the gig.

If you're fortunate enough to be playing a job sanctioned by the musicians union, there will be provisions made for players getting ill. Unfortunately for all musicians, the great majority of nightclubs and bars do not fall under union jurisdiction. Consequently, the general rule of thumb for bar gigs is that unless you're at death's door or break a limb, you're expected to show up. Believe me, there are few things less pleasant than being in a smoky, extremely loud bar with a 102°F fever and a bad sore throat.

Another hazard you must guard against is falling asleep at the wheel. If you typically have to drive long distances to your gigs, you're going to be doing a lot of late-night driving, and the odds are that you'll often be very tired. I've had a number of scary occurrences when I've dozed off for a second and woken up as my car was starting to head off the road. The best way to avoid this is to try to get a lot of sleep the night before a gig. Unfortunately, this isn't always possible, so you may have to try some other things to keep yourself alert on those long drives. It helps to keep your alcohol consumption to a minimum on the gig. Not only will this help keep you from getting drowsy, but you'll also avoid the possibility of being legally drunk when you leave for home after the gig. Besides all the obvious dangers to yourself and others from drunk driving, if you were to get arrested for DWI you could lose your license for a while and have no way to get to your gigs. In any case, if you do find yourself dozing off at the wheel, try opening the window, cranking the radio, and stopping for a soda. If none of those solutions works, you may need to find a safe place to pull over and sleep for awhile.

Another driving-related dilemma you'll face as a bar musician is the problem of getting to gigs in dangerous weather conditions. Here's an example of what can happen: I once had a gig at a club that was about an hour-and-a-half away from home. Normally this would be no big deal, but on this particular night there was a major snowstorm. I called the club before leaving and they assured me that the gig was on. Finally, after a very slow and dangerous drive, I arrived at the club and set up my gear. We played one set to an empty house (only a musician would go out in such bad weather) and were informed by the club owner that they were canceling the rest of the night and we would only be getting half of our money.

More recently I had a freelance private party gig that was about an hour's drive from my house. On the night of the gig there were horrendous thunderstorms that knocked down countless trees, caused many power outages, and forced major sections of the main highway to be closed. I called the country club where the party was taking place and was shocked to hear that the gig was going on as planned. I then heard on the radio that the state police were advising all motorists to stay off the roads. At this point I decided that the $125 I was going to earn was not worth risking my life and my car, and I made the choice to stay home. My decision jeopardized my future work with that band, but I still feel that I made the right choice.

What these stories illustrate is the quandary gigging musicians find themselves in when you they have to get to jobs in dangerous conditions. You must make a tough choice, weighing the financial impact of blowing off the gig against the dangers you'll face trying to get there.

When you're "in" a band rather than freelancing, the pressure to show up at all costs is much stronger because you have a number of musicians who are dependent on you to make their money. Not only will this peer pressure manifest itself in bad weather or when you're sick, it will also be present when you're choosing which gigs to accept. Some band members want to take each and every gig that's offered, while others would rather be choosy and not always take those Thanksgiving or Christmas night gigs. You have to come to some sort of agreement about those kind of issues or you'll be in for a lot of internal dissension. Everyone in a band is coming from (at least slightly) different financial situations, and therefore have different needs and expectations when it comes to accepting work. Learn to compromise. Believe me, it's worth it in the long run.

GETTING INTO A BAND

Unless you're a solo act, your first priority when starting out as a working musician is to get into a gigging band. Later on you might choose to work freelance (more on that later in this chapter), but the best way to launch your career is to get into a working band.

Surveying the Scene

Just as in any other job-hunting situation, the key to getting into a bar band is to network. Not only do you need to make contacts, but you've also got to demonstrate to people how well you can play. Before you can really get started, you need to familiarize yourself with the clubs in your area that feature the type of music you play. In many places there are groups of clubs featuring the same musical style that become de facto *circuits* or *scenes.* The successful bands on that scene will probably play in most, if not all, of the clubs on the circuit.

In most urban and suburban areas, you can find some sort of alternative newspaper that features club listings. *The Village Voice* in New York and the *Boston Phoenix* are two examples of such papers. If you look in music stores you can often find freebie music papers that are basically glorified club listings. If you're hooked into the Internet, there are plenty of Web sites devoted to concert and club listings that may be of help in your search (see Appendix for examples of these sites).

Taking Stock of Your Contacts

Once you have an idea of what's happening in the clubs around you, you should think about the people you already know who may be able to help you along in your search for a gig. You may be pleasantly surprised at the length of your list. Think of anyone you know who is remotely involved with the live music scene. This can include friends, friends of friends, former music teachers, people you know who work at the music store, and so on.

Write all the names down and systematically call them. Tell them what you're trying to do and see if they know of any bands or singers looking for musicians. Getting a direct introduction from someone you know is almost always more effective than dealing with strangers. However, if you can't come up with any names, or if the ones you come up with don't lead anywhere, the following sections will give you some advice as to how to develop your own leads for getting into a working band.

Using the Classifieds

In the same newspapers that provide club listings, you'll usually find a section of musician's classified ads. Using the classifieds is the most direct (although not always the most successful) method of getting into a band. When you answer an ad you'll most likely get called to go to an audition, where you can show your stuff.

A few words of caution regarding classified ads: Many of the ads are for bands playing original material that are trying to get signed and are not aiming specifically for making money on the bar circuit. If you're looking for paying gigs, these bands are probably not for you. Ask about the goals for the band and whether they're currently working. If they say something like, "No man, but after we get a record deal we'll be touring a lot," you should thank them and hang up. You want to find bands that are actually out there doing gigs. It's often very difficult to judge whether a band has a realistic chance of getting signed and you don't want to waste a lot of time in a spec project that's going nowhere. Having said that, joining an original band is an option you should consider if you're getting nowhere in your search for a working band. Despite the fact that you'll be doing a lot of uncompensated work, it can help you make some connections and get more experience.

If your search of the classifieds does land you an audition with a working band, you've got a shot at getting into the circuit right away. Try to find out before the audition what material you'll be expected to play, and do whatever you have to do to familiarize yourself with it in advance. If you're comfortable with the songs, you'll play better at the audition and you'll stand a much better chance of getting hired.

On the day (or night) of the audition, allow yourself plenty of extra time and make sure not to be late. When you arrive, look good, be friendly, and try to act as confident as possible. If there are other players auditioning for the same position, keep your cool and don't get unnerved or distracted by them. Focus instead on doing the best job you can, and hope that your talent will win out for you.

Publicizing Yourself

Just as in the business world, most of the job openings in bands don't get advertised in the classifieds; instead, they're filled by word of mouth. In order to maximize your opportunities you need to start making contacts, and the best way to do that is to make yourself known on the circuit. Think of yourself as a new product on the market that needs to be advertised before anyone will know to buy it.

Passing Out the Cards One thing you should get right away is some business cards. They don't necessarily have to be flashy; just make sure they have your name, instrument, and phone number on them. Always carry some cards with you, and be sure to put one up in any music store or rehearsal studio where you see a bulletin board.

Whenever you meet another musician or someone related to the business, give him or her a card. Handing someone a card gives you a good opening to mention your search for a band. After you've met somebody and spoken to him or her for a few minutes, you can hand over your card and say something like, "By the way, I'm looking to get into a working band, so if you hear of anyone looking, please call me or give him or her my number."

Sitting In and Jamming One of the best ways to develop contacts is to hang out at the clubs where you'd like to be playing. By getting to know the musicians at these clubs and sitting in with them, you may be able to start making a reputation for yourself. Sitting in is a particularly common occurrence on the jazz scene. According to New York–based guitarist Mark McCarron, "There is still somewhat of a tradition in jazz of being able to sit in. And it just means that you have to know the standard tunes, so that when you get up there you know what is going on. Jazz people take a lot of stock in the person knowing the music."

No matter what style you play, sitting in is the best way, short of actually being on a gig, to show off your abilities as a live player. Begin by making a list of the clubs that feature your kind of music and start frequenting them. Talk to band members and try to get a sense of what's happening on the club scene. If you develop a rapport with any of the musicians, you might eventually want to ask them if you can sit in for a song or two. If they say no, politely thank them. If they say yes, make sure that it's a song that you know (at least a little), then go up there and kick some butt. Remember that unless you're just going up there to sing, you'll probably be playing someone else's instrument and that might hinder you somewhat. If you play well you'll have earned the respect of the players in the band, and you'll stand a much better chance of getting recommended for some gigs.

Another good way to network is to go to organized jam sessions at clubs. Check the club ads in the newspapers and ask around to see if you can find one. The Internet is also a good place to find listings of jam sessions (see Appendix). Jam sessions seem to be particularly popular at blues and jazz clubs, but you can find them in other types of music as well.

The problem with jams is that they attract all types of musicians, both good and bad. Whom you end up playing with is usually a matter of luck, and it can be a major bummer if you wait all night to play only to find yourself onstage with a bunch of hacks. No matter how good you are, bad players will always drag you down to their level, so whenever possible try to play with the best musicians in the joint.

In any case, going to jam sessions gives you the opportunity to make some good contacts and show your stuff. Don't forget to bring plenty of business cards and hand them out liberally.

Making Your Demo You might also consider putting together a demo tape of your playing. Ideally, you can use portions of live tapes from previous bands that you've been in, as long as these tapes show off your playing and have reasonably good fidelity. It's probably best not to use entire songs, but rather segments of the songs that spotlight your ability. If you don't have any such material on hand and you have access to recording equipment, consider making a studio demo.

Either way, you want to end up with a tape containing relatively brief examples of your best playing. Unless you have access to digital editing equipment, edit your song sections to fade in and out, as this allows easy transitions from one piece to the next. Keep the spaces between pieces very short (no more than half a second) so that your listener doesn't have a chance to hit the stop button before a new piece starts. Assume that whomever is listening has a short attention span and edit accordingly.

If you want to be super-aggressive, hand out tapes whenever you give someone your business card. Anything that shows off your playing and helps people remember you is a valuable tool in your search for work.

Bear in mind that this type of demo isn't a necessity for getting work, so you don't need to spend a large amount of money to hire a commercial studio to record it for you. If, between you and your friends, you don't have the equipment to record your own tape, focus your energy on other avenues of publicity.

Getting Work as a Freelancer

Once you've earned a reputation as a good player, it's sometimes possible to work as a freelancer rather than in just one band. This gives you more freedom to take only the gigs you want. Conversely, when you're in a band full-time, you generally have to play whatever gigs get booked, regardless of how inconvenient they might be for your schedule.

I've done a lot of freelance gigs where I filled in for regular band members who are sick, out of town, or have taken another booking. You'll also find that some bands have a core group of regular members and use freelancers only when they want to expand their lineup for selected gigs.

You'll find freelancing to be more common on blues and country circuits and anywhere the material is more standardized and less rehearsed. Your ability to freelance on a consistent basis will probably depend a lot on which circuit you're on. The bulk of freelance opportunities occur with cover bands because freelancers are much more likely to know at least some of the repertoire. Even if their material is all covers, many bands will send freelancers a tape and/or some charts in advance so that they can familiarize themselves as much as possible with the songs and the arrangements before the gig.

As a freelancer, you need to know a lot of material and have very good ears so that you can follow along with songs you've never played before. You also need to be able to take direction and fit in with the band. It's important that you have a good idea of what's expected of you in that particular type of gig and follow it to the letter.

There are also opportunities for freelancers to play showcase gigs with artists who are looking to get signed. These jobs often consist of one or two paid rehearsals and a gig. These can be fun because you're almost always playing original material in decent clubs. More important, you're often playing with good musicians, because when someone's putting a showcase together they generally try to hire the best people available. These are excellent situations to make contacts and try to enhance your reputation.

At or before the first rehearsal for this type of job, you'll probably be given charts of the material, so the ability to read (at least chord charts) is very helpful. Often the artist will send you a tape and expect you to familiarize yourself with the material prior to rehearsal. If you're not comfortable reading charts, make sure to spend a lot of time with the tape. When you get to that rehearsal you want to be able to play through the songs confidently. If you consistently have trouble following the music, you run the risk of making yourself look bad in the eyes of the very musicians you're trying to impress.

BAR BAND SURVIVAL GUIDE

Here are a few tips to help make your bar gigs more enjoyable and stress-free:

• Arrive early at all your gigs. Allow yourself enough time so that after you set up, you still have a half hour or so before the show starts. This gives you a chance to relax and focus before the gig starts and also allows a little buffer just in case you hit traffic on the way to the club.

• Always be nice to the waitresses and bartenders. Even though you're also an employee at the bar, tip them and treat them well. If they're on your side they can make your life a lot easier. In some cases, their opinions can even influence whether you're hired back or not.

• Go easy on the drinking. Nobody likes to watch a drunk onstage. Under no circumstances should you smoke a joint before or between sets. Contrary to popular myth, it does not help you play better; it only makes you lose your focus. I'm not suggesting that you become a choirboy (or girl); just treat your gig like the job that it is and things will go a lot more smoothly.

• Make sure the front person of the band talks to the audience during the set. Develop a rapport and, whatever you do, don't be stand-offish. Never insult anyone in the crowd, regardless of how dumb a request they might make.

• Use a set list and work hard to keep the time between songs to a minimum. It looks very unprofessional to watch a band discussing their next song for two minutes before they play it.

• No matter how mad you are at each other, *never argue onstage.* It looks incredibly unprofessional. Work out your problems at rehearsal, or when nobody's there to see you. When you're in front of your audience, it's important to present an image of unity.

• Always bring spares for anything that routinely breaks while playing, such as strings, picks, sticks, and drumheads.

• If at all possible, test the PA before most of the crowd comes into the club. I doubt that many people want to hear the inevitable feedback that occurs when monitor levels are set, or the bass player saying "check one, two" thirty times. If you want to appear professional, make sure the system is set and squared away well before the show starts.

Getting Along With Your Fellow Musicians

After you've spent a great deal of time and effort getting yourself into a working situation, you want to make sure that you don't get into conflicts that might lead to your getting fired.

Musicians by nature have strong egos, and when you put four or five of them together in a band the disagreements can be monumental. This is especially true in a group where everyone has equal say in the decision-making.

Although there's no way to avoid having differences of opinion, you can help the situation by being conciliatory rather than confrontational. Pick your battles and be willing to compromise. In short, be professional. I've seen too many situations where a good band is torn apart by internal dissension. You'll have a much better chance of advancing your career if you're able to get along with your fellow players.

You'll probably also find that a lot of bandleaders and front persons can be extremely hard to get along with. Their egos are often the largest in the band, and they often have somewhat quirky personalities. If you want to keep your gig, you need to figure out a way to get along with them. I learned that lesson the hard way many years ago, when I was working with a lead singer who was a few notches past quirky, perhaps even bordering on unstable. During a club set he kept telling me to change my volume (both up and down) over and over again. I finally got tired of it, and just as we finished the last song of the set, I quietly told him to piss off. We were still onstage when he picked up his guitar and twirled it threateningly in the air while screaming curses at me. Meanwhile, everyone in the club was staring at us. Needless to say, it was not a very pleasant situation.

GETTING GIGS FOR YOUR BAND

Until now, we've concentrated on how an individual musician can get into a band. This next section is dedicated to helping existing (or future) bands get more work.

Putting Together a Press Kit

Before you can start looking for bookings, you need to put together a press kit. In order to do so, you'll need the following items:

Logo Besides being attractive, a good logo conceptually represents the musical style and attitude of your band. It will be on all your promotional materials, including photos, letterhead, and tape labels, so make sure that it's strong. Maybe someone in the band knows a graphic designer who can design your logo for you.

If you don't have any friends who are able to design a logo and have no money to hire someone, you can do a low-budget logo using just a personal computer and printer. Find a *display typeface* which has some characteristics that fit your band's image and use it to render your logo. If you have access to any clip art and can find an appropriate image to go with the name, consider incorporating that into the design as well.

If you use a hand-drawn or handlettered logo, have it scanned at a computer service bureau so that it can be inserted into all your word-processing documents pertaining to the band. If the logo is computer-generated, make sure it can be converted to a format that's compatible with your word processor and any graphics programs you're using to put your publicity together.

8-by-10 Photo A good publicity photo is always an important element in creating a professional look for your band. Usually at least one of the band members knows a photographer who can be cajoled into doing a photo session. Try to arrange it so that the setting of the photo is appropriate for the musical style. For example, if you're a country band you might want to consider a rustic outdoor setting. If you're a rock band, an urban backdrop might be best. Whatever you do, try to be original. You don't want your photo to be one of those ubiquitous, cookie-cutter publicity shots that are completely forgettable. You want something to stand out in this photo that people will remember. On the other hand, don't get so artsy that your photo is hard to fathom.

When you do get your photos printed, go to a photographic house that's accustomed to printing publicity shots. They'll arrange it so that your prints will feature a white strip along the bottom that contains your logo and contact information.

Song List This one's pretty self-explanatory. Have a list printed out on your band letterhead with your songs listed either in alphabetical order or by style (for example, "Ballads" or "Up-Tempo

Rockers"). As innocuous as it might sound, it's very helpful for a club owner to see a song list when evaluating a new band.

Band Bio Here you want to provide a succinct listing of pertinent information regarding your band, such as names of band members and the instruments they play, where you've appeared, and any name acts you've opened for. Make sure your contact information is clearly visible. If you're friendly with any well-known musicians in your area, consider asking them for a quote, then display any such quotes prominently on your bio.

Press Clippings On a separate sheet (or sheets) you might want to put reprints of any press clippings your band has gotten. Probably the easiest way to generate press clippings is to get reviewed by college newspapers. If you're going to be playing at a college, contact the paper there and ask them to review your gig. Since one of the main reasons that college papers exist is to give journalism students experience at writing, they're often eager for the opportunity to review your show.

Business Cards It's always good to include business cards in all publicity materials that you distribute. Above your contact information should be your logo and a three- or four-word description, such as "Red Hot R&B."

There are some labeling programs for computers that allow you to print your own business cards, but I don't recommend going that route. By necessity they require flimsy stock (the real heavy stock won't feed through most printers), which makes the final result look somewhat cheesy. It's not all that expensive to have your cards commercially printed, and the results are much more professional-looking.

Demo Tape A good-quality demo is an essential item when looking for gigs. If your band has not recorded yet, now is the time to consider it. If the band can come up with the money to do it in a professional studio, go for it. If not, it's likely that someone in your band or one of your friends has a home-studio setup. The problem with recording at home is that you won't have the high quality of equipment that you would in the studio. The flip side is that when you're recording at home, you don't have to watch the clock the way you do in the studio, and consequently you can spend a lot more time on everything.

If the home studio you're recording in has an Alesis ADAT or a Tascam DA-88 (or another modular digital multitrack that's compatible with one of those two standard formats), you can record the basic tracks in a professional studio that uses the same format and do the overdubs and mixes at home. This allows you to get a much better drum sound than you probably could in a home studio, yet saves a lot on costs. It also gives you the option of bringing your multitrack masters back to the studio to mix. Although it's more expensive, the results of getting your tape professionally mixed might be worth it.

Another option is to do a live tape. Although the sonic quality is not as good as a studio demo, recording live does have some advantages. For one thing, some club owners and agents give more credence to a live tape because it's more likely to be an accurate representation of what a band can do in a performance situation, since a good-sounding studio demo may be more reflective of the producer and the engineer's skill than the band's. An additional advantage of recording live is that you can usually do it for less money than it might take to record in the studio.

The various methods of taping a live performance vary greatly in quality and degree of difficulty. The best method (from the standpoint of sound quality) is to use a multitrack deck (preferably digital) and have an engineer in a truck outside the club or in an isolated room. You'll need mic or direct-out feeds from all the vocal mics and instruments, which can be sent to the remote location from the live mixing board via a *snake,* which is a very long multi-connector cable that allows you to connect two or more pieces of gear that are far apart. Assuming that your tape deck is only eight tracks, the engineer will have to do a submix on the drums and possibly the background vocals in order to fit everything into the available tracks. Nonetheless, you'll still have enough separation of the individual elements to do a mix at a later date.

Another way to go is to have the remote engineer record a live mix directly to a DAT (digital audiotape recorder) instead of a multitrack. This will save you time (and money) because you won't have to go through the mixing phase. The downside of using this method is that you've got less control over the final product because the engineer will have already made the mixing decisions while he was recording your performance.

An easier but lower-quality option is to have someone in the audience with a portable DAT and a good-quality stereo mic. The advantage of this approach is that it's much less of a big deal to set up and therefore may allow you to record more than one show. You then have the luxury of choosing from different versions of the same songs. The biggest problem is that you're liable to pick up a great deal of audience noise on the tape. Though it's nice to have the sound of people cheering and clapping between songs, the sound of people sneezing, laughing, or ordering from the waitress is not something most bands would want on their demo tapes.

A last resort is a DAT made directly from the tape-outs of the mixing board at the club. The problem with this is that levels are likely to be out of whack because the board is set for the mix in the club rather than the one going to tape. Any instruments that are loud coming off the stage won't need to be pumped through the board as much, and will therefore be under-represented on the live tape. Nevertheless, it's worth a try because you might get lucky with the mix, and at worst you'll have a good way to evaluate and critique your own performances.

When it comes to mixing, there are a few points to keep in mind regardless of whether your tracking was done live or in the studio. If you're going to be mixing at a commercial studio, let the engineer set up the mix to the point where he thinks it's right. You can then make small changes to suit your taste. Remember that most engineers have learned through experience what sounds good in a mix, so you should put a lot of weight in their opinion. You don't want to spend a lot of money tracking only to walk out with a lousy mix.

If you're mixing at a home studio, you won't have the benefit of a professional engineer (unless you hire one, which is a great idea if you can afford it) but you will have the luxury of time. Ideally, after you finish mixing a song you should leave all of the settings in place and wait until the next day before you listen again. Mixing is an intense process, during which you can easily lose your objectivity; taking an overnight break is the best way to recover it.

If you can't wait until the next day, at least take an hour or two off. I can almost guarantee that it'll be beneficial. If after your break the mix still sounds good, and it sounds good on other systems besides the one at the studio, you've probably done a good job. Even on a good mix you're still likely to notice that some minor adjustments need to be made.

One method to help you make your mix sound better is to find a CD of a band that plays the same kind of music as yours and compare your mix to a similar song on that disk. Try to match the equalization (tone settings, known as *EQ)* and the relative volume levels between instruments as much as possible, and be especially careful to get the bottom end (bass) sounding similar. Using this method gives you perspective and helps you avoid having a tape in which the levels are completely out of whack.

If at all possible, do your final mix on to a DAT and include at least three songs. If you have more than that, put the best three at the top, as it's unlikely that a club owner will have the time to listen to any more than that. If you have access to a computer-based digital editor, you can play around with the order of the songs until you're completely satisfied.

Once you're done mixing and you're happy with the sequence of the songs, it's time to make copies. For a band trying to get gigs playing cover material, it may not be cost-effective to have CDs pressed for your demos. Although CDs are a lot more impressive, they're pretty expensive to reproduce commercially. If you do want to use the CD format but don't have a lot of money to spend, here are some suggestions. If you or a friend has a recordable CD-ROM drive, you can make a limited run of CDs for the cost of the discs (around $7 per disk at the time of this writing). It's very time-consuming to make copies in this way, so you probably won't be able to make too many.

Another solution is to find a duplication house that can make a small number of copies for you. Look in the classified sections in the back of magazines such as *Electronic Musician* and *Keyboard.* I was able to find places that would do five CDs for $100. If you spent $300 and had fifteen CDs made, you'd probably have enough to cover most of the clubs you're targeting. Consider it this way: If you get just one gig from your efforts, you'll most likely come close to covering most of the cost of "burning" (pressing) your CDs.

Whether you use CD or cassette, try to have your logo, a list of the songs, and a contact phone number printed on your cassettes or disks (or on labels affixed to them). Many duplication houses offer help with graphics as part of their services.

If you're using cassettes and having them copied at a duplication house, make sure that they make your copies in real time. High-speed duplicators are acceptable for voice-only tapes, but they sound like cardboard for music. Also, arrange for your copies to be made on the best-quality high-bias cassettes they have.

Videotape (Optional) A video makes a good supplement to a CD or cassette because the club owner can see the band as well as hear it. If you know anyone who is a videographer, or if you have access to some good-quality gear, you may be able to make a live video without spending too much money. Like the demo, keep your video short and only include your best material on it. You may even want to consider using only sections of the songs in order to keep the attention of the viewer. Remember, it's not MTV; you just want to show off your band's capabilities in the most efficient and effective way possible.

Another strategy for getting a video made is to contact your cable TV company to see if there are any local access music shows in your area. It's sometimes possible to get booked on one of these shows and get a video copy of your appearance. An edited version of this can serve as your band video.

Although a video is not essential to get club bookings, it can certainly be helpful. If it doesn't cost you too much to get one made, go for it. If not, you can get gigs with other types of publicity.

Your Finished Press Kit Once you've assembled all this material, you've got yourself a press kit consisting of your 8 x 10 photo, song list, band bio, business cards, press clippings (if you have any), demo, and video (optional). Now it's time to get some gigs!

One word of caution concerning costs: As much as you might want to have the best-quality tape, slick graphics, and a flashy video, don't spend more than you can possibly recoup from the gigs you're going after. Your expenditures should make sense from a business standpoint.

If your band is already working, take an extra cut of the pay and create a band fund that pays for promotional expenses.

Pounding the Pavement

Once you've put together your press kit, make a list of the names and phone numbers of appropriate clubs that are within about two hours' driving distance. You probably won't want to consider anything farther than that on a consistent basis, because the traveling time will be brutal.

Before you begin calling, do some research. Ask any working musicians you know for information regarding these clubs. Try to find out who does the booking at each club, what the club pays, and what its like to work there. Write all of this down on your list so that you're armed with as much information as possible when you call. For certain clubs, this information is published in directories such as *The Musician's Guide to Touring and Promotion,* or can be found at sites on the Internet (see Appendix, "Playing Live"). At any given club, you'll invariably find that it's difficult to reach the person in charge of booking, whether it's the club owner or someone else on staff.

After you've done as much research as possible, it's time to start dialing. Systematically call each club and ask to speak to the person who books the bands. It's best to call in the afternoon when the club is quiet and the people who work there are less busy and frantic. Most likely you won't reach the appropriate person on the first try, but make sure to ask for his or her name, when the best time to call back would be, and the name of the person with whom you're speaking.

You may have to be pretty persistent, but eventually you should be able to reach the booking person. One trick you can use is to always ask for him or her by first name only. This may cause the person answering the phone to assume that you're a friend or acquaintance and put you through more readily.

When you've finally reached the booking person, succinctly explain your band's situation and why you think you'd be a good draw for this particular club. Mention that you would like to stop by to meet them and drop off a press kit, then try to set up an appointment. If he or she is resistant, say you'll drop one by the next time you're in the area. Stop by the club the following week at the same day and time that you spoke on the phone. With a little luck, the booking person will be there and you might be able to meet. It's more likely that someone will remember your name after you've met face to face, as opposed to just talking on the phone.

You can also use this "ambush" method for clubs where you've had trouble reaching the booking person on the phone. Try stopping by (in the afternoon) in the hope that he or she will be around. At the very least, leave your press kit.

Keep in mind that booking people are inundated with requests for bookings, and may not have much patience for you if you become a pest. You want to be persistent, but don't cross the line or you may never get a booking there.

When you do go in for an appointment, try to play your demo or video while you're there. Even if they seem to like it, don't expect a prime booking immediately. If you've impressed the owner (or other booking person) enough, you might get offered an off night that they need to fill. If you do well on that gig, then you can reasonably expect some better bookings.

Remember that even if the people who run the club are bowled over by your stuff, they may not have any open dates to give you right away. In that case, you should make a point of calling or sending a postcard every month to remind them of your band's existence. Mention other places in the area where you've played since you last spoke. If you come up with any new recorded material, send a cassette. If you remain persistent, you have a much better chance of eventually getting some gigs. One important point: Once you've finally reached the club booker, it's imperative that you know the future availability of your bandmates, so that if you're offered a gig you can take it without hesitation. If you're unsure and have to check with everyone, you might lose the gig before you're able to give an answer.

If at all possible, try to talk to some of the other bands that play in the clubs you're targeting to find out what a typical night's pay is. That way, if you're offered a gig you'll have a ballpark idea of what to ask for. Some clubs have a standard rate (depending on the night of the week) that they pay all but the best draws, while others negotiate separately with each band.

One of the obstacles that you're likely to run up against is that even if the club is impressed by your tape and publicity materials, the club owner may insist on seeing you live before you get a booking. If you don't have any other gigs, this puts you in a rather difficult position. Depending on the club you're trying to get into, it can be worth your while to take a freebie gig somewhere else as a venue to showcase your act.

Even if you do have somewhere for the club owner to see you play, it can sometimes be maddening to motivate him or her to make the date. If he or she doesn't show up, don't get angry (at least not in his or her presence); just bite your lip and extend an invitation to another gig.

Audition Nights

Occasionally you'll find clubs that have audition nights for which any band can sign up to do a set or a few songs. You don't get paid for these auditions, but conceivably they can lead to a paying gig. You then have to decide among yourselves whether it's worth the trouble. If you do decide to do an audition, try to make sure that the club owner or booking person will be there when you play so that you're not wasting your time.

Once you've got the gig, invite as many friends as possible to come down and hear you. This will ensure that you have a responsive audience. It'll make the band feel more at ease to have some friendly faces there, and if your friends buy a lot of drinks, the owner will be happy, too.

Things To Watch Out For

Club owners, as a group, are not held in very high esteem by most working musicians. In some of the bands I was in, we used to joke that they were only slightly higher than amoebae on the evolutionary scale. The reason for this resentment is that club owners have historically treated musicians rather shabbily. Because of the intense competition for gigs, owners often exploit bands, many of whom are so eager to work that they don't even realize they're being taken advantage of.

If a club owner offers you a gig that pays nothing but will give you lots of "exposure," your alarm bells should start going off. Many club owners use the carrot of publicity to cajole bands into playing for nothing. Remember, if there's a decent crowd in the bar and the club is making money, you should be too. Only take a free-bie gig if it's a benefit for charity or if it's absolutely in the band's best interests (such as an audition night). All bets are off if you're an original band that's trying to get gigs to showcase its own music. In that case, the only gigs you may be able to get are at clubs where getting paid is not part of the equation.

Even when you're trying to get paying work, the specter of the freebie gig is never far away. I remember a club in New Jersey that used to have something called a "jamboree" every couple of weeks. They'd book five or six bands that worked at the club to play a set each on a Sunday afternoon or evening. Only the house band (which had to provide amps and drums and stay there all day) would get paid. The club owner made it clear that the jamborees were mandatory if you wanted to keep working at his club. Conse-quently, many of the bands ended up playing more free gigs than paying ones! Why the musicians put up with it is beyond me, but it goes to show how exploitable people are in this business. It would have been one thing if the club had produced a jamboree twice a year and donated the proceeds to charity, but the money from these shows was going directly into the pocket of the club owner.

Be wary of "door" gigs as well. These are gigs for which the band isn't guaranteed any money but instead gets all or a percentage of the admission charge. If you're going to do a gig like this, make sure you have one of your friends either taking the money at the door or counting the paid admissions. I've heard many stories of bands get-ting shorted when the club purposely miscounted the door. Assum-ing that you're in a band whose prime motivation is to make money from gigs, you should only do a door gig if you know that you'll be able to draw in enough people to make a reasonable amount. Oth-erwise the gig becomes a dreary exercise in frustration.

It's only fair to point out that while there have been many abus-es of musicians perpetrated by club owners, there are plenty of friendly, honest club owners out there. Your best approach when dealing with a club is to keep an open mind, but watch your back.

In the interest of fairness it should also be mentioned that many musicians abuse their privileges and try to take advantage of the clubs in which they play. This can take the form of starting late,

Q&A **LOU ROSS**

NATIONAL ASSOCIATION OF CAMPUS ACTIVITIES

The Lowdown on College Gigs

In this interview, NACA official Lou Ross provides some insights into the college music scene.

Are fraternities and sororities still having a lot of parties for which they hire live music?
Yes, they are. Although there was definitely a drop-off in the number of live music acts that were hired for quite a while, it seems to be on the upswing again. More acts are being hired again to play at schools. . . . Fraternities and sororities are still booking bands, still doing house parties and things, and still going nuts.

What types of venues do touring indie bands typically play at colleges?
There are a lot of different types of venues, as you might expect. Some people are just putting them in cafeterias. Other people still have pubs, so to speak; actually, there are a few colleges that still serve alcohol. A lot of them are going nonalcoholic—pubs, coffeehouses, those types of things. . . . Some of them have ballrooms, or large, multipurpose rooms where they might do a band. And there's still a high number of outdoor events that are held when the weather is good enough for that. . . . Then, as you move up in price, some people have small auditoriums on campus, things like that. . . . It seems like a lot of folks are still booking a lot of local acts on campus. . . . It seems like the local acts are getting an opportunity to play.

Because their prices are lower?
Yeah, exactly. And also the production end of things. Because a lot of the students now are used to buying comedy and novelty things ["interactive" entertainment such as "human bowling," inflatable obstacle courses, and Velcro walls]. Obviously, with comedians, you

taking overly long breaks, performing while intoxicated, or not making an effort to put on a good show. If you expect to be treated fairly, it behooves you to act in as professional a manner as possible.

Getting College Gigs
Another area where you can find gigs is at colleges. Make a list of the colleges in your area and research them. Call the main office and ask

give them a microphone and they're ready to go. The novelty things are pretty much self-contained. So there's not a lot of desire, or maybe even funding, for the production necessary to put a band on. So some of the local acts that can come in with their own sound and lights or whatever, just bring it in and perform. It's a lot easier that way. [When] putting a band on the road, probably one of the most difficult things is dealing with the sound and light situation.

Are these road bands mostly booked through agents?
I think probably the majority of them would have to be, but there are still some folks who are representing themselves and having good success with it.

Tell me a little bit about what NACA does.
We're an association of colleges and universities, and our members look to us to seek out educational needs. We do a lot of workshops and seminars and help students and staff learn about their jobs on campus. We do specific things like how to book a band, how to negotiate contracts, all the way to more issue-oriented things like AIDS awareness and sexual harassment. But then we also have this link to the entertainment industry, with agencies and performers who are also members, which try to reach colleges through our mailing list. We do eleven conferences and regional shows, then one national convention every year. And then each of those shows has an educational component, as well as an exhibit hall . . . where the exhibitors are again the entertainment folks. You can book anything you can think of there: jugglers, hypnotists, lectures, and films, as well as music, comedy, and other types of entertainment.

Can individual bands contact you and get listed with you?
Yes. And other bands will contact us looking for agents who can help them in the college market. . . . We'll provide them with a list of agencies in the market as well. We can help them get direct access themselves, or we can give them some information to help get an agent.

who handles the booking for college events. Also, find out whether there are any on-campus pubs, coffeehouses, or other establishments that feature live entertainment.

Obtain a list of the fraternities and sororities at the college and contact them as well. Ask for the names of the entertainment chairpersons for each organization. Frat houses and sororities often have parties, for which they sometimes hire live bands.

Once you've compiled a list of names at each college, use the same type of systematic publicity campaign that you did with the clubs. Your chances of getting booked will be enhanced if you keep track of all the correspondence, calls, and meetings that occur during your search for gigs. If you're systematic in your record keeping, you won't forget important dates, meeting times, and follow-up calls, and you'll generally be more productive (this same principle applies to club gigs as well).

For further assistance in getting college gigs you should contact the National Association for Campus Activities, or NACA. This organization can give you information regarding college bookings as well as a list of agents that handle campus activities. They also have conventions and shows at which member bands can exhibit and try to pick up bookings. For more information, call NACA at (803) 732-6222 (see Appendix for a complete listing); see also the interview on pages 70–71 with NACA official Lou Ross.

ONCE YOU HAVE SOME GIGS

Once your band starts working, you have to take some steps to build and maintain your following. The people who come out to see you on a regular basis are the key to your success on the bar circuit. Club owners measure a band's worth not by musicianship (many club owners wouldn't know good musicianship if they heard it), but by the amount of cash in their registers at the end of the night.

Creating a Mailing List

Once your band starts working on a regular or semiregular basis, you need to do all you can to create momentum that will keep you headed in a successful direction. One of the tools that can help with this is a mailing list.

If you put together a list of friends, acquaintances, club owners, and people you've met at gigs, you'll have enough names to start your list. Send out a monthly mailing of postcards that list your upcoming gigs and any interesting band news, such as the release of a new demo.

You can also hand out flyers at your gigs that list the same information as your postcards. Just be sure that the club owner doesn't object to your promoting gigs that won't all be taking place at his or her club.

Another way to generate publicity for your appearances is to put up flyers. You can either print up, or have printed, a generic flyer with the band's logo and maybe a photo. You can then write or print the appropriate information for each particular gig and make photocopies to put up.

Look for bulletin boards at colleges, music stores, laundromats, and copy shops. Having your flyers around town helps keep the visibility of the band high. Avoid putting them up on public property such as lampposts and telephone poles, or you run the risk of attracting the ill will of your local magistrates.

Refining Your Material

Once your band has begun working on a steady basis, you'll have played enough gigs to start getting a sense of what works—and what doesn't—on your song list. Make it a goal to systematically learn new songs so that you can weed out the bad stuff and keep your sets fresh and current (where applicable). If there are people who regularly follow your band, you don't want to bore them by playing the same material every time they see you. You also don't want the band members to get bored, or the result will be lackluster performances.

Work, too, on the segues between songs, the onstage patter, and all other aspects of your "act." The more professional you appear, the more likely you are to get more work. Try to watch other bands perform, especially the successful ones, and see how they relate to the audience. Make it your goal to be as entertaining and audience-friendly as possible. This helps assure that you'll build a large and loyal following.

Being an Opening Act

One way to generate good publicity is for your group to be an opening act at a club that books well-known artists. There are plenty of medium-sized to large clubs that bring in name acts on a fairly regular basis. If you're already working at one of these clubs, ask the owner if you can be an opening band. If you haven't worked at the club yet, mention that you're interested in opening slots when you speak to the owner.

Being an opener is a good way to expose your group to a large crowd, plus it looks great in your band's press kit. You don't usually make much money, but this is one instance where the benefits more than compensate for the low pay.

As an opening act, you should expect to be treated like a second-class citizen when it comes to sound checks, dressing rooms, advertising, and other extras. Don't take it personally; that's just the way it goes when you're second banana.

The most important thing when you're opening for a name act is to not get too nervous or hyped up. The first couple of times I played on the same bill with a national act, I was extremely tense and did not have good gigs. I was trying so hard to prove to the headlining band what a great guitarist I was that I ended up doing just the opposite. Just treat it like another gig and you'll come off much better and more naturally.

Booking Agencies

For the majority of local bar gigs, there are no booking agencies involved. You do occasionally find a club who uses an agent, though, and since they also handle most of the corporate private and party gigs, it's probably a good idea to contact any agencies you can find in your area. Usually an agent charges a commission in the neighborhood of 15 percent when they book you on a job.

Agencies can be very useful for booking out-of-town gigs and tours. The following section will detail those kinds of bookings.

Touring with a Band

There are bands that travel all over the United States and Canada to play at medium-sized to large clubs. Most of these bands don't have major label record contracts, and they don't make great money, but they do get to spend almost all of their time touring. Many clubs on this circuit book cover bands, but there is also a growing number of venues in cities and college towns that hire "indie" bands to play original music.

As mentioned earlier, one type of venue that's experienced heavy growth in recent years is the casino lounge. Throughout the United States, there are many more gambling establishments than there used to be, and virtually all of them hire bands. In fact, many bands play on tours that go from one gambling facility to the next.

In less populated parts of the country there often aren't enough quality local bands to play at the clubs, so traveling bands fill the void. Playing in a traveling band is a grinding way to make a living, and the pay is not great, but if you like life on the road it can be fun.

If you want to get in on the traveling circuit, your best shot is to get hooked up with a booking agency. (The one exception to that is the indie rock circuit, on which bands commonly book their own tours.) Once you've played for a while in your local area and refined your act, you may be ready for the road.

The best way to get yourself out there is to convince an agency that your band has what it takes to be successful at touring. You need to be polished and commercial, and have good equipment and reliable transportation. Investigate the reputation of an agency before you agree to let them book you. Not all agencies are alike, so you want to make sure you're hooked up with a dependable one. When you're out on the road, your happiness and livelihood rest squarely in the hands of your booking agent.

Also, be very wary of signing exclusive booking agreements unless the agency guarantees you a specific amount of work in the contract. In addition, there should be an escape clause for the band in case the agency doesn't deliver the amount of work it promised. If an agency wants you to sign an exclusive contract, you should have a qualified entertainment attorney review it for you first.

If you do need to hire such a lawyer, be sure to get a recommendation from someone you trust (never use anyone suggested to you by the booking agency). Attorneys are very expensive, so you want to make sure your money is being spent for competent representation. A bad attorney can blow the deal or negotiate unfavorable terms for you, so be careful.

The most important part of the booking agent's job is to book your band in decent and appropriate clubs. Many of these gigs are for five or six nights consecutively, except on the college/indie rock circuit, where they tend to be one-nighters. In the case of multiple-night engagements, it's essential that the band and the club be compatible. If your agent has overhyped your group to a club owner and promised stuff you can't deliver, you could be in for a long week. Worse yet, you could be fired after a day or two

PROFILE | **THE ZOOKEEPERS**

An Inside Look at a Working Band on the Road

The Zookeepers are an independent band from Los Angeles that play their own material. Guitarist Patrick Vernon describes the music as "upbeat rhythm and folk party rock." Theirs is an interesting story because all the members work day jobs, yet they manage to do a lot of touring throughout the western United States.

The Zookeepers started out as a local band but soon discovered that the road offered a lot more than the nonexistent pay and difficult conditions of the L.A. rock scene. As Patrick explains,

> It was two years ago when we first left L.A. We did a seventeen-day tour. We did almost twenty shows in that seventeen days, and that opened our eyes to the fact that people elsewhere like music, as opposed to L.A., where it's really jaded. Everybody here [in L.A.] is connected in some way, or has friends who are connected in the entertainment business, so people watch you wondering whether you're deserving of a deal rather than whether they like you.

Unlike many acts, The Zookeepers book all their own gigs and don't use an agent. According to Patrick, "We're fully independent. We've released our own CDs; I do all our booking." Just about all of the band's material is original, yet they manage to play about half their gigs in clubs that normally hire cover bands.

> Our little niche has been to try to find venues that often have cover bands play three or four hours. We have enough original material, and we're upbeat and danceable enough that we can convince these folks that we'll entertain their crowd. . . . Actually, the other half of our income comes from colleges, and those are booked by calling them up. . . . It takes so much time to book colleges. But they'll book you [especially] if you're coming into town and you're from somewhere else. Being from L.A.

is maybe a little bit helpful when we're calling Corvallis, Oregon, or Coeur d'Alene, Idaho.

To book their tours, Patrick makes a lot of phone calls and sends out a press kit.

We have reviews and our demo, and we have a CD. I think it helps to have a CD; I think it's helped that we have a full-color poster in the pack. We took the plunge and spent the money to get a full-color poster. It's a heavy investment, about $700. But three or four gigs easily pay for that, especially college gigs.

The band makes a big effort to get airplay in the cities they play. "We visit college stations everywhere we go and work it. We do a lot of radio interviews, especially in the smaller towns, where we're able to get on radio stations, and sometimes clubs will even produce radio spots with our music."

Contrary to the conventional approach, The Zookeepers focus their energy on gaining popularity from touring rather than on trying to get a major record deal. Their strategy is to build their fan base from the bottom up, rather than from the top down. "I spend all my time booking. I figure it's more worth my time to try to get a $600 gig than to get 'Billy' from Atlantic records to listen to our CD, which it's highly likely he will not be interested in."

The Zookeepers sell their CDs onstage and on consignment with record stores in some of the towns they play. They also generate publicity from their Web site *(http://www-scf.usc.edu/~rvernon/zoo. htm)*, which features concert listings, photos, sound clips from their songs, and stories from the road.

Traveling so much without giving up their day jobs results in a grueling schedule for the band members. "We really concentrate it," Patrick explains. "This week we leave Wednesday night, we have a show in Corvallis on Thursday, a show in Portland on Friday at noon, a show in Eugene on Friday night, and a show in Corvallis again on Saturday, and then we drive home and work. And next weekend we drive back to Oregon and do a few more shows and then drive home and work. We did shows last weekend in Las Vegas and now we're at work, Monday morning."

and end up stuck with four or five or even ten idle days before your next booking. While this scenario might not sound bad at first, you have to realize that the band will be far from home and have no funds coming in to pay for food and lodging during those days. Because most bands on this level don't usually operate with a large cash surplus, unexpected periods of unemployment can be financially catastrophic.

Another important part of the agent's job is to make certain that your tour is routed properly. Since you'll be driving to all the gigs, you want to make sure that the distances and travel times between them are reasonable.

Here's an example of bad routing. I was once in a road band that finished playing a week in Rock Springs, Wyoming (in the south-western corner of the state), on a Saturday night, and was due to start playing in Prince Albert, Saskatchewan, on Monday night. We left directly after the gig Saturday night and had to drive straight for thirty-six hours in order to arrive in time to set up on Monday.

Using the sources listed in the Appendix, you should be able to obtain a fairly extensive list of booking agencies. Call around and find those agencies that book club tours. If they handle bands that play the same kind of music as yours, and they're not too far away, ask to set up a meeting. If that's impossible, at least get a name to whom you can send your band's press kit. Follow this up with a call a week or so later; with luck, they'll have listened to and liked your material.

Bill Hughes, who is an agent with Good Music Agency (GMA), a Minneapolis-based agency that books bands all over the Midwest and West, explains what he does when a band first contacts him:

> If we haven't heard of them and they sound fantastic over the phone, we'll usually arrange to meet with them and see them in rehearsal or something like that. Otherwise we ask for a promo kit with a photo, a demo tape, a song list, maybe a short bio . . . and a video if possible. And then we review that and evaluate whether or not we should go further on approaching the act. And the decision to pursue the act is based on . . . number one, does it fit into what we're doing? . . . and number two, what is the quality? Because if the qual-

ity is exceptional, we think it's a pretty surefire hit, we'll link up with the act and we'll create a market for them.

Although agencies tend to get somewhat inundated with promo material, it's in their self-interest to check everything out that comes in because they don't want to miss out on a good, money-making act. According to Bill Hughes, "We get a lot more probably than we can use, but that's our business and it's always welcome. And when we get it, . . . each thing will be assigned to a particular agent to follow up on." He says that it's important that the demo tape is a pretty close reflection of what the band can produce live. "We'll take that into consideration too, if it's a studio tape, and whether they've got the same players in the band that they did in the studio, and how much production is on the record."

One thing to consider before taking your band on the road is that if you're away too long, you can lose a lot of momentum back home. While you're out traveling, other bands will have taken your slots at the clubs back home and people can tend to forget about you. If your band has a good following and is working steadily, you should think long and hard before going on any extended tours.

WORKING AS A SOLO ACT

For those guitarists and piano players who are willing to play alone, working solo can present an intriguing option. It gives you the opportunity to play out, often for better pay, without the annoying personality issues that are such a part of being in a band. In addition, you can sometimes make quite a bit more money than you would as a sideman. However, there are some special considerations that go along with solo work that you should bear in mind when considering this approach.

In the old days, 99 percent of solo gigs consisted of a pianist or guitarist playing by themselves and singing (except for pianists hired to play instrumentally). If the guitar player were really versatile, he'd also have a harmonica on a rack, à la Bob Dylan.

Nowadays, many solo acts use MIDI sequencers in conjunction with synths and samplers to sound like a full band, albeit a somewhat wooden one. Although this has been a boon to some, it's hurt many musicians who once worked in clubs that hired bands, but now use only "one-man band" solo acts. Nonetheless, it has created an opportunity for the enterprising singer/entertainer who is not afraid to sink some money into equipment.

Another area of opportunity for keyboard players in which no equipment purchasing is necessary is piano bar gigs. Much of this work tends to be at cabaret clubs in large metropolitan areas (see "Getting Cabaret Gigs," in Chapter 5).

Buying the Gear

You'll need quite a bit of equipment to be a solo act, even if you're not trying to be a one-man band. This is because in many situations you're required to bring your own PA. Twenty years ago, you practically needed to be a weight lifter to carry around a PA system. Today, however, there are many companies that make compact, good-sounding speakers and small but efficiently powered mixers. You can put together a decent-sounding small club system for under $1,000.

If you want to go the "one-man band" route, you're also going to need some combination of synths, samplers, drum machines, and sequencers. There are many keyboards on the market that are self-contained, with instrument sounds, drum sounds, and a built-in sequencer. All you have to do is program in your songs, choose your sounds, and off you go. Not all solo artists favor this method because it can be limiting (see "Profile/Cory Morgenstern: 'One-Man Band,'" pages 82–83). If you're a guitar player, however, it's the only way you're going to achieve the full-band sound.

One of the pluses of using sequences is that you don't have to do the sequence programming yourself. If you look in the back of *Keyboard, Electronic Musician,* or any other music technology magazines (see Appendix), you'll find advertisements for companies that program Standard MIDI File (SMF) sequences for most popular music. Although this is an additional cost, it saves you from having to do a lot of tedious programming. There are also plenty of sites on the Internet where you can download SMF sequences for free (see Appendix).

Getting the Work

To get gigs as a solo act, you need to use essentially the same methods described earlier in this chapter for booking bands.

Because you're a solo act, you'll be targeting a different universe of clubs, and you'll find that there are a lot of restaurants where you can work as well. You should also contact agents regarding corporate and party work.

In order to function as a solo, you'll need a large repertoire of very recognizable songs. It's probably wise to spend a couple of months learning material before you try to do any gigs. Good solos know many more songs than they actually need to play a three- or four-hour gig. This is due to the fact that requests are a big part of doing solos, much more so than in band gigs. You want to be able to handle as many requests as possible, because happy patrons make for happy bar owners, and happy bar owners make for more gigs. Tips are also much more common in solo work, and you'll get a lot more if you can honor most of the requests.

Playing requests can be somewhat problematic if you're doing a "one-man band" act. If you don't have a sequence programmed for the request, you won't be able to do it. One way to get around this is to make a list of all your material by category, then put one on each table and some at the bar. This will cause most people make their requests based on your list rather than asking you for something you don't know. You can also put your name and phone number on the sheet—you might get more work because of it.

Something to bear in mind if you're thinking of going into solo work is that there's a lot more focus on you at all times than there would be in a band. You need to constantly be "on" and able to interact with the audience. You have to be an entertainer in addition to being a musician. If you're hired to do a solo instrumental job, like being a background pianist in a hotel lobby, it's a different story. There you can blend into the scenery more easily and not be as much of an up-front presence. But even in that situation people are going to make requests, so you'll be interacting with the audience to some degree.

PROFILE | **CORY MORGENSTERN**

"One-Man Band"

Cory is a keyboard player and singer who, in addition to fronting his own original band, Soular System, has become extremely successful as a solo act in the New York/tri-state area. He's developed contacts with numerous wedding bandleaders who call him with solo gigs. He describes most of his jobs as being

> All the smaller jobs that nobody bothers dealing with because they're after the big band jobs. . . . I have an ad that I run in *New York* magazine and I get a lot of work that way. . . . I'm the guy that everybody calls at the last minute. I've got a beeper, a cell phone. They know I jump. I book a lot of last-minute work. I get a lot of cancellations from other musicians, but I [also] get a lot of my own work.

Cory is very busy year-round, but especially so during the holiday season. He describes one stretch where his workload was almost overwhelming:

> One December, I peaked at fifteen dates in one week that I did all myself. I did two a day for seven days, and on the seventh day I did three. I did a twelve-to-two in a restaurant, then I came back and did a five-to-eight in same the restaurant . . . then I did another private party from nine to one. And that night somebody found me asleep, slumped over my equipment in the elevator in my building, riding up and down.

Cory spent the first part of his career gigging in bands, but after a while got pretty tired of dealing with the eccentric personalities of some of the musicians. He tells a particularly bizarre story from the 1970s, when he played with a disco band:

> There was actually an incident where the lead singer was blowing balls of fire during the song "Fire" by the Ohio Players. One night he set his face on fire, and I ran out from behind my keyboard and put his face out in my polyester shirt. He went to the hospital and I said, "That's it, I'm out of here."

He hadn't seriously considered doing a solo act until he had a conversation with a successful musician that he respected. "He said, 'Learn how to work solo, because you can always work solo, and . . . you don't have to depend on anyone else.' . . . It was a real revelation to me, the thought of becoming a solo artist."

Because much of the work he gets are parties that are looking for a full-band sound, Cory has developed a "one-man band" approach with the help of some cool technology. "I have a Korg I-5, which is an interactive synthesizer that plays about eight different things: drums, percussion, bass, three different accompaniment parts, . . . you play the right hand over it, and you trigger the chord in the left hand. . . . It also tracks inversions, so you can play some pretty complicated bass lines." Morgenstern compares this method to other ways of achieving a one-man band sound.

> From a keyboard player's point of view, there are three ways of doing this. One is the old traditional way, . . . which is having a drum machine and a keyboard that plays a left-hand bass and a right-hand keyboard sound. Then you have what I do, which is using a keyboard that has arrangements, where you can switch songs at a moment's notice. You can change the key, the tempo, and the arrangement. I can go from a twist to a waltz instantly at the correct tempo. . . . The third way is [to use] sequences, . . . which I don't care for, because the sequence goes from point A to point B and you have no control over it.

When asked what it takes for someone to be a successful solo act, Cory mentions three categories: "Being able to play, being able to sing, and being able to entertain. And I would say I'd rather have somebody that was a seven across the board, instead of a ten entertainer and a two player or a ten singer and a one entertainer."

For musicians who are just starting out, he advises:

> If you want to be in the music business, you've gotta keep in mind that it's a business and that you're gonna have to make money, so you're gonna have to figure out what you're willing to do to make that money. And it may not always be exactly the way you had planned it. You may have to adapt, and you may have to deal with a lot of circumstances. You've gotta be realistic.

CHAPTER 4 | **WORKING WEDDINGS, PARTIES, AND OTHER PRIVATE AFFAIRS**

❖

If you're looking to make better money than you can on the bar circuit, playing private parties is a good alternative. In New York these kinds of gigs are called *club dates.* In southern California and some other parts of the country they're known as *casuals.* No matter what you call them, working a wedding, bar or bat mitzvah, corporate event, or country club can earn you almost twice as much as a typical bar job, and sometimes more. In New York, union scale for a four-hour, Saturday-night job is $200 per musician. In the Midwest, a typical non-union wedding job pays around $100 to $125.

Besides the money, the working conditions tend to be much better at private parties. Instead of smoky bars, you play in clean catering halls, restaurants, and hotels, generally in nice parts of town. Most of the time you even get fed. In addition, the hours are generally much better and you're usually home earlier than your nightclub-playing compatriots.

Despite all these advantages, this kind of work has had the reputation of attracting a lower caliber of musician than some other segments of the industry. That's changed quite a bit in recent years, due in large part to the decrease in recording work. Especially in New York and Los Angeles, where the amount of session work has diminished considerably, many disenfranchised studio players have now started crowding into the same wedding circuits that in the past they would have ridiculed.

To further complicate things, a lot of wedding couples and bar or bat mitzvah parents are now hiring DJs instead of live bands. This has come to pass for a number of reasons, one of which is economic. DJs can deliver danceable, recognizable music for a fraction of the cost of a live band. According to John England, a guitarist who has worked extensively in the New York club date circuit (see "Profile/John England: Club Date Guitarist and Vocalist," pages 96–97), "A DJ can work for $600 a night and make a lot of money, whereas a band has to charge $2,000, and nobody, except maybe the booking agent, makes as much as the DJ."

Financial issues aside, the unfortunate fact is that many people simply don't care if the music is played live or not. According to Chip Riedeberg, who leads a big band wedding and party group called Swing Set in the Raleigh/Durham, North Carolina, area, "There are some that still care, . . . but I guess a lot of them are so used to their stereos and TV and all, that they don't know a hell of a lot about live music." This apathy toward live music that Riedeberg refers to may also have something to do with the fact that a sizable amount of current popular music is created without the use of live musicians. In addition, live music is broadcast on television so much that the novelty of it may have worn off somewhat.

A trend that makes live musicians doubly nervous is that there are some people who can afford to hire live bands but instead are paying comparable money to DJs. These DJs are not just spinning CDs, they're providing an entire extravaganza, replete with lights, dancers, and monstrous sound systems. In the New York area, bandleaders have created some of their own problems by charging outrageous prices for live music, which have forced many customers to go the DJ route.

Nevertheless, there's a lot of good work to be had if you can reconcile yourself to the fact that on these gigs you won't be playing original music or furthering your chances for a record deal. If you're simply looking to make some decent bread playing your instrument, private parties might be for you.

THE GIGS THAT ARE OUT THERE

In most parts of the country, the majority of the wedding and party work goes to bands that specialize in those kinds of gigs. They generally have set lineups, although sometimes they'll have a "core" group of regular members, and hire freelancers as additional pieces when budget and circumstances permit. In some of the larger cities, New York in particular, there's a much more robust freelance scene, in which musicians who aren't members of a specific band get called for individual gigs by various bandleaders.

In order to get gigs, you'll have to do a little detective work to find out what types of bands are working in your area (see "Breaking In," later in this chapter). Before we examine how to get the work, a little information about the gigs themselves will provide you with some context. To this end, the following are capsule descriptions of the various types of private party gigs.

Weddings

Wedding gigs are found everywhere in the country. The larger the population in a given area, the more wedding work there's likely to be.

A wedding band usually consists of bass, drums, guitar, keyboard, and often a saxophone player. Sometimes you'll have a larger lineup that includes a horn section, but that is the exception rather than the rule. In each band, there's a *front person* who generally does the bulk of the lead singing and also functions as the master of ceremonies for the reception. This person announces the entrance of the wedding couple, the first dance, the throwing of the bouquet, and the cutting of the cake. Some bands have both a male and a female lead singer so that they're able to cover a wider repertoire.

A typical wedding gig runs around four hours, not including any overtime that you might get. Generally, you'll start off playing background music for the cocktail hour and the dinner. This is usually where you play the more mellow material as well as the older jazz standards. After dinner comes the dancing part of the evening, at which point the band starts to rock out more.

You should keep in mind that there are some negatives to this kind of work. When you play at a wedding you're the "help," and you get treated that way. The band is more like window dressing than the center of attention. Unlike a bar gig, where the band is the featured attraction, the musicians at a wedding (or any other private party) are there to perform a service, just like the waiters and bartenders. It can be somewhat deflating to your musical ego when you're told to take a break because the salad is being served.

Another thing that differentiates wedding jobs from nightclub work is that you have to play for an audience with an extremely wide age range. Consequently, the musical tastes are very diverse and the band has to play a varied repertoire in order to satisfy everyone. The problem is that while you're playing Gershwin standards to please the older folks, the kids and young adults are annoyed. When you try to appease the young crowd by playing rock and roll, the old people put their hands over their ears or leave the room. I remember just such a situation at the first wedding I ever played. We'd just finished playing a rock tune when the bride's inebriated father approached the stage, followed by the bride herself. The dialogue went something like this:

Bride's father: "Turn the f---ing thing down."

Bandleader: "Huh?"

Bride's father: "I said turn the f---ing thing down."

Bride (whispering to the bandleader): "Don't worry about what he says, keep playing rock and roll."

Bandleader: "Huh?"

The rest of the gig went downhill from there, ending with the bride's father accusing us of trying to steal a bottle of vodka as we were leaving (it was actually an empty vodka jug filled with water for our overheating truck). This story also illustrates another problem at weddings—the drinking.

Coping with drunks is a problem live musicians have always had, but it can be particularly bad at weddings because there's usually an open bar. Occasionally the band has to deal with belligerent and obnoxious guests and members of the wedding party, and that can make for some pretty unpleasant situations. The worst drinking-related incident I ever encountered at a wedding was one in which the band was only peripherally involved. It all took place after the guests had eaten dinner and the dancing portion of the evening had begun. Apparently, relations between the two sides of the newly joined family were somewhat strained to begin with, and when someone on the groom's side was overheard making a disparaging remark about the bride, all hell broke loose. A challenge was made to step outside, and before long we were playing to an almost empty hall as most of the guests ran out to the parking lot to join in a knock-down, drag-out brawl. Meanwhile, someone in the wedding party ran up to the bandstand in a panic shouting, "Keep playing, keep playing! Whatever you do, don't stop playing!"

Naturally, most weddings are happy, peaceful occasions and do not feature after-dinner rioting. Most of the problems musicians encounter on wedding gigs are a bit more mundane.

Corporate Parties

New product announcements, conventions, annual sales meetings, and company picnics are some of the occasions for which companies stage events requiring live music. Bands are usually booked through agencies for this kind of work, although sometimes party planners will hire as well.

The gigs are usually three to four hours long and pay equivalent money to wedding jobs. The working conditions are generally quite good, and because the events often take place during the day the hours are usually pretty favorable.

Many of these gigs go to "specialty" acts, such as country, Caribbean, or oldies bands, that are hired to fit in with a theme of a particular event. There are also occasions for which a more traditional or "wedding"-type band gets hired. In resort areas where the hotels cater to conventions, bands and individual musicians are frequently hired for affairs such as dinners, dances, cocktail hours, and presentations.

One of the problems with these kinds of gigs is that the agent, fearful of alienating a lucrative corporate client, often sends one of his or her staff to the gig to "baby-sit" the band. It's been my experience that these representatives are often overly concerned that something the band does is going to offend the clients. Consequently they spend their time badgering the band to take shorter breaks, making sure that (God forbid) the musicians don't eat anything, and generally making a pain in the ass of themselves.

On some corporate gigs (as well as some wedding and bar or bat mitzvah gigs), the band is hired to play what's called a "continuous engagement," which means that the band never takes a full break during which everyone stops playing. Instead, you take turns taking breaks while one or more of the other members of the band continue to play.

Country Club Gigs

In the wealthier sections of most towns, you're bound to find country clubs, tennis clubs, and yacht clubs that hire live music for their various events. As with corporate parties, these events tend to be "theme"-oriented, such as a country-western or Caribbean night. Naturally, the bands that are hired for these events play the type of music that fits with the theme of that particular evening. Unfortunately, this doesn't leave a lot of room for a typical wedding band that plays a little bit of everything. Luckily, there are some non-theme events for which the more traditional bands get hired.

One of the good things about country club gigs is that they rarely last as long as they're scheduled to. Due to the fact that the guests are usually middle-aged or older, they tend to not want to stay out too late. As a result, it's not unusual to finish an hour early on one of these jobs. They also generally pay quite well, on par with weddings.

Bar Mitzvah Gigs

Having a live band at a bar or bat mitzvah was once a common occurrence. Now, unfortunately, many of these gigs (which are generically referred to by musicians as "bar mitzvah gigs") have become the province of DJs. Aside from the economics, what has happened is that the musical taste of the kids has diverged so far from that of the grown-ups that it is very difficult for a band to satisfy both anymore. It's much easier for a DJ to spin a CD of kid-pleasing, current pop music than it is for a traditional bar mitzvah band to try to play it. Sometimes, however, a big-budget bar or bat mitzvah will have both a DJ for the kids and a live band for the older people.

Bar and bat mitzvahs are structured pretty similarly to weddings, in that they also include a cocktail hour, meal, and dancing. What's different is that the bands not only have to play music that the kids will like, they have to entertain them as well. The DJs also have an advantage when it comes to entertaining. For the same

Q&A | **ROB TAUBE**

CLUB DATE MUSICIAN

Bar Mitzvah Gigs

Rob Taube is a guitarist/keyboardist and vocalist who has worked extensively in the New York bar mitzvah and wedding scene since the early 1990s.

Tell me what happens at a typical bar mitzvah gig.
It differs from a wedding in some of the ceremonies that have to be done. Instead of a cake-cutting, there is a candle-lighting at a bar mitzvah. That's where the young boy or girl lights candles on the cake and calls different people up to light the candles. Sometimes he or she will recite a little poem about each person that comes up. Generally the band plays short snippets of songs that have some relevance. Say it's Aunt Bessie from Georgia, then they'll play "Georgia On My Mind."

Is this all worked out in advance?
Yeah, when the people [clients] are responsible. A lot of times they throw stuff at you. But generally the bandleader will meet with somebody who's fairly responsible and will plan it ahead of time. In this the client plays a strong role, because they obviously have to tell you who is from where and what needs to be done. If they do it a week or two in advance, you can usually get enough of the song to do it in one or two minutes, one or two verses, however long it takes the person to walk from their seat to come light the candle.

Does a bar mitzvah start like a wedding, where there is often a cocktail hour? Do you play more quieter standards then?
You play whatever you want during the cocktail hour because people pay the least attention to you then, so it's a good place to practice.

And then a meal is served?
Before the meal is served, the guests come in, then usually the family is introduced separately, just like the bridal party and the bride and groom at a wedding. . . . The family members come in either one at a time or all at once, however they want to do it. And then they usually dance the hora, . . . and depending on how traditional they are . . . you may do some other Orthodox songs. . . . Then there is the phenomenon called "kids' games" at bar mitzvahs, during which the children get out on the dance floor and play certain games; musical chairs is a good example. Or in New York it's a game called "Coke

and Pepsi," where the band plays some type of preferably current funky type of music. The kids dance and then you call out the names of different soft drinks. . . . It's all a permutation on musical chairs. Sometimes they'll want to do limbo, so you'll have to play Caribbean music for fifteen or twenty minutes, generally Caribbean oldies like Harry Belafonte standards or "St. Thomas." Then it's up to the client as to how much of the kid stuff you do and how much of the adult stuff, but generally it's a multigenerational affair, and the generations tend to span a wider range than at a wedding, because at a wedding it tends to be the families and friends of the bride and groom and their parents and there aren't so many kids. So you really have to do a mixture, and you wind up doing a lot of big-band stuff as well as hip-hop. A good bandleader knows how to mix it up and how to read the crowd. . . . The rule is always the same: If you're playing a song and no one is dancing, then you dump the song and try again with something else.

What about breaks? Are bar mitzvah gigs continuous?
There are usually just one or two people on [band members playing] during the part of a meal when the caterer will not want dancing. Then just the keyboard player will do a number and everybody else will leave and hang out somewhere. If you're the keyboard player and you happen to be doing the number and people get up and start to dance to it, the caterer will often come over to you and give you the "fist-in-the-air" sign, which means "Get out of this." . . . And so a practice has sprung up called the "no-tempo song," which I really hate. A good example would be "Misty." You're doing it, but you're doing the whole song rubato so that people won't dance, they won't hear the rhythm and they won't dance.

Because dancing would disrupt the meal?
Yeah, because waiters are trying to get out there [and serve the] food, they're trying to cross the dance floor; they need that area to coordinate the meal.

How would you recommend getting into the circuit?
I guess it's a matter of developing some kind of repertoire or some type of performance that you do real well. . . . So I'd say it's different for different people. If you're a drummer you have to have a flawless groove and you have to be totally flexible and change tempo and groove at will; somebody else's will, usually. And you have to be able to play things loud or soft. . . . It's a lot like being a studio drummer, I suppose, except that you have to do it on the spot. What I've found is that very rarely do you run into a bad drummer because they

simply don't get hired. You gotta develop that kind of groove, then you have to get a recommendation from somebody. It would usually be that you're replacing another person who plays the same instrument and can't make a gig for some reason, an emergency situation. So June or New Year's Eve is usually a good time to break in, because they're gonna need extra people. So if [you're] a good musician and you've just come to town and you're looking for work, get your first job on New Year's Eve or on a Saturday night in June because there are gonna be people begging for somebody. They'll take almost anybody, and if you're good, you'll get the callback. If you're a guitar player, you have to know all the oldies stuff and you usually have to sing. You rarely see a non-singing guitar player.

Are the guitar players looked upon to do the rock and roll?
Yes, and if you're a keyboard player, you somehow have to know everything: Broadway standards, the whole Cole Porter–Gershwin book, Jerome Kern, all that stuff. You have to know French waltzes, Viennese waltzes, you know, fake versions of all of them. You have to know jazz standards, and I'm not talking about nightclub jazz, I'm talking about "All Of Me" kinds of things. And the way to learn them probably is to tape a club date and see what's played. Or tape two or three of them and then learn all that stuff. . . . You have to know how to stay out of the way and cover everything at the same time. It's very hard to be a keyboard player.

What kinds of sounds do keyboards typically have? Do they use a piano sound or synth sounds?
There are two opinions on this: Some people like to use all kinds of synth sounds, other people really hate them. I'd say the safest way to go is to get a really, really good piano sound. Then you're safe; you can play everything with that.

money or less than a band charges, DJs can provide not only music, but also a magician and/or dancers. Because the DJs have so much to offer, the bands are left at quite a disadvantage. Consequently, the DJs have increased their market share significantly in the bar mitzvah market.

PREPARING YOURSELF

The skills you need to be a successful private party musician are in many ways the same as for the nightclub circuit. First and foremost, you need to be an unselfish ensemble player. You also need to have decent chops on your instrument and a good musical head on your shoulders. If you're a lead singer as well, you'll enhance your market value quite a bit. Even if you just sing harmony, it will help. Without question, however, the most important aspect of preparing yourself for these type of gigs is to learn a lot of songs.

Learning Repertoire

In the words of New York club date guitarist Richard Frank, "No one has ever come up to me and complained on a job that I was playing a song that was too familiar."

Much more than in a bar situation, a band that plays private affairs must be able to perform a very wide cross section of standard tunes. You need to be comfortable playing everything from Cole Porter to Elvis to Alanis Morissette. As an individual musician trying to get work on this scene, you'll be a much more desirable commodity if you already know a lot of the material.

In addition to just knowing the tunes, you need to know how to play in the "idiom" of each song. Let's say you're a guitar player and the bandleader calls "The Girl from Ipanema." You should know not only what the chords are, but also what a guitar typically does in a bossa nova. Further, you're expected to know how to set your tone so it sounds right for that particular idiom.

If you're in a wedding band that rehearses regularly, you'll have a better chance to learn a lot of the material after you join the band. Nevertheless, you'll be more likely to get into a band in the first place if you can demonstrate a good knowledge of the repertoire. If you're on the freelance scene, you've got to determine what the repertoire needs are and learn a lot of it in advance. The best way to do this is to talk to people who play your instrument and are already on the circuit. You might even consider asking one of these players if you can take some lessons from them. Who knows, if you can impress them enough they might end up recommending you for some work, or letting you sub for them.

Suggested Repertoire List

In order to give you an idea of the kinds of tunes you'll need to know, a typical song list for a wedding band is shown on the following page. Obviously the repertoire will vary from band to band and from region to region. Nevertheless, by learning the songs on

BASIC PRIVATE PARTY REPERTOIRE

JAZZ AND BIG BAND
Chattanooga Choo Choo
In the Mood
All Of Me
Misty
What a Wonderful World
As Time Goes By
All the Things You Are
Autumn Leaves
It Had To Be You
Unforgettable
The Way You Look Tonight
Isn't It Romantic
Cheek to Cheek

COLE PORTER
Night and Day
I Get a Kick Out of You
Got You Under My Skin
Just One of Those Things
Anything Goes

DUKE ELLINGTON
Don't Get Around Much
   Anymore
Satin Doll
Take the "A" Train

GEORGE GERSHWIN
Someone To Watch Over Me
Love Is Here To Stay
Embraceable You

FRANK SINATRA
New York, New York
Summer Wind
My Way

BOSSA NOVA
A. C. JOBIM
The Girl from Ipanema
Meditation
One-Note Samba
Wave
Corcovado

1950s: ROCK AND POP
Still of the Night
Under the Boardwalk
Help Me Make It Through
   the Night
Great Balls of Fire
Johnny B. Goode
Blue Moon
You Send Me
Stand By Me
For the Good Times
Save the Last Dance for Me

ELVIS PRESLEY
Can't Help Falling in Love
Jailhouse Rock
Hound Dog
Blue Suede Shoes
All Shook Up

1960s: ROCK AND POP
Unchained Melody
Proud Mary
Mony Mony
Do Wah Diddy
Pretty Woman
Louie Louie
Mac the Knife

THE ROLLING STONES
Satisfaction
Honky Tonk Women

VAN MORRISON
Brown Eyed Girl
Have I Told You Lately (also
   covered by Rod Stewart)

THE BEATLES
Twist and Shout
I Saw Her Standing There
Birthday
Yesterday

MOTOWN AND R&B
My Girl
Heard It Through the
   Grapevine
Shout
Midnight Hour
Sugar Pie Honey Bunch
Dancin' in the Streets
Respect
Ain't Too Proud To Beg
I Feel Good
When a Man Loves a
   Woman
Dock of the Bay
Knock on Wood
Mustang Sally
Stop in the Name of Love
I'll Be There
I Want You Back

DISCO
YMCA
Boogie Oogie Oogie
I Will Survive
Hot Stuff
She Works Hard for the
   Money

Disco Inferno

1970s AND '80s ROCK
Old Time Rock and Roll
Margaritaville
Peaceful Easy Feeling
Pink Cadillac

ERIC CLAPTON
Wonderful Tonight
Lay Down Sally

COUNTRY
On the Road Again
Country Roads
Crazy

SPECIALTY TUNES
The Anniversary Waltz
Daddy's Little Girl
Through the Years
Sunrise Sunset
Thank Heaven for Little
   Girls
Happy Birthday

SPECIALTY DANCE MATERIAL
CHA CHA
Never on Sunday
China
Tea for Two

MERINGUE
Compadre Pedro Juan
St. Thomas
Spanish Eyes
Besame Mucho
More

TANGO
La Cumparcita
Hernando's Hideaway

WALTZ
Tennessee Waltz
Moon River
Always

POLKA
Beer Barrel Polka
Pennsylvania Polka

MISCELLANEOUS
The Macarena
The Electric Slide
Hot Hot Hot
Havah Nagilah

this list you'll have a leg up on your competition when it comes to getting into a band. If you can't learn everything, try to learn at least some from each of the categories. If you're not in or around one of the major cities, you can probably get away without learning all of the jazz standards, but don't skip the category entirely. Within each category and subcategory, the songs are listed in order of their importance.

I also suggest that you learn the songs in the keys of the original artists. You probably won't have most of this stuff on CD or record, but between your collections and those of your friends, you should be able to find a lot of it without having to buy too much. If you have an oldies radio station in your market, you can probably tape a lot of the old rock and roll standards, and request any others that you need to hear.

When learning the jazz standards, you can find legal "fake books" that include the sheet music for most of the tunes. If you're unfamiliar with the jazz idiom, it would probably be a good idea to take some lessons so that you know at least the basics of how to play in that style. I guarantee you'll look foolish if you've been a rock and roller your whole life and you try to play jazz tunes without knowing how. Conversely, musicians who've only played jazz can sound pretty lame when they attempt to rock out.

Although this list is by no means a complete one, you certainly can't go wrong learning any of these tunes. You'll probably need to know some current Top 40, which changes too often to include in a list. Try to remain up to date and you'll at least be familiar with whatever tunes the band you work with plays.

Attire

At most wedding and bar mitzvah jobs, the male band members are required to wear tuxedos and the females either tuxes or formal dresses. There are some exceptions to this rule, but if you're thinking seriously about playing weddings you'll eventually have to pay a visit to your local formal wear store.

The clothing requirements for corporate and country club jobs will depend on the event. If it's a dinner dance at a country club, it will probably mean black tie for the band. At an outdoor company picnic, the dress code probably won't be as formal. As previously

---

PROFILE | **JOHN ENGLAND**

Club Date Guitarist and Vocalist

John England is a guitar player and vocalist who, until his recent move to Nashville, successfully freelanced on the New York club date circuit. He originally started playing gigs in his home state of Indiana, but moved to New York and had to establish himself in a whole new scene. "When I first came here I didn't have any work at all. I played in an original band. They actually did some things; I made some money with them. But that kind of ended. I was broke, I had no gigs, I didn't know what to do. Then I saw these guys playing the subway. So I borrowed a friend's Mouse amp. I was so broke and desperate that I had to try it." England discovered that by singing popular songs, he could actually make some money in the subway.

> It was a real cool thing, and it taught me a lot, . . . especially in repertoire, the things I could do as a singer. . . . It's like market research when you're playing the subway, it's so direct and obvious. You play a song, and if people like it you make money. . . . I started out doing things like country rock and old rock and roll, which I really like. I really got into sixties R&B back then, Stax and Otis Redding and that kind of stuff.

While his subway playing helped with his repertoire, it was from playing with a band that John got his break into the club date business. "I was playing in some original bands and one of the guys who was a singing guitar player was playing with a club date band. He got fixed up doing jingles and wanted to get out of the band, so he suggested that I fill in sometimes."

Once he got his foot in the door, John was able to successfully build his club date career. His ability to be versatile helped him out quite a bit.

> When I was in Indiana I studied jazz and aspired to sound like Wes Montgomery. The club date bands that I've worked with mostly, not exclusively, are ones who have at least one foot in that kind of camp, playing New York society music. And that's an advantage I've had over other singing guitarists, who are more sort of rock-and-roll people. They don't know what to do, or they get in the way, and people have to tell them just not to play at all.

Until his move to Nashville, John averaged about two to three club dates a week in addition to other musical projects that he was involved in. He feels that freelancing has been a good thing for his career.

> I've always wanted to be a freelancer and not get tied down to one commitment. When you're freelancing you can take the dates you can and then about the other ones you say, "Well, I'm sorry, I can't make it. I'll try to find somebody else if you'd like." But you're not promising all your Saturdays to some guy who may not be able to fill them.

He's also found that, despite their bad reputation, wedding and party gigs are an enjoyable way to make a living in the music business.

> I don't think it's demeaning work. Maybe I'm romantic but I think there's something noble about it. . . . You're playing and singing for your living, and I think that's fantastic. . . . In my experience, you're playing great music. Because if you're playing standards, whether it's Motown or rock and roll or Cole Porter, you're not playing the crappy songs that Motown recorded, you're playing the great ones. I think that's very interesting and satisfying.

When it comes to getting gigs, John's advice is to get to know a musician who's working and playing the same instrument as you. When this player gets more calls than he can handle in the busy months of the year, you might get called upon to sub. "Of course," he says, "that first year, you're only working in June and September. But if you knock their socks off, they'll put you on the list. . . . Maybe they'll even like you better."

John goes on to explain that once you get a gig, you need to continue networking. "You want to get to know all the musicians on the gig. . . . You want them to consider you when they need to recommend someone and you want to know who they're working for."

John has some advice on how to be successful on a club date. "I always tell people that there are priorities on a club date: Get there early, dress appropriately, know the tunes, know the repertoire. And then, after that, it's sing great and play great. . . . Be able to do different styles of music well, and be easy to work with. Be flexible."

He makes a very important point that when you're playing a private party, you mustn't lose sight of the ultimate purpose of the gig.

> The musician has to realize that even though he's thinking about the music, the bandleader has a different set of priorities. It's not an absolute music situation; it's music in the service of the party. And sometimes the bandleader might do things the musician doesn't understand, but you have to kind of go with the flow.

stated, a lot of corporate and country club events will hire "specialty" bands to fit the theme of a particular event. So, for example, a golf club having a country-western night would probably hire a country band and expect that they'd be wearing western attire.

BREAKING IN

Trying to identify where the private party work is in your particular area can be much more difficult than it is for the nightclub circuit, for the simple reason that the gigs are private and therefore not advertised to the general public in the same way. As a result, you'll have to dig a little deeper to get information.

Identifying Contacts

Just as in other segments of the music business, the first thing you should do when trying to get wedding band work is to think hard about anyone you know who plays or has played on the wedding circuit. As I've stressed in earlier chapters, nothing substitutes for personal contacts when it comes to getting work in music (see "Building a Network of Contacts" in Chapter 1). Call any musical contacts you have, even if they're not specifically associated with the private party circuit. They might know people who do play those kinds of gigs.

If you studied music in school, contact your old classmates and teachers; maybe some of them will be able to help you. Once you've exhausted all the personal contacts, you'll have to start developing some new ones.

Making Contacts by Playing

If you accept the premise that the best way to get gigs is to get recommended, then you're going to have to get out there and do some playing in order to build a reputation. On the surface it seems like a catch-22 situation: You need contacts to get the gigs, but the best way to make contacts is on the gigs. The only way to overcome this quandary is to play in as many other musical situations as you can, even if some of these are nonpaying, original bands. Eventually (and it will most likely take time), you're likely to meet some musicians who can help you get hooked in to the private party circuit.

It's also a good idea to keep your eyes on the musicians' classified ads. Every so often you'll see a working wedding band advertising for players. If you're looking to get into a "set" band rather than a freelance situation, the classifieds might provide you with a solution. (For tips on auditioning, see "Using the Classifieds" in Chapter 3.) You can also find musicians' classifieds on the Internet. A Web site called the Wedding Music Information Source *(www.nuwebny.com/wedmusic/index.htm)* has classifieds specifically for wedding musicians.

Whether on paper or in cyberspace, you might want to consider running your own "musician available" ad to try to get things going.

Creating New Contacts

In addition to the above-mentioned steps, you can also attempt to create new contacts by doing some cold calling. This is definitely not the best way to go about networking, but if just one of the people you call ends up giving you work, it'll be worth the effort.

Here's one way to go about making new contacts: Take a look in the yellow pages under "orchestras." You're likely to find a number of listings for bands that play weddings and parties. Call them up and explain concisely why you're interested in working with them. Ask if they ever need people on your instrument. Even if they say no, get the name of the person you're talking to and send a follow-up letter with a business card and any other self-promotional material you might have. You might even try sending a cassette with some examples of your playing on it (if they're good quality). About every six weeks, call and touch base with this person. Be sure to call in late November or early December, when he or she will be focusing on New Year's Eve. Many bands are scrambling to find enough people to cover their gigs at that time, so it's also a good time to get your foot in the door. Another productive time to call is just prior to or during the month of June, which is the busiest part of the year for this kind of work.

Yet another way to find wedding bands it to get copies of wedding publications such as *The Wedding Pages* (see Appendix), which have all kinds of advertisements for wedding-related goods and services, including bands. In addition, if you have any friends or relatives who are getting married, ask them if they can inquire at the hall they're hiring about the names and numbers of bands. If you're a union member, you might also ask at the musicians union for the names and numbers of wedding and party band-leaders and contractors.

Working on the New York Club Date Circuit

Because it's somewhat of a unique scene, there are certain things you should know if you're trying to get private party work in the New York area.

Although it's not nearly as busy as it once was, the world of New York club dates encompasses everything from parties for the rich and famous at posh New York City hotels to wedding gigs in catering halls on Long Island. In the New York area, the agencies that book most wedding and party work are referred to as *club date offices.* These "offices" are usually run by bandleaders who hire freelancers for various parties and weddings. In some cases, they have a stable of set bands that they send out to jobs.

If you're looking for work with one of the so-called *society offices,* which book engagements for New York's upper class, the gigs have a unique set of rules and customs that you should know about. First of all, the repertoire is much more heavily weighted toward the old standards, à la Cole Porter or Gershwin. In addition, much of the work is freelance, and someone new on the scene is expected to know the material and play it in the "correct" way.

The easiest way to attain this knowledge is to have someone teach it to you—all the more reason to go the subbing route to try to get into these gigs. Guitarist Richard Frank, who's been freelancing on the New York club date scene for years, tells how he learned the material.

> The first thing I did when I got into the club date business was ask around and find out who was the best "straight" [non–rock and roll] guitarist, the best guy playing standards, and whether he taught. As luck would have it, he did teach, so I took lessons to figure out how to play a club date as a straight guitarist, so that all the years I spent learning how to play the guitar wouldn't be a waste. . . . It's a special way of playing and a special way of handling the tunes . . . the little licks that everybody plays on certain tunes, the little tag endings, the little riffs; the bass line that all the really experienced society bass players are gonna play, . . . and, of course, which tunes.

WEDDING AND PARTY MUSICIAN'S SURVIVAL GUIDE

• Leave yourself plenty of time to set up. You don't want to be tuning up and sound-checking when the guests are arriving.

• Be friendly to the banquet manager and staff. You'll need their goodwill to make the job go smoothly and to ensure future gigs.

• If you don't like being hungry for long periods of time, bring a snack with you, because you can't count on getting a meal. Ninety percent of the time you do get to eat something, but for that other 10 percent it's a good idea to have a sandwich packed. If they do let you eat, keep a low profile on the buffet line and don't be a pig.

• Don't grumble or complain out loud when your bandleader calls out a song you find boring or dumb.

• Remember, networking is the key. If you're freelancing, make sure to exchange business cards with all the musicians on the gig who you've never met before. If your band was booked by an agency, the only business cards you should hand out to guests are those of that agency.

• Keep your volume under control; there will probably be a lot of older guests there who are not enamored of high-decibel music.

• Handle all requests from guests politely. If the band doesn't know a particular song, suggest something similar that you do know.

• Do not order any alcohol from the bar unless you're specifically told it's OK. Even then, go real easy.

• Always remember that you're there to perform a service, not to be a star. Be sensitive to the needs of the wedding party and the guests at all times.

• The band should play a good mixture of old and new standards. You can rock out late in the gig, but keep it mellow during the cocktail hour and especially during the meal.

• Unless you're instructed by the client or banquet manager to do otherwise, the breaks should not exceed 20 minutes.

• If a drunken guest gets belligerent, try to handle him or her nicely. It never looks good for the band to insult a guest.

> I immediately made a list of the tunes I really needed to know right away, . . . that were inescapable components of every job, like "New York, New York."

Also remember that if you're trying to be a guitar player on the freelance scene, you're probably going to have to sing. Frank has this to say about it: "In my field, the freelance thing, the guitar player is thought of as the guy who's gonna handle the rock and roll, and he has to sing. There are very few non-singing guitar players."

FORMING YOUR OWN BAND

If you're thinking of forming your own wedding and party band, here are a few tips to keep in mind.

Deciding on Your Instrumentation

For just about any gig, you're going to need bass, drums, guitar, and keyboard. You'll probably also need a sax and, if budget permits, another horn or two. One of the players will have to front the band and be a lead singer. If you want your band to be more versatile, you should have both male and female lead singers.

The front person will have to know how to MC the various wedding events, such as the cake-cutting, the garter toss, and so forth. If you're trying to get bar mitzvah work, the front person should know how to handle all of the appropriate ceremonies, such as the candle-lighting and the kids' games.

Assessing Your Equipment Needs

If you're going to be the leader, you'll need to supply the PA. You won't need a monstrous system, but you'll want something that's good quality and that can easily handle a large banquet room or small ballroom. A well-made powered mixer should suffice, because you won't need to mike any of the amplified instruments. The only things you'll want to put through the PA are vocals and maybe sax or horns.

Generally, most wedding bands do not own lights and are not expected to bring them to their gigs.

Putting Together Publicity Materials

Similarly to a nightclub band, it will help to have a promo kit to sell your group. Probably the most important item in your kit will be a video. Wedding couples love seeing videos of prospective bands, preferably a wedding promo video that shows your performance at an actual reception, and has clean sound. The best way to keep it interesting is to use short excerpts from several songs, rather than performing all of them in their entirety. This tends to keep the viewer's attention more effectively than a video with a bunch of three- to five-minute numbers. You should be able to find a video production facility that will edit your tape for you. Be sure to shop around, because prices will vary greatly. If you can't afford an outside facility, you can edit it yourself using two VCRs, as long as the deck you're editing onto has a *flying erase head,* which allows for smooth transitions between edits. This method should only be used if you have no other options, because the results will likely be less than professional.

You'll probably also want to have a cover sheet printed on the band's letterhead that describes the band and the services it can offer. You might even want to include some quotes from satisfied clients, since a wedding band is unlikely to have any press clippings. In addition, you can print up a song list (also on your letterhead) so that the bride and groom can see what your repertoire is and choose any special requests that they may have.

The other thing you'll probably want to have in your promo kit is an 8-by-10 photo of the band. Unlike a nightclub band, you should strive to have your publicity shot look as conventional as possible. An unusual-looking photo might make the bride and groom (not to mention their parents) nervous and jeopardize your chances of getting booked.

Getting Gigs

Unless you know a lot of people who are planning to get married, or your cousin is a banquet manager, you're going to have to spend some money on advertising and publicity in order to get your band onto the wedding circuit. One thing you might want to do is to book your group into some *wedding showcases.* A wedding or bridal showcase is usually held at a local hotel or catering hall. In it, many bands play live for the benefit of the future brides and grooms. This is a way to start getting your band's name around and to possibly pick up some gigs. The problem is that you generally

PROFILE | **ERIC SUTTMAN**

Wedding Band Leader

As the leader of a wedding band, you not only need musical ability but good business savvy as well. For the past fifteen years, Eric Suttman has successfully used both sets of skills while leading his band (The Eric Suttman Band) in the Dayton, Ohio, area. "Dayton's not a huge market," he says. "There are probably four or five bands that are the primary wedding bands in the area."

Suttman does all his own booking, rather than depend on agencies to get the gigs.

> I do all mine myself. . . . In this area, the way to do it—probably one of the main ways—is to stay tight with the banquet managers in the different halls. They get to see every band that comes through. . . . Often the bride and groom will ask him or her if they have any suggestions for music. So if you stay on a banquet manager's good side, on his or her "A" list, that's a good relationship to maintain.

For Suttman, the most important piece of promo material for marketing his band is a video. "I've got a videotape of the band that's short: It's five minutes long, with twenty-two tunes on it. It's a whole bunch of twenty-second clips. You don't need to hear more than twenty seconds of 'My Girl.'"

Eric finds it problematic when the bride and groom insist on hearing the band live before deciding whether to book them.

> To be honest I really dread that, because when a couple comes out to hear you at a job they usually allow themselves somewhere between fifteen and thirty minutes to stand in the back of the room. Well, if I know that a bride and groom are looking for a crankin' rock band to have a good swingin' party, and they show up during the dinner set when we're doing background quiet music, they'll say, "Oh no, man, this isn't what we're looking for." If they had just been there two hours later they would see us doing that stuff.

Suttman thinks that versatility is the key to a wedding band's success. "I describe us as a chameleon-type band. We're able to fit into every situation. If it's a really classy big-band evening, we can be that all night. If people want grungy rock and roll, we can do that." Most of the time the band has to do a little of both. "Within a wedding reception," he says, "there are three main parts: the cocktail hour, the dinner, and the dancing. The first two need background music, so you don't want to play stuff that makes people say 'Let's get up and dance.' You just want to provide atmosphere, so we play the jazz standards at that time, and more of the rock and roll and the current stuff during the dance part."

Suttman uses a combination of freelancers and regular players for his gigs. "My whole approach is the five-piece band," he says. "I'm at every job, and my frontman vocalist is at every job. Then [for] the other three parts—guitar, sax, and drummer—I have a pool of musicians that I call to do a job, depending on who's available. . . . I basically have two or three main people on every instrument that I can call. . . . As a bandleader, I want to work with good musicians who don't have attitude problems." He says that some players he's hired get snobby about playing some of the necessary wedding material. "If I call 'The Beer Barrel Polka,' they play it with a real chip on their shoulders. . . . There are good musicians who, as they get better and start becoming jazz-heads, start sneering at that stuff. And then when they are really working full-time, they realize, 'Hey, I'm doin' this full-time, I'm gettin' paid, I'm gonna have fun doin' it, I'm gonna play it the best I can.'"

Eric agrees with the notion that the best time to get into a wedding band is during the really busy times of the year. "There are certain nights of the year [in June and October especially] when everyone's working and I'm scrambling to find a sax player and I end up having to call someone who's a friend of a friend of a friend." It sometimes means working with people who don't know all the material. "I usually work with musicians who can play something if they can hear it in their heads . . . as long as they have a concept of what the song is." His advice for getting a foot in the door is simple: "Find out who the bandleaders are and just make calls about once every six months. Say, 'Hi, I'm here if you ever need me, and make sure my number's on your list.' Otherwise, out of sight, out of mind. I'm sure I've forgotten about good players myself."

Although the pay scale for Dayton is not nearly what it is in New York (Suttman's players get between $100 and $125 for a Saturday night), the conditions are good and the dress code is more relaxed. On some gigs the musicians don't have to wear tuxes, which is a fact that Suttman is glad about. "Frankly, I get tired of people asking me to fill their wine glasses on the break," he says.

have to pay to be included in these showcases, and it can cost upwards of several hundred dollars to participate. There's no guaranteed work when you do a showcase, so it comes down to whether you're willing to risk the money.

Another publicity method that's highly recommended by wedding bandleaders is to advertise in the local wedding directories. They're distributed through jewelry stores and other businesses that cater to people getting married. You can take out a display ad for your band that will be seen by many potential clients. Chip Reideberg, a wedding bandleader in North Carolina, finds this kind of advertising indispensable. "Without that I would have fifty percent less business," he says. Some of the directories even provide advertisers with lists containing names and addresses of future wedding couples printed on address labels. This gives your band the opportunity to send promo material directly to the homes of people in your area who are getting married.

You can also include your band in wedding music listings on the Internet. It's hard to say how effective it will be, but according to the Wedding Music Information Source Web site (see Appendix), some 2,000 people a day look at their listings. Of course, that 2,000 is spread throughout the United States and even the world, so it would be hard to gauge the impact in your local area. Nevertheless, for the relatively low annual fee of $19.95 (at the time of this writing), it sounds like it could be a good deal. In addition, as the Net's popularity increases, such sites will likely become more of a standard resource for prospective brides and grooms.

Yet another route you can take toward getting private party gigs is to go through a booking agent. They are crucial for getting corporate gigs, and many agencies handle weddings as well. (For tips on contacting agents, "Booking Agents" and "Touring with a Band," both in Chapter 3.)

Without a personal contact, the best way to get hooked up with an agency is to start by phoning them and trying to set up an appointment. In most cases you'll have to send some promotional materials before they'll agree to see you. Follow up in about two weeks with a phone call. Be politely persistent (call every two weeks or so) until you've gotten an appointment, a turn-down, or an offer to book you.

As was mentioned in "Touring with a Band" in Chapter 3, you shouldn't sign an exclusive agreement with an agency unless you've had it looked over by your attorney, and the contract guarantees that the agent will get you an certain amount of work. Even then, I would shy away from exclusives unless the guaranteed work level was very high. In all likelihood, an agent booking private parties won't ask for an exclusive anyway; he or she will probably offer you gigs on a one-shot basis.

CHAPTER 5 | PLAYING FOR BROADWAY SHOWS, MUSICAL THEATER, AND CABARET

❖

Being an orchestra member for musical theater is an entirely different experience from performing with a band. Instead of being onstage, you're usually hidden from view, and instead of being the center of attention, you're playing a supporting role to the actors and actresses onstage.

Unlike a bar or wedding gig, you're following a conductor, and most, if not all, of your parts are completely written out. There's very little room for improvisation, and you've got to play the same music night in and night out. Until you're really comfortable with your parts, the pressure can be intense. To be successful you must learn to play with a minimum of mistakes and never lose your place in the score.

On a per-show basis, the pay for playing in a musical is usually higher than for playing in clubs. Because shows tend to have somewhere between four and eight performances a week, you stand to make pretty decent money for a musician. If you're lucky enough to get hooked up with a long-running show, you can have a steady income that lasts for years. In addition, because most of the better theater music work is unionized, you often can qualify for pension and health benefits.

Another type of gig that is different from playing in a bar or wedding band is being a back-up musician for a cabaret singer. The aesthetic sensibilities are more akin to the theater than to any styles of popular music, and the structures and conventions of the gigs are also different. Conversely, because cabaret jobs by their nature occur in nightclubs, the pay, lack of unionization, and poor working conditions are similar to what you'd find in mid- to high-end bar band work.

WHERE THE WORK IS

Although you can find musical theater in many parts of the country, New York is the capital by far. Broadway is without a doubt the mecca for show music in this country. In fact, theater music, and Broadway in particular, is one of the few areas of the music industry that's been booming over the last few years. For a musician, the opportunities in New York are far greater than anywhere else. Broadway dominates the nationwide theater scene in other ways, too. Most important, it determines which shows will travel to other parts of the country, because the shows that tour are generally those that have made their reputation on Broadway.

Playing on Broadway

Having a steady show on Broadway is a plum gig for a musician. The base pay is in the neighborhood of $1,100 for an eight-show week. If your part, or *chair,* calls for playing more than one instrument, it's considered a *double,* and entitles you to extra pay.

In addition, the union contract allows regular players a lot of latitude for sending in substitutes, thereby freeing them to pursue other musical projects and keeping their personal lives reasonably intact. Thus, it's rare for a musician on Broadway to play all eight shows every week.

As you might expect, the competition is fierce for Broadway gigs. However, for an accomplished musician, it's achievable. As in any other sector of the industry, the keys to getting work are to be good and to get to know a lot of people in the business.

New York also has quite a few smaller theaters that are considered as *Off-Broadway.* The distinction between Broadway and Off-Broadway is technically based on the seating capacity of the theater. Because they play to smaller houses, Off-Broadway shows have a lower pay scale, but they can still provide steady work for musicians. Due to space and budget considerations, you're more likely to find a small ensemble than a large orchestra in the pit of an Off-Broadway show.

Yet another designation in the New York theater scene are the *Off-Off-Broadway* shows. These are smaller-scale productions that occasionally have a small band, or, more often than not, just a piano.

Playing Shows in Other Major Cities

Although they can't compare in numbers to New York, most major cities have a handful of theaters that put on union-scale, Broadway-type productions. Often these productions are touring companies of Broadway shows. Outside of New York, you won't find a lot of theaters of this caliber. Los Angeles has four, Philadelphia has three, and Chicago has five. To put it in perspective, there are over twenty Broadway theaters in New York, and at the time of this writing, fifteen of them are showing musicals.

The pay for these shows is quite good, but it's rare to find one that runs for an extended period of time in one city. In any given location, these productions usually last from a few weeks to a few months. An exception to this would be *Phantom of the Opera,* which ran for four-and-a-half years in Los Angeles, and at the time of this writing is in its third year in San Francisco.

It's rare to find musicians outside of New York who are able to make a living exclusively from playing musical theater. There are some in Los Angeles, but they're the exception to the rule. Los Angeles percussionist and contractor Bonnie Boss describes one group of musicians that do very well on the theater scene. "There's a circle of players that are good woodwind doublers; that's something specific to theater pit orchestras that you have to have. . . . They can handle all these crazy parts, like the Marvin Hamlisch shows where you've got four reed books, but they're all playing like five different instruments." When it comes to rhythm-section players, however, Boss doubts that anyone in Los Angeles is playing strictly musicals. "I don't really even know of anyone that does musical theater exclusively." Many successful southern California musicians play musicals to supplement their studio or orchestral work, but their careers aren't centered around it.

In the San Francisco area, there's a small group of theater players that work pretty steadily. According to Gordon Messick, a trombonist who's been playing shows in the Bay area since the early 1960s,

> I would say there are probably about forty to fifty [musicians] in San Francisco . . . [for] whom the theater is their primary source of income. Some of those people, maybe even a majority, have to supplement their incomes from time to time. At certain times the theater will be real good, so they'll work and do well for a year or so, but then they'll have periods of two or three months at a time where no show is available and they have to do club date and casual work. Of course, that's sort of the standard all over the country, even in New York.

Playing with Broadway Touring Companies

If you don't live in New York, your best chance for playing in a high-level production is with the traveling road company of a current Broadway show or a revival. According to the American Federation of Musicians, there are more of these touring companies than ever before. One of the reasons for this is that Broadway is doing so well. Also, due to the high cost of staging the original productions, investors usually don't begin to see any profits until a show has established itself and sent out one or more road companies. Because the overhead on the road is substantially lower, the profit margins are generally much higher. In fact, the November 1996 issue of the union's monthly newspaper, *The International Musician,* reports that traveling companies account for 66 percent of the revenues that Broadway producers take in. In addition to the national road companies, some shows even stage international productions. At one point recently, *Beauty and the Beast* had more than ten road companies touring around the world simultaneously.

Touring companies stay in one town anywhere from a few days to a few weeks, and occasionally for months at a time. In most cases, it's too expensive to tour with a full orchestra, so they travel with only a handful of key musicians, which typically include a drummer, a keyboard player/associate conductor, and possibly a lead trumpet or other instrument that management may not feel confident in hiring locally. The rest of the orchestra is filled in with local players who stay with the production only as long as it's in that particular city. Being one of these *pickup players* is best way to work on a Broadway-level production if you don't live in New York.

Because most shows travel with a drummer, it's rare for a local drummer to find any work as a pickup player, though traveling shows often do use local percussionists. For keyboard players, the market is also somewhat limited because so many of the shows travel with their own. Nevertheless, there are enough second keyboard parts and subbing opportunities to keep local pianists relatively busy. The largest amount of pickup work available is probably for string, woodwind, and brass players, as well as guitarists and bassists.

Occasionally a show will tour with a totally self-contained orchestra, and therefore not need to hire any pickup players. This happens when the producers decide that due to musical complexity, the show will require a prohibitive amount of rehearsal time in each city it travels to. In such cases, it actually becomes more expensive to use locals. As usual, these decisions are not based on musical considerations as much as the bottom line.

Assuming that pickup players are being used, it's the responsibility of the local contractor to hire them. By definition, a *contractor* is usually a musician who's hired by the producers to recruit the rest of the orchestra. When the touring company gets to town, the local musicians will rehearse and play the show under the direction of the conductor who travels with the company. Sometimes they'll get only one day of rehearsal before the first show. If it's a complex show, there will also be a dress rehearsal with the cast. Occasionally the music will be sent ahead to the next city so that the local musicians there can look at in advance. In any case, pickup players, like any other theater musicians, need to be able to read music well.

Playing Other Theater Gigs

Once you get below the level of theaters that put on traveling road company productions, you get into a whole different class of work, usually non-union, with significantly lower pay scales for the musicians. In some cases, there are productions that use tapes in place of live musicians. As Bonnie Boss observes,

> The producers don't care enough about live music, and unfortunately, the more that happens, the more the audience

becomes anesthetized to it. The producers aren't there to watch audience members lean over the pit and say, "Wow, look at these people, isn't this neat, isn't this cool." I've even been sitting in the pit when people have walked by and said, "Oh, there *is* an orchestra in there." Because they're so desensitized to live music, and they don't understand what it lends to the performance. They really don't get it. They don't get the magic that happens at every performance.

The smaller independent shows that do use live players are usually short-run productions at suburban regional theaters or smaller theaters in big cities. Chicago has a particularly robust independent theater scene that doesn't offer a lot of steady, high-paying work, but it does have a lot of opportunities. Ben Sussman and Andre Pluess are cofounders of Stagenotes Music, a company in Chicago that arranges, contracts, and musically directs such shows. According to Sussman, "We find that in Chicago there are a lot of small theaters that want to do original musicals or even preexisting musicals on a very small scale. I think Chicago kind of has a reputation for grassroots theater. There's a special free paper here called *The Reader*; it runs at least as many theater listings of small shows as movie listings." He says that the typical run for an independent musical at this level is about six weeks and the typical pay for a run of that length is around $55 per musician, per night.

There are also summer stock productions in various parts of the country. You can find listings for these in the spring in theater trade publications such as *Backstage,* as well as theater sites on the Internet (see Appendix). Some of these productions have union contracts, but many are non-union.

Summer stock can provide a very good training ground for theater musicians. Jan Rosenberg (see "Profile/Jan Rosenberg: Broadway Keyboardist and Conductor," pages 118–119), who is now a successful Broadway keyboardist and conductor, recalls a particularly busy summer stock experience:

Back in 1983 I went out to the Pittsburgh Civic Light Opera Company and was associate conductor for one summer. That was a whole other incredible experience. . . . That summer we did *Pirates of Penzance, Oliver,* and Stephen Sondheim's *Follies,* which was the first show that season. I think we also did *Showboat, They're Playing Our Song,* and *Music Man.* You do this season where you're rehearsing one show all day long, for eight hours. You have an hour or two off, then you go back and you play another [different] show at night. . . . Great, great training.

In addition to summer stock there are dinner theaters, which also tend to be predominantly non-union. In some places you can find regional theaters that put on independent productions that sometimes include live musicians. The pay for these types of theaters tends to be one-third or one-half the union scale for a large production.

Sometimes you can also find decent-paying work in community theaters. Gordon Messick gives an example from the San Francisco area:

Around here there are some community theaters that are actually sort of half-professional, half-amateur. . . . And the orchestras tend to lean a little bit that way also. They'll have sort of a core orchestra of amateurs that they can get to rehearse for thirty hours or something. And then when it gets close to performance time they'll hire a few ringers—professionals—to come in and play some key chairs.

Even if you have to start out by taking work that doesn't pay well, the process of playing the shows will help develop your abilities, your résumé, and your connections.

PREPARING YOURSELF FOR THEATER WORK

In order to be a theater musician, you need to be an accomplished, versatile player. Despite Broadway's propensity for up-tempo, two-beat show tunes, you may be asked to play any style, from rock to jazz to classical, within the course of a given show. The more authenticity you bring to your performance, the better your chances of being hired again.

Reading, Reading, Reading

One skill that you'll need almost more than any other is the ability to read for your instrument. As previously stated, most musical scores are heavily written out, and you need to be able to play your part exactly as notated. If you're a string, reed, or brass player, chances are you're already a good reader, so this won't be an obstacle to you. For rhythm-section players, however, it can be a different story.

There's an old joke that goes, "How do you get a guitarist to turn down? Put some music in front of him." This joke was borne out of the reality that many guitarists, especially those coming from a rock and roll background, don't read well, if at all. This is also true for many bass players and drummers. You can be the greatest player in the world, but if you can't read you're going to have big problems playing for musical theater.

If your reading skills are very weak, I'd suggest making a concerted effort to improve them before you start looking for professional theater work. It's a bit of a quandary because the best way to improve your reading is in a working situation, but you don't want to take on something that you can't handle. You've got to remember that contractors have their own reputations on the line when they hire players, so naturally they'll be very hesitant to hire you back if you make them look bad for any reason, including a lack of reading skills. When you consider the fact that in most cities there are only a handful of contractors that hire for musical theater, you can see how damaging it could be to your career to alienate any of them.

Perhaps the best solution for those with reading deficiencies is to practice regularly and often (preferably under a teacher's supervision) and to try to get experience in nonprofessional reading situations such as jazz workshops and amateur community theater productions. That way you can improve your skills without damaging your reputation.

Learning How To Follow a Conductor

Another skill that is absolutely of the highest importance for theater musicians is the ability to follow a conductor. The conductor of a musical has an immense amount of responsibility, which includes a lot more than just conducting the orchestra. He or she also must watch what's happening onstage and make sure that the music is correctly following the action. If something goes wrong onstage, such as an actor forgetting the lyrics of a song, the music must be adjusted to avoid a complete train wreck. In turn, the musicians need to be able to follow the conductor precisely and without hesitation.

If you've never worked with a conductor before, it takes some getting used to. Despite the fact that there's supposed to be a standard way in which the hand motions of a conductor work, you'll find that each one handles them somewhat differently. You'll also find that the conductor's demeanor has a huge impact on the morale of the orchestra. Because they're under so much pressure, some conductors are quite testy and tend to jump all over you if you make a mistake. Others are a little more tolerant. Either way, you want to always stay on their good side. If a conductor doesn't like you, he or she can make sure that you never work on one of their shows again.

Ideally, you'll have had some experience playing with a conductor at the high school or college level before you get into a professional orchestra situation. If you haven't, it's a good idea to educate yourself about the basics of conducting so that you have a better idea of what's going on. One approach is to take a class in conducting to learn the mechanics of it. Tim Berens, a Dayton-based guitarist, did exactly that. "When I took that class," he says, "I finally figured out what those beats meant. From that point on I could follow the conductor."

Understanding Your Role as an Orchestra Member

If most of your performing background has been with bands, you'll find that playing in a theater orchestra (also known as a *pit orchestra*) is a very different experience. You're a cog in a wheel playing somebody else's compositions, and you rarely have the opportunity to express yourself musically. It's more of a "job" than playing in a rock band, but in most cases it pays a lot better.

If you're a rhythm-section player and have spent most of your career playing in bands, crossing over to the world of theater music will probably be a big transition for you. You'll not only have to adjust to playing with a conductor, but to limiting your playing to what's in the score. Reed, brass, and string players, on the other hand, are much more likely to have had orchestra or big-band experience, and therefore won't find the pit orchestra to be such an alien environment.

The drummer in a show has an especially awesome amount of responsibility. He or she must play forcefully at all times (a tentative drummer will never last), yet be flexible enough to follow tempo adjustments that the conductor makes based on what's happening onstage. It's not an easy line to walk, and there are many good drummers who have failed at playing musicals because they couldn't get comfortable with following the conductor. Drummers who've spent most of their careers playing in bands are used to being in control of the tempo, and many find it hard to give up that control. Yet, to be successful in a show that's what you need to do.

Here is a case in point that I remember from a Broadway show I played on. A well-known drummer with a reputation as a stellar studio musician came in to sub the show, and there was quite a bit of excitement around the pit, as many of the musicians looked forward to hearing him play. Unfortunately, when he did play the show he was a complete disaster. Despite the fact that he was a world-class drummer, he was either unable or unwilling to take direction properly from the conductor, and consequently bombed big-time. Meanwhile, there were other subs for that drum chair with much less in the way of chops, who nevertheless succeeded at playing the show because they understood their role and were able to take direction.

Whatever instrument you play, you need to approach being in a pit orchestra from the perspective that you're a small but important piece of a big puzzle. If you're looking for individual glory, you're unlikely to find it playing in musicals.

Special Opportunities for Keyboard Players

If you're a keyboard player, you have a unique set of opportunities in musical theater that no other instrumentalist can claim. Pianists not only get hired to play shows, but they often get quite a bit of rehearsal work as well. Most rehearsals are done with a piano only because the cost of bringing in a full orchestra to rehearse on a regular basis is prohibitive.

Broadway shows typically have pretty full rehearsal schedules. There are understudy rehearsals that occur regularly, as well as

> PROFILE | **JAN ROSENBERG**
>
> # Broadway Keyboardist and Conductor
>
> **T**hrough talent, perseverance, and networking, Jan Rosenberg has built a successful career as a Broadway musician and conductor. She's been a keyboardist and/or associate conductor for numerous Broadway shows, including *Tommy, How To Succeed in Business, My Favorite Year, Cats,* and *Starlight Express.* She's also subbed on many other shows.
>
> "Like most pianists, I studied classical music throughout high school," she says, but what she really enjoyed was musicals. "I got the theater bug in high school; I actually played piano for it. I also played piano in the high school choir and for rehearsals in the school productions. Actually, in my senior year I might have conducted, too. God knows how."
>
> Rosenberg studied music in college and continued to play for school theatrical productions.
>
> > I think I always knew in my heart that theater was where I wanted to be. Unlike most musicians, I think pianists have other expectations about the theater. You're much more involved with the actual production than just going into a pit and playing. . . . You're in a process, there's a whole rehearsal process, working with the actors, the singers, the dancers.
>
> After college Jan began her career in New York and landed her first show on an audition that was listed in *Backstage* magazine. She jokingly describes it as an "Off-Off-Off-Off-Way-Off-Broadway thing." She played piano and served as musical director. "And I just started from there, to meet people, to play at auditions. . . . I got my first subbing job through a friend of a friend. The show was the revival of *Peter Pan* with Sandy Duncan." She feels that she got the opportunity to sub as a result of "taking the steps of just getting out there and meeting as many people, doing a lot of Off-Off-Off-Broadway stuff."
>
> In addition to doing a season of summer stock, she began subbing on some other Broadway shows, including *Evita, The Mystery of Edwin Drood,* and *Me and My Girl.*
>
> > My first show that became my own was the first national touring company of *Cats.* I did the road thing for twenty-one months. That was at the end of 1983. I went out and was the first keyboard player on that. I left in August of 1985, and by that December I had my first chair on Broadway, for *Starlight Express.*

Rosenberg agrees that subbing is the best way to get into the Broadway scene, but cautions, "It's hard to sub if people don't know you." One way she recommends making contacts is to try and get work playing piano for actors and actresses who are auditioning for parts. She also suggests doing Off-Off-Broadway as well as cabaret (see "Getting Cabaret Gigs," later in this chapter)."I did a ton of cabaret because they [the cabaret singers who are frequently actors and actresses] always have friends, and [recommendations are made by] word of mouth." She also recommends patience. "In the theater business it takes a while to get established. It took me a good five, six, seven years to become truly established."

If you do get an opportunity to sub a Broadway show, Jan has some advice on getting prepared: "Watch a show, record it. Sometimes go back and watch the show again. The reason for that is that keyboard players have a slightly more difficult time because we're not playing our own instruments. With synthesizers being in the pit so much, you rarely ever find an acoustic piano anymore." She goes on to explain that because the synth setups vary for each show, it's important for a sub to get used to making the *patch changes* (changes from one sound, or "patch," to another) that are called for in most keyboard parts.

> So you go home and practice your part on the piano, and then you go to the theater whenever you can to practice. . . . You need to learn how to make those switches, and what the actual keyboard feels like. Again, like drummers and the rhythm section, a lot of times your conductor really relies heavily on you—sometimes your chair could very well be the glue of the show—so it's often good to go back a second time after you've learned the book and watch the conductor. . . . You don't have a section to hide under, so it requires a great deal of practice.

Rosenberg's scariest moment in theater came when an earthquake hit during a performance of *Starlight Express* she was conducting in L.A.

> It happens to have been in the biggest part of the show, when the most special effects occur: A laser beam opens, a big musical crescendo goes on, this whole technical thing. . . . So I look out in the audience, I see half of them leaving the theater, the other half thinking that it was part of the effect. . . . I was looking at the band and the band was ready to jump, and I'm thinking: "The stage management will call me to stop if they want me to stop.". . . It really put the business in perspective for me at that point . . . I kept thinking to myself, "For all I know, all of Hollywood Boulevard could be leveled right now, and I'm an a theater conducting a show about trains. Where is reality?" Sure enough, it was about a five-point-five.

periodic dance rehearsals. On long-running shows there are auditions as well as rehearsals for replacements in the cast. Pianists are also hired by actors and actresses who are auditioning and need an accompanist, a route that some pianists have used to get their foot in the door.

Being a keyboard player in a musical can mean a lot more than just showing up and playing for each performance. You often have a real opportunity to get involved in the nuts and bolts of the production. Another advantage is that if you have conducting skills, you may eventually wind up as an assistant (or associate) conductor. Like any other musician, conductors can't be at every show and it's usually the player in the first piano chair (also known as "keyboard 1") who subs for them. According to long-time Broadway pianist and conductor Ethyl Will, "Somehow when you're a keyboard player *and* the assistant conductor, you're almost more like management. You're not really just a sideman; it's a slightly different job, because you really have to work with the choreographers, the cast, and the stage managers." Kathy Sommer, who holds the keyboard 1/associate conductor chair for the Broadway production of *Beauty and the Beast,* defines the job this way: "As the associate conductor, you're basically responsible for whatever the conductor needs you to do to help the ship sail smoothly: playing dance rehearsals, teaching vocals to understudies, giving notes, stepping in to conduct the orchestra whenever called upon, and basically doing whatever's necessary. It's an extra pair of hands and an extra person who's aware of everything that's happening."

BREAKING INTO THEATER WORK

As in any sector of the music business, getting work as a theater musician is based as much on who you know as what you know. You need to find your way into a working situation and use that as a springboard to build your reputation and name recognition. Getting theater work requires that you meet as many people as you can who can potentially recommend you for work. As I've stressed elsewhere, the best kind of contacts are working contacts: Any musicians you've met while on a gig. They're the ones who'll have the most credibility when they suggest your name to a contractor or other potential employer.

Devising a Strategy

Many successful theater music careers have developed in a random fashion, with luck and chance playing a big role. Unfortunately, for each success story there are a lot of careers that never got off the ground because the musicians didn't know where to look for the work and had no plan for how to get it.

First, you need to figure out what you want out of being a pit musician. Do you want to be full-time and devote your career to it, or do you just want to supplement your other gigs? If your answer is the former, then you should probably plan on moving to New York (if you don't live there already) with the ultimate aim of ending up on Broadway. In any other part of the country, theater music isn't likely to provide you with steady employment for a prolonged period of time, so you'll have to supplement with other types of gigs or a day job.

This brings up a key point: Because success in music is so highly predicated on making contacts and networking, it's somewhat self-defeating to work in one area of the country with the intention of moving to another eventually. When you move to a new place you'll have to start from square one in terms of contacts. Therefore, if your aim is to work on Broadway, it makes sense to move to New York as soon as you can so that the time and energy you spend making contacts doesn't go to waste. The only exception to this is if you've had little or no theater experience and feel you need work on your skills and your résumé before heading to New York. There are a lot of smaller theater venues around the country where you can accomplish that goal, in summer stock, community theater, regional theater, and dinner theater.

If you're a keyboard player, you're in a much better position to succeed in theater music full-time. You not only can play shows, but you can also get work as a rehearsal pianist and as an accompanist for acting auditions and cabaret. More importantly, you've got more upward mobility than other pit orchestra members due to the fact that many keyboard players go on to be associate conductors and sometimes even *musical directors* (conductors).

You also need to assess your skills to see if you're ready to play Broadway or other high-level theater situations. If you're a good player and your résumé includes significant theater or orchestral experience, your skill level is probably high enough to jump directly to Broadway work and be able to handle it. Otherwise, you might want to consider getting some other theater experience first. It is possible to make the jump to Broadway without a lot of experience, but it's harder. In my case, I played for one college production that lasted a grand total of two shows before I subbed for the first time on Broadway, so it can be done.

Starting out as a Sub

The best-case scenario for getting into the theater circuit is to have a friend who is involved with writing, producing, directing, or contracting a show who can get you into the orchestra as a regular player. For most people, however, the only way to get started on the scene is as a sub.

Everyone involved with theater music with whom I spoke agreed that subbing is the most common way that musicians get started playing on Broadway or other high-level theater scenes. Although it varies from city to city, union theater contracts generally allow players to sub between 40 and 50 percent of the performances during any given year that their show is running. While most do not sub out that much, many do have other musical projects going on and need to use subs quite often. A Broadway show has eight performances a week, which is a lot for one player to do if they have anything else going and/or a family life. On Broadway, most players in long-running shows have two, three, or more subs that they call in from time to time. Typically, a sub will get called in a few times a month. The musician whose "chair" it is (the regular) has to keep all the subs working on a fairly frequent basis to keep them from getting rusty. The regulars also have to tread a fine line in terms of how many subs they have. They want to have enough so that there's always someone available, but they can't have too many or the subs won't play enough shows to remain sharp.

In many situations, a sub must be approved by the contractor or the conductor. Subbing is highly stressful and does not usually provide steady work unless the regular player takes some significant time off or you're being called to sub by musicians on a number of different shows. Nevertheless, once you start doing it you'll have your foot in the door and can begin developing a reputation.

Finding Sub Work

Getting yourself into a position where someone asks you to sub for them is the hardest part of the process. Ideally, you'll have musical acquaintances who'll ask you to sub for them. This scenario generally only happens to musicians who've been playing professionally in the same geographical area for a number of years and have developed a large number of contacts. Even if you've been working in another sector of the music business, there's so much crossover between different scenes that you have a good chance of knowing or at least knowing of someone who's a theater musician. The key is to make a reputation for yourself so that your name gets around. According to Kathy Sommer, you need to do "anything that gets you out there in somebody's face, so that they see and hear what you sound like as a player, and get to know your skills as a musician. I think that's the idea. I don't think it's a matter of sending your tape around, that's for sure."

I got my first Broadway subbing opportunity through a band leader whom I did occasional gigs for. Another musician we both knew was playing in a show and the band leader clued me in that this guy was looking for subs.

Think long and hard about who you know in town that might be involved with playing for the theater. If you studied music in college, try to find out if there are any alumni from your school who are working for musicals. Sometimes the college connection can help you get in the door. Ethyl Will recalls that a school contact helped her get a big break early in her career: playing at Radio City Music Hall. "The contractor was an old Eastman grad who loved to hire Eastman people. . . . When he heard that I had gone to Eastman he hired me to sub in the orchestra, and for me that was a really big deal."

If you don't have any direct contacts, you might have some friends or acquaintances who know someone who's playing in the theater scene and can give you a recommendation. Ultimately, your goal is to find musicians who are working in the theater and play the same instrument as you do. Once you get someone's name, contact him or her and ask if he or she is looking for subs. Perry Cavari, a very busy Broadway drummer (see "Q&A/Perry Cavari, Broadway Drummer: On Working as a Sub," pages 134–136),

ADVICE FROM THE CONTRACTORS

Contractors play a very important role in musical theater. They're the ones who hire the regular players, and, in many cases, approve the subs. On Broadway, they're often referred to as *musical coordinators,* and they generally don't play in the orchestra. Because they don't, each show has what's known as an *in-house contractor,* who is an orchestra member and functions as an assistant to the musical coordinator. The in-house contractor also takes care of the payroll and associated paperwork and also coordinates the subs. Outside of New York, there's usually just one contractor for a show, and this person hires the musicians, does the paperwork, and is often a member of the orchestra.

At separate times I spoke with four different contractors from various parts of the country about shows, how new players get hired, and various other pertinent matters. Since they're so intimately involved in the personnel issues for musicals, I thought it would be informative to compare their thoughts on a variety of questions. I spoke with John Miller, a bass player and one of Broadway's most successful musical coordinators; Stu Blumberg, a trumpeter who contracts for some of the larger Los Angeles theaters; L.A. contractor and percussionist Bonnie Boss; and Neil Wetzel, a reed player who contracted the Valley Forge Music Fair until it closed in early 1997. I asked each contractor what he or she felt is the most important thing for an aspiring theater musician to do in order to get work. It was universally agreed that subbing was the most direct route in. John Miller describes the process that players must go through in order to become subs:

> They should make sure that they meet the players who play their instrument. It's far more important to meet them than someone like me. . . . They've got to throw themselves to the wolves. They've got to eventually have the conductors hear them. Ideally what they want is to have the conductor say, "This is the best sub I've ever heard." What they don't want the conductor to say is, "I never want this guy to ever come into any of my pits again." Usually it's a gray area in between. But unless they get to know players who play their instrument, life will be very tough for them. No matter how many tapes or résumés and phone calls they make to someone like me, I think it's basically kind of insignificant.

Bonnie Boss echoed several of the points that John Miller made about subbing.

> Yeah, that's about the only way. It's hard to even become a sub. Really, it seems like the best way to become a sub is to meet the people. You almost have to play with the people who play the same instrument as you so that they can hear you, so that they have the confidence to recommend you as a sub, because it's very hard to get into anything in L.A., playing-wise.

Stu Blumberg agreed that subbing was the best avenue in, but added a caveat:

> It's very hard to get in without being heard, I will say that much. Someone can call you and talk to you on the phone. And I have to say that when people call me I try to be as accommo- dating and as polite as I can because it's a horrible thing to have to call someone and introduce yourself and say, "Gee, could you hire me if you can?" Fortunately, I've never had to do that, but I try to put myself in that person's position and I wouldn't want to have to do that. And it takes just as much energy for me to be a jerk as it does to be nice. And there's no reason for me to be a jerk.

When asked if subbing is a viable way of getting hooked into the the- ater scene in Philadelphia, Wetzel replied, "It is, but on a much more limited basis than in New York. It's not the type of scene where you could do a whole lot of work. . . . But it is a good way to get your name known."

Because they hire the musicians for shows, contractors hear from a lot of players who are looking for work. Wetzel said this:

> As a contractor I've gotten résumés, or had inquiries. Then I check it out with other people. I ask other contractors, "Did you ever hear of this person? Did you ever use them?" You go as much on recommendations as on people contacting you. . . . When I first wanted to play at the Forrest [one of the principal theaters in Philadelphia], I contacted my friend who was play- ing there. I asked him if I could just come in and sit in the pit, get to know the contractor. . . . It was a little bit after that when I first got called to do a gig. But it probably wasn't until some- body said, "Why don't you try Neil Wetzel?" You know it wasn't the fact that I was just there, although it helped to get my name known. Finally, I'm sure I was recommended by somebody.

Boss had this to add on the subject:

> When people call me up and tell me they're available, and I always try to be really polite to everyone because I know where they're at. I do ask for a résumé because you need to know something, you have to have some sort of frame of reference. People do send me tapes, but you know I don't have time to sit around listening to people's tapes. So those for me are a waste. But I do look at résumés because you can get quite a lot from that.

Miller recalls an episode that illustrates how, for a contractor, hearing someone play is worth a lot more than résumés or tapes:

> There's a great story of someone who was calling me up periodically, sending me letters, tapes, and résumés for a good three years, so I recognized the name as being a pain in the butt. When I stopped by one of the shows I was doing, I heard a sub playing and I thought he sounded absolutely great. I said, "Who is this guy?" They said, "Oh man, this guy's tearing this place up." I said, "What's his name?" And he was the same guy who'd been writing me all the time. I immediately gave him a show. He sounded unbelievable and he was the nicest guy in the world and the conductor loved him. That's what you want.

On the subject of what it takes to be a successful player in a pit orchestra, attitude was a quality that was mentioned repeatedly. According to Boss,

> There are some people who are perfectly good players, but either they're flaky or they're not in place when they're supposed to be, or you're wondering whether they're gonna show up. Or they're whiners, or they've got attitude problems, or they drive everybody around them nuts. There's just a lot of stuff that has nothing to do with music, so you really have to be

recommends this tactic if the musician you've contacted doesn't need any subs at the moment:

> The best way of doing it is to tell people you'd like to look at it [the player's written part, known as "the book"], even though they may not need you. Get in, be personable; of course, you should feel that you have the ability to do the job. Then maybe one day down the line they'll say, "You know, I need a new guy to come in." And if you can get a book and

careful with people. Especially [in a] pit orchestra. I'm very sensitive to who's sitting in the pit, because there are some pits that are really small and if people aren't getting along, oh boy, does it escalate. . . . I find that the people who can deal the best are the ones who are a just little more laid back, a little calmer, and can have the ability to accept what goes on and to roll with the punches a little bit.

Miller described, in a nutshell, the ideal theater musician: "It's not complicated: Sound great, be of good cheer, and show up on time." He went on to say that some musicians have trouble with the artistic constraints and the taking of direction that necessarily go along with being a theater musician:

Some people have an easy time with authority, some people don't. I don't think anyone took violin lessons to play in a Broadway pit, to play the same music eight times a week without being noticed. So some people are angry that they're playing Broadway shows, and some people feel it's beneath them. That's OK, you'll just have a tough time working—certainly a tough time working for me.

Blumberg put the role of a theater musician in perspective:

All we are is the accompaniment to what's going on, and it's our job to make it [sound] as pristine and as good on a regular basis as possible. The most important thing is that the people in the audience have an enjoyable night of theater. Now we can't control the subject matter or the content of what we're doing, but we can do it to the best of our abilities. And that's the kind of player that I like to hire. I myself put a hundred percent effort into every show that I play, or even just contract and don't play. I like to think that I hire the same kind of players, who don't just phone it in.

work on it, it's a good learning experience and maybe one day they will need you.

If you have absolutely no contacts, you can try to identify the musicians who play your instrument in a particular show by asking around at the union (provided you're a member). They probably won't give out that information officially, but you should be able to find someone who knows about the personnel. You might also attend any union meetings that emphasize the subject of theater music in order to try to make some contacts. Unfortunately, even if you're able to find out the names of musicians whom you could potentially sub for, it's hard to get taken seriously when you're approaching someone without a recommendation. According to Kathy Sommer:

> I get a lot of résumés from people, a huge number from pianists. Every once in a blue moon you look at somebody's credits and say, "Oh, that's somebody I'm interested in." But it generally doesn't happen like that, because when you're playing on Broadway you don't want someone who's too green. You need somebody who's had some experience. Someone you can count on.

Another approach is to find out the names of contractors and get in touch with them. Again, you can use the musicians union as a resource to get the names of the contractors. Contact them and offer to send a résumé. If you can impress them enough, they might give your name to theater musicians who need subs, or at least give you some names to contact (see "Advice from the Contractors," pages 124–127).

Yet another excellent way to get connected is to take lessons with a working theater musician. If you're good enough, they'll recognize it, and you'll have a good chance of being asked to sub. In addition, they'll probably be able to give you the names of some other people to contact.

I'd advise against trying any of this unless you're very sure that your skills are at a high level. As the old cliché goes, you have only one chance to make a first impression. This is particularly true in the area of theater music, where even in a large scene like Broadway a bad reputation can get around quickly. It's even worse in a smaller city where there's a handful of theaters, one or two contractors, and only a couple of people for whom you could potentially sub. If you're insecure about your ability to cut it in a big-time show, you might want to aim your energy toward getting work in lower-level productions such as community theater, where you can work on your skills without as much pressure. As your abilities and confidence grow, you can start casting your net higher and higher in search of better work.

Preparing for Your First Subbing Job

Once you've gotten over the big hurdle of initially landing some subbing work, you've got to make sure you do a good job or your career as a sub will come to a screeching halt. The following section will guide you through the process of learning to sub a show.

Watching the Book The musician you're subbing for will almost certainly ask you to come in and observe the show from the pit. In New York this is referred to as *watching the book;* in Los Angeles it's simply called *auditing.* In many cities, the regular musician actually pays the sub to audit the show. In a city other than New York, where a sub may only get two or three opportunities to play during a four- or six-week run, paid audits came about as a way to help ensure that players put in some time learning the show.

On Broadway, on the other hand, this practice is unheard of. Gordon Messick explains: "Because of the long-running shows, a sub feels that he's glad to have the job and he'll make the money up in the long run."

When you do come in to observe for the first time, you'll sit next to the regular player and watch. Because pits are usually crowded to start with, squeezing in an extra person can sometimes mean you're sitting in a pretty cramped spot. I auditied one show where I had to sit on top of a guitar amp for three hours.

Unless the regular player already has one made, the main thing you need to accomplish while watching the show for the first time is to make a good-quality tape of it from start to finish, which you'll later use for practicing and reference. Ideally, the tape recorder you use will record in stereo so that you'll be able to hear the parts clearly and distinctly. Since you'll be sitting next to the player you're going to be subbing for, his or her part will be the loudest thing on your tape. This is good because it will allow you to hear everything that he or she is doing, even when the band is cranking.

Bring a few 90- or 100-minute tapes with you and keep an eye on how much tape you have remaining on a given side. Since you only get forty-five or fifty minutes a side, you'll have to flip the tape over at least once during an act to make sure you don't miss anything. Don't wait for the side to run out; preemptively flip the tape when you're a few minutes away from the end of the side, during dialogue rather than music. It's very important that you record every last bar of music, so be diligent. If there are long stretches of dialogue between certain songs, you'll be tempted to shut off your recorder to conserve tape, but I wouldn't recommend it. You won't know when the next song will be starting and you run the risk of missing the intro. In addition, dialogue can act as a cue for the start of the next number.

Don't expect to find AC power available for plugging in your tape deck. In many pits you'll find that all the outlets are in use. Plan on recording with batteries and put in a fresh set before you head over to the theater. You might even want to bring a spare set. If you find AC, great; if not, you're covered.

Besides making the tape, try to get a good feel for the setup of the player you're subbing for. If you're a guitar player, note what types of guitars the regular uses, any effects that need to be turned on and off, and anything about the setup that's unusual. For keyboards, note how the patch changes are made and how they're notated in the score. When you practice at home, you want to try and recreate the pit setup as much as possible. This is especially important if there are multiple instruments, known as "doubles," on the part. Set up your practice instruments similarly to how the regular has his or hers set up in the pit, so that the conditions at the show are simulated as much as possible. There are instances in some shows where players have to switch instruments very quickly. By practicing these changes at home as you're playing along with you're tape, you'll be learning not only how to play the music but how to make the switches smoothly. Pianist and conductor Michael Rice relates this anecdote about preparing to sub a Broadway show:

> One of the hardest things for a keyboard player to do is to get down the mechanics of a synthesizer. That's a major job. When I've rehearsed a book, and it may have been *Jerome Robbins's Broadway*, . . . I put up a little piece of paper on my piano and drew buttons to simulate the keyboard [in the pit]. And I actually hit those little pieces of paper when it was time to do it. And it really helped. I felt like an idiot at home, but it helped.

Drum subs have an even more compelling reason to make their

practice setups the same as the one at the show. If they don't, they'll be practicing hitting toms and cymbals that are in completely different places than the ones at the show. I guarantee that that's a recipe for disaster.

The third thing you need to do when auditing a show for the first time is to watch the conductor. The more you get used to the conductor's moves, the better prepared you'll be to play after you've learned your part.

Practicing the Show Before you start listening to the tape from the show, make a backup copy of it, if possible, and knock out the erase tabs on the original so you can't accidentally wipe anything. Rewind the tape to the beginning and zero the counter. Listen through the tape while looking at the music and write down the counter numbers for the start of each piece of music. Be sure to make a note of when you have to flip the tape. When you've listened to the entire show, you should have a list with the titles of all the musical numbers and their counter readings. This will make your practicing immeasurably easier, because you won't have to search through the tape for specific pieces of music.

Now you're finally ready to start learning the show. What works best for me is to start at the beginning and learn one piece at a time, in the order in which they occur. When you've got one piece learned, move to the next and learn that one. At some point in each practice session you should start at the beginning of the show and play down as much as you have learned. It's really helpful to do this, not only as a review of the material, but to get used to the flow of the show and any switches you might have to make.

When you're looking at the written music, it's especially important to check for any comments that the regular player has scrawled on the part. One of the things that he or she might note are dialogue cue lines at the beginning of a song or section. These indicate that when you hear that particular piece of dialogue, you should look at the conductor because the music will start right away, or shortly thereafter. If the regular has drawn what looks like a pair of glasses, this means "Look at the conductor." It's often accompanied by the word "Watch!"

If the part you're subbing for includes doubles, look carefully for the notations in the music indicating when to switch instruments. In addition, keyboard players should look out for patch changes and guitarists should watch for effects changes.

After working with the music for a while, you'll probably also start recognizing phrases that the orchestra plays just prior to your entrances and in other significant parts of a given piece. These so-called *cue licks* will help you keep your place and give you a frame of reference. If you have really long *tacets* (rests) in your part, knowing the cue licks just prior to your reentrance will give you the luxury of not having to count along with every bar all the time. This allows you to relax momentarily when you're not playing, which can help alleviate the stress.

As you're learning the show, there will likely be notes, phrases, or sections that you have questions about. Sometimes you'll find that what the regular played when you taped the show was different from what's written. Make a note of all these questions and ask the person you're subbing for about them. Another potentially helpful source of information is one of the regular player's other subs. Since they had to learn the part in the same manner as you did, they might have some good insights for you. Just be aware that if they're at all insecure they might view you as competition and not be very terribly forthcoming with information.

Everyone's learning time varies, and some parts are more difficult than others, but it's safe to figure that it'll take you a number of weeks to master the entire show. Once you've gotten to the point where you've learned all your parts, I'd recommend that you take another week or two to practice along with the tape. If you run the entire show twice a day you should be pretty comfortable with it by the end of that time. You want to be as relaxed with your part as you can before you play your first show, so don't be overeager to call the regular player and say that you're ready. You may think it'll look better to have learned the show quickly, but if you go in and make a lot of mistakes you probably won't get asked back. It's much more sensible to take some extra time and really lock in your part before that first show.

Playing Your First Show When you call the regular and let him or her know you're ready, they'll most likely give you a date to do your first show. When you've got that date booked, arrange to audit one more time shortly before the day you'll be playing. Use that audit to watch the conductor closely and try to get a handle on his or her style. Especially if there are any points in the show where you have to come in by yourself, you want to be able to "read" the conductor's baton motions so that you'll enter correctly.

If you're going to be using the regular player's instruments, make sure to find out where any spare parts, such as strings, cables, drumheads, and so on, are kept. You don't want to hunt for that stuff during a performance.

When you come in for your first show, the most important thing you'll need to do is relax. Subbing for the first time is a highly stressful experience, and if you're too keyed up you're not going to play well. Arrive an hour early so that you have plenty of time to set up, tune up (if you play a stringed instrument), warm up, and get accustomed to the instruments if you're not using your own. You'll also need time to fill out the paperwork that the in-house contractor gives you.

When I subbed the first time on Broadway, I had butterflies in my stomach beforehand and wondered how I'd ever get through the show. Somehow I managed it, but it felt like the longest three hours of my life.

Even if you make it through your first show with flying colors, you'll need to keep your concentration level equally high for subsequent performances because it's easy to have a letdown. Many subs do well on their first show only to have problems on their second or third. This was true in my case. After having my first two shows go well, I had a disastrous third that almost wrecked my confidence. Luckily, I managed to pull myself together after that and become a successful sub. In fact, things went so well that when the person I was subbing for decided to leave the show, I became the regular.

Subbing Outside of Broadway There is not nearly as much subbing work to be had outside of New York because there are fewer shows running, generally for much shorter durations. It's only when a show runs for more than a couple of months that any regular opportunities for subbing occur. Nevertheless, even if you

Q&A | **PERRY CAVARI**
BROADWAY DRUMMER

On Working as a Sub

At the time of this writing, Perry Cavari is the drummer for the hit Broadway show *Victor/Victoria*. He's played on numerous other shows as both a regular and a sub, including *Tommy, Crazy for You, Beauty and the Beast, The Will Rogers Follies, Kiss of the Spider Woman,* and *Evita*. Cavari has done a lot of subbing and has some very useful and specific advice for musicians (especially drummers) who are looking to sub.

Would you say that the only way to get in is to start out as a sub?
I wouldn't say it's the only way, but it's by far the path most taken. I know a lot of players who have gotten their shows by knowing the composer, the arranger, the lyricist, the orchestrator, or the writer. But if you're not fortunate enough to have those connections, you have to get on the horn, you have to make some calls, you have to start subbing. Subbing for people who have a track record, the Broadway guys, makes a lot more sense than subbing for someone who might have one show in his career because he knew a writer. Another way is to contact contractors and explain to them that you're willing to take or sub a road show. Because a lot of the people who are on Broadway right now were doing road shows. . . . Contractors will not give a new player work unless they've heard you or gotten a recommendation from someone who has. Of course, sending a résumé and a tape is required.

What do they look for on a résumé?
Musical background, everything you've done. It's hard for contractors; they have to protect their own [interests]. Their position is that they have to provide professional people who fulfill the service needed. And even though a tape is something that they'll hear along with a résumé, they really need some hands-on information. They want to hear from a conductor they know: "Oh yeah, I've worked with her; she's very good," or, "He's subbed this, he's subbed that." Because their reputations are on the line.

Describe what it's like to be a sub.
Subbing is one of the hardest and most thankless tasks in the music field. . . . Subbing drums or a piano chair is probably the most difficult. With drummers, even if you're a better player than the person you're subbing for, your feel is different, your timing is different, your volume

is different. All these little factors make the whole show feel different. My advice is: When you do sub, don't be a hero. Do exactly what [the player you're subbing for does]. When I learned all the books I subbed, I actually wrote in what cymbal to hit and where. I taped it [the show] a number of times. If I saw he did the same thing in a particular spot every time, I did that. In another spot, if I taped it three times and he did three different things, then I know in that spot you have a little freedom. But I would still pick one of the three things he did.

Do you have any other little tricks for learning a book?
Having subbed so many shows, I have a system of my own. My particular one is that I go in a minimum of three times, but usually it's three. The first time I do nothing but try to make a decent tape and just get a feel for what's going on. Then I go home and before I sit at the drums, I sit at a table with a pencil and a tape and transcribe everything that's not in the book that the regular does. Then, by the time I'm finished with that, I have a good feel for the show. Then I start practicing it. Then I'll go in again, I'll tape it again but I'll watch the drummer. All I want to do is see how he does things. Then I'll go home again and I'll practice and practice and practice. Since I have two tapes, I play the overture on one, for example, then I switch tapes and I play the overture again. Then I do the next tune. So now I'm doing everything twice in a row. And if there are any little differences between or nuances in each tape, you're learning both of them. I go over the hard numbers again and again and again. The third time I go in, I'm just watching the conductor. Then I'm ready to play it. And I tell subs, . . . "When you feel you know it, and you're ready to call me and say I'm ready, take two more weeks to practice." Because slow things fly by you. And if you should stumble and a conductor is starting to turn and comment to you, it's very high-stress. You have to stay cool and know exactly where you are. And more times than not I've said, "If I didn't know the show as well as I did, there would have been a train wreck."

Have you had a lot of train wrecks?
Fortunately, no. Have I ever made mistakes? Absolutely. In this business, if you make a mistake as a regular player, you get a smile. If you make it as a sub or as a first-timer, you may not work there again. The business has changed, too. Years ago, you learned the book, you came in and played. Now, you learn the book and you hear comments like, "He doesn't do this, he doesn't do that." They want to hear the sub do exactly what the other person's doing. . . . If I was a conductor, my feeling on a sub would be, "Let's get through it from beginning to end with no one getting hurt." Some conductors have that approach, they know

it's a different human being. Others expect it to be perfect, so it's a very hard situation to be in.

What do you think are the factors that make a show either easy or difficult to play?
I don't consider any show easy. The easy ones are hard. What makes it difficult in my eyes is that, first of all, you're following a conductor. Now as the drummer, you look up and the conductor's one place, the band's somewhere else, and you're in command of analyzing the situation. Go with the conductor and you're moving the band, which is part of your job. But sometimes the conductor is conducting the stage, which is getting a little behind and doesn't necessarily want the band to move—and you have to interpret. That's the key word. You have to interpret the conductor in a way that isn't a roller coaster, but yet you're doing your job, which is to follow the conductor and keep the band together. That's one of the hardest things, because it's not like doing a record date or anything else where you just go in and it starts and ends at the same place. Things move around a lot. Flexibility is the key word. Another thing that's difficult about subbing is that you're playing other people's equipment. . . . When I go in [to watch the show for the first time] I look at the setup, and I set up a set of drums exactly like it at home. If he has fifteen cymbals, I set up fifteen cymbals. If he has his toms flat and low, I set up mine flat and low, because the last thing you want to do is have to get used to a different set unexpectedly.

When you go in to actually sub, do you ever adjust any part of the regular player's drum kit?
I try not to move anything. The only thing I will adjust, and that's only if it's drastic, is the seat height. Because as a sub it makes it easier for you, and the regular player doesn't have to come back and adjust cymbal heights and stand heights. Try to learn to use everything that way. If you have to bring your own pedal, OK. I try not to do anything.

Do you have any advice specifically for first-time sub drummers?
You have to be overly prepared and my advice to the subs is: Know the tempos. When the conductor's hands come down, play, and play strong. If the tempo's not exactly right, you'll be adjusted. But don't come in tentatively and search for it. You won't last.

What's your advice for young players starting out as theater musicians?
Do anything you can—high school productions, regional productions—because the experience is unparalleled to anything you can do at home with a tape.

only get to sub a couple of performances of one show, it's worth doing because it's a great experience and it opens a whole world of contacts up for you. To get this work, use the same methods described under "Finding Sub Work," earlier in this chapter.

Breaking into Other Theater Work

If you're looking to get started doing theater music work outside of Broadway or other high-level urban theater scenes, you will most likely have to break in through methods other than subbing. Venues such as summer stock, regional theater, community theater, and dinner theater generally don't have a lot of subbing opportunities, if any. Many of them don't even have full orchestras (if they have musicians at all), and if they do, the combination of limited runs and lower pay make subbing a much less frequent occurrence. The reason is that if you're the regular player and you're only making $50 or $60 a show, you need to do all of the week's performances in order to make it worthwhile.

In order to get into these types of productions, you're going to have to send out some résumés unless you have some contacts. Look in theater industry publications such as *Backstage* to find listings of what shows are being produced and where. Contact theaters or production companies and find out who contracts the various shows. In some of the smaller, non-union situations, there may not be an official "contractor"; the musical director of the show might be the one who puts the band together. In any case, find out who does the hiring and call to ascertain the procedure for getting into the orchestra. If you're unable to reach the person, call back once a week or so until you do. They'll probably tell you to send a résumé. Perhaps you'll find a situation where they're looking for someone who plays your instrument. Keep in mind that it won't be easy to get work without a recommendation. There is no question that you'll be more successful in obtaining work if you can call up and say, "So and so suggested that I call," or "I'm a friend of so and so."

If your résumé is totally lacking in theater experience, you might want to try to find high school and college productions you can play in. Some high school productions will hire outside musicians to fill key chairs. Contact the drama departments at local

THEATER MUSICIAN'S SURVIVAL GUIDE

• Never, ever arrive late. Short of a major earthquake or equally serious catastrophe, no excuse is considered valid for being late for a show. Failure to arrive on time could very well lead to your termination. Make a habit of getting to the theater well before show time. This minimizes the chances of an unforeseen transportation delay. It also gives you sufficient time to warm up, tune up, or do whatever preparation you need to do.

• Make sure your instruments and any equipment you might use are functioning and ready to go well before the "five minute" warning call is given. This way you'll have time to deal with any unforeseen problems before curtain.

• Don't let the monotony of playing the same show over and over again dull your ability to play well. Make it a personal challenge to yourself to play each successive show better than the last.

• If you're subbing, make sure to leave things in your playing area the same way you found them. If you adjusted seat or stand heights, changed settings, or moved anything around, put it back the way it was. It's likely to annoy the regular player if he or she arrives in the pit and has to readjust things that you've changed. This might cause them to use you less and other subs more.

• Be deferential to the other members of the orchestra. If you come off cocky or obnoxious and annoy the other musicians, you can bet that word will get back to the person you're subbing for. Furthermore, many of these musicians might at some point be in a position to recommend you for work, so try to get on their good side.

• Always play forcefully. Indecision never sounds good in a pit orchestra. You should be comfortable enough with your part to be able to play it with energy and strength.

• Be courteous with the stagehands and other members of the theater staff. Having them on your side will make the time you spend there a whole lot easier.

schools to find out if this is a possibility. Even if they don't pay, you might want to consider volunteering just to get the experience.

GETTING CABARET GIGS

Cabaret is linked to the theater in a number of ways, the most obvious of which is that its standard repertoire is largely made up of show tunes. Although a cabaret show usually only consists of one singer and a pianist or small ensemble, cabaret shares a sensibility with the theater in that the acts frequently have a director and some sort of lighting design. More important from a musician's standpoint, many cabaret singers are actors and actresses (both aspiring and working) and therefore represent a good networking opportunity. In fact, there are many musicians who move back and forth between the theater and cabaret worlds.

With very few exceptions, pianists are the only musicians (not including the singers) who can make steady money in cabaret. For them it also presents a great opportunity to develop contacts in the theater world. For other rhythm-section players, it's a different story. Some acts do supplement piano with a small rhythm section consisting of bass, drums, and maybe guitar, but the opportunities are more limited. Michael Rice, who in addition to playing on Broadway has worked extensively on the cabaret scene, had this to say about the amount of work for non-piano players: "I think they'd have a lean winter if they sat around waiting to get called to do a cabaret gig." For pianists, however, the outlook is much brighter, because piano is a fixture in the cabaret sound. Another advantage for pianists is that, just as in the theater world, there's money to be made rehearsing with the singers and helping them develop their acts.

Cabaret clubs are generally found only in large urban areas. Due in large part to its vibrant theater scene, New York City has the country's most happening cabaret circuit. At the time of this writing there are over thirty clubs there that feature cabaret acts, either exclusively or part of the time. These clubs range from Rainbow and Stars, the most prestigious cabaret club in New York, to small piano bars.

Although it's mostly non-union, cabaret work pays pretty well compared to other nightclub work. Generally, the musicians negotiate a deal directly with the singer, who pays them out of his or her proceeds from the job. Typical pay in New York is around $100 to $125 per gig. For players who are in demand, especially pianists, it can be closer to $200 per gig. The gigs are usually only one or two sets long and they often have paid rehearsals in the days or weeks preceding them. Another advantage for the musicians is that these gigs can occur on any night of the week, not just Friday and Saturday. Weekday gigs are not as plentiful for musicians as those on the weekend, so consequently they're highly prized.

For a keyboard player, a piano bar gig can net them close to $200 per night in a combination of salary and tips. These gigs consist of playing show tunes and other popular material, often by request. The downside of piano bar work is that the gigs often last close to six hours, which is two hours more than the typical bar band gig. They're also grueling from a repertoire standpoint because the pianist must handle a very large number of requests.

As in any other segment of the business, you need to have contacts in order to get work in the cabaret world. If none of your friends or acquaintances is involved in that scene, you've got to make your own connections. One way to do this is to hang around at the cabaret clubs and get to know some of the performers. The clubs are pretty informal, so you shouldn't feel too intimidated talking to the singers and musicians when they're on their break. Ask them if they know of any singers looking for musicians and perhaps, if you can convince them of your credentials, they'll give you a name or two to call. In the process of your conversation you might discover that you know some musicians in common, which would help establish you in their eyes as well. For piano bar gigs, you need to contact club owners similar to the way you would when trying to get bar band work. (See "Pounding the Pavement" in Chapter 3.)

In New York there's an organization called the Manhattan Association of Cabarets and Clubs, or MAC (see Appendix). They have information on the clubs in the city that feature cabaret, and would be a good starting point for networking.

Another route is to try to get work as an audition or rehearsal pianist for actors and actresses. They make up a large percentage of cabaret singers, so they're a logical place to start. Look in the trade papers for ads, place your own ad, or even put up signs at acting schools or college drama departments.

CHAPTER 6 | GETTING WORK PLAYING CLASSICAL MUSIC

❖

If you're interested in working in a symphony orchestra, or if you're a student contemplating a career as a classical musician, the following chapter will describe how to get work in this segment of the business.

One of the advantages that a classical musician has over his or her pop and jazz contemporaries is that there is more of an established career path for achieving success. A classical player who is extremely talented and follows the prescribed road has a relatively good chance of making a decent living. While nothing is guaranteed, getting from point A to point B is a lot clearer in the classical world than in other segments of the business, where the path to success is more dependent on chance and less precisely defined. Sheer talent counts for more in classical music than in pop, where charisma, looks, and savvy are also decisive factors. There are all too many instances in the pop world where someone with a lot of appeal but very little talent has been able to make it. This rarely happens in classical music. Nevertheless, for all but the most extraordinarily gifted, success does not come easily. You must devote yourself completely to your instrument and you also have to network.

THE WORK THAT'S OUT THERE
Aside from being a featured soloist, an objective that few players ever attain, being a permanent member of a big-city symphony

orchestra is the ideal job for many classical musicians. The pay is good and the prestige is enormous. In addition, many orchestras offer the players tenure after a specified number of years of service, which means that they can keep their position, or *chair*, for life. As a result of this tenure system, chairs only open up when a tenured member retires or dies. Consequently, the amount of vacancies are somewhat limited. Couple this with the fact that there are many more qualified musicians than there are chairs, and the dilemma that a classical player faces upon leaving school and entering the job market is obvious.

To make matters more difficult, not all orchestras pay what's considered a "living wage." Although just about all of the work is unionized, an annual salary depends on the prestige of the orchestra and the number of events that are played in a given season. A typical orchestra will not only play a number of large concerts, it will fill out its calendar with park concerts, children's concerts, and other smaller events. An annual salary can be in the neighborhood of $80,000 for a principal chair in one of the most prestigious orchestras, such as the New York or Los Angeles Philharmonic, but it can also be in the high teens or low twenties for smaller orchestras, such as the Fort Wayne Philharmonic. These salaries generally are based on union scale for performances and a lower scale for rehearsals. Some orchestras use a different system in which musicians are paid the same rate whether it's a concert or a rehearsal. They define either of these events as a *service*.

For those musicians who don't have regular chairs, there are other methods to make money playing, though none are easy. Many become freelancers and work with as many orchestras as they can. There are plenty of smaller orchestras that don't pay nearly enough to constitute a living wage, so the players in them are by necessity freelancers. There are also opportunities to work for the larger orchestras on an occasional basis by getting on what's called their *sub list*. This is a list of available musicians to be called in when players are either sick or unavailable, or when a particular composition calls for more pieces than are in the regular orchestra. The subbing system is completely different in symphony orchestras than it is for musical theater. In contrast to musicals, symphony musicians generally don't have their own personal subs for when they can't make a show. Instead, the orchestra has its own hierarchical list of subs for each instrument that get called on an as-needed basis.

Besides symphony orchestras, there's some work to be had playing in smaller ensembles and chamber groups. For the most part, however, freelancers cannot make their money solely from live performance of classical music. They generally have to supplement their income from a variety of other sources.

In the past, recording work was a staple for freelance players but the volume of it has been greatly diminished by the advent of synthesizers, samplers, and MIDI. The crème de la crème of studio string players who were making six-figure incomes in the 1970s and '80s have found their work more than cut in half, and others who were getting sessions on a less regular basis are barely working at all anymore. Nevertheless, there's still work to be had, especially in the jingle field, but it's a lot harder to get than it used to be.

Just as many rock and pop studio players have had to gravitate to theater music to make up for lost recording work, so have a lot of classical players. According to New York violinist and contractor Dale Stuckenbruck (see "Q&A/Dale Stuckenbruck, Violinist and Contractor: Career Advice for Classical Musicians," pages 152–154), who is a veteran of both symphony orchestra and Broadway work,

> Many of the people from the recording field have come into the best thing in New York, which is Broadway. They've also come from the freelance [classical] scene . . . and now they've all merged into the Broadway scene. Broadway has become the thing. I know concert masters who would frown on Broadway; they're all doing Broadway now. It's the only thing that's making progress that they can actually live on. I got involved early on and I've been extremely lucky.

Another way for classical players to earn money is through private party work. Strolling violinists, string quartets, harpists, and guitar and flute duets are often hired for weddings and other events. New York–based freelance violinist Laura Seaton (see "Profile/Laura Seaton: Freelance Violinist,"pages 144–145) says that not only can this kind of work bring in decent income, "it's also a nice way to meet people and actually have them hear you in a small setting." To get party work, you either have to hook up with a leader who'll

---

PROFILE | **LAURA SEATON**

Freelance Violinist

When it comes to the importance of networking, classical music is no different than any other segment of the music business. The story of violinist Laura Seaton illustrates that, if you're good enough, you can use one contact to start yourself on the road to a successful career. Seaton is a busy freelancer in New York City, playing not only orchestral jobs but many commercial recording sessions as well. She also has a jazz background, and her versatility has enabled her to handle the wide variety of styles required of a session player. "I've done tangos, jazz spots, and country spots," she says referring to the commercials she's played on. She's also played or recorded with such artists as Hall and Oates, Carly Simon, and Elvis Costello.

Seaton was a performance major in college, then went on to get an advanced degree in London as well as a masters in music performance with a jazz minor at Indiana University. After she completed her graduate work, she decided to move to New York to try to get established in the music scene there. Just prior to her move, a friend gave her the name of a cellist to contact when she got there. She describes what happened next:

> So I called her when I got to New York . . . and she said, "There's this group you should really come check out. We're playing at an outdoor concert soon, and you can meet the leader." The leader was Marin Alsop, who's now having quite a conducting career. So I went to the concert, and got introduced, and Marin was interested because I said I was an improviser. And that was 1984, when there weren't as many string improvisers around, and at that time it was an all-woman group. So she and this other woman, Diana, invited me to play chamber music with them, and Marin really liked my playing. She was a very busy freelancer, really established, so she was one of my first col-

---

hire you, or get out and pound the pavement for it yourself, which is very time-consuming.

GETTING THE PROPER SCHOOLING

In the classical music field, it's imperative that a musician get the correct kind of education, for two reasons. First and foremost, you leagues who would give my name out. "I can't do it, but call this person." . . . That's always the best way. . . . In that first year I met some key people whom I'm still working with to this day.

Once she started getting some work, Seaton's network of contacts began to mushroom. She tried not to turn any work down in that first year, and all that effort paid off in some valuable connections. One gig she took got her started doing sessions on the commercial music scene.

I did a chamber music job, and one of the violinists was quite an established session musician. He needed a sub for a film date because he had a jingle. So I went in and subbed for him. . . . My stand partner was a contractor. I think on a whim, basically, just from talking to me, he hired me for some jingles.

The more Seaton played, the more people she met, and things really started to take off.

That first year I also met David Soldier, who was starting an avant-garde string quartet called the Soldier String Quartet, which I worked with for eight years. We did avant-garde improvisation, rock and roll, and new music of every genre. This group opened doors for touring in Europe, and I returned many times with the quartet and as a soloist. Musically, that was a whole new realm for me.

Since that first year back in 1984, Seaton has built on her success to the point where she now has a solid career as a freelancer that's been rewarding both financially and artistically. Her advice for newcomers in the scene is that they need to have more than just ability to make it.

Talent is a large part of the equation—it definitely is. You've got to be talented, you've got to be good. But you also have to be a person whom people want to work with. If you're bringing too much attitude, like you're the best thing that happened to the violin since Heifetz, I don't think you're going to go very far.

need to receive the proper training in order to mold and enhance your talents in the appropriate way. Second, your teachers can be very important to your résumé. If you go to the right schools and study with teachers who are held in high esteem, you'll greatly enhance your chances of getting past the screening phase at auditions, and therefore will have a much better chance of getting into a good orchestra. In addition, there are times when well-respected teachers will help a young player with his or her career, if they are sufficiently enamored of the student's abilities.

The key is to get into the most prestigious school you can, and within that school to study with the most esteemed professors. Unlike the pop field, classical music has a very rigid and tightly defined career path that is based on talent, schooling, and hard work. Who you know also has a lot to do with your ability to succeed, but you can make a lot of valuable contacts if you're in the right school. Graduating from an institution such as Julliard, Eastman, Yale, or the Manhattan School of Music goes a long way toward establishing your credentials. If you've already completed

---

RELATED WORK: POPS ORCHESTRAS

In an effort to expand both their audience and their revenues, many orchestras also put on "pops" concerts at which they perform repertoire outside of the classical genre. Often, many of the more important players from the symphony orchestra will choose, for a variety of reasons, not to take part in the pops programs. This creates opportunities for musicians whose names are further down the sub list. Although they are not as prestigious as symphony gigs, pops shows can not only make you money, but contacts as well.

Another interesting fact about pops concerts is that they are the one area of orchestral work in which rhythm-section players, especially guitarists, can sometimes find gigs. To play pop material, an orchestra will often need a guitarist, a drummer, a bassist, and a pianist who can play nonclassical parts. Ohio-based guitarist Tim Berens, a veteran of many pops orchestra gigs, gives this example:

> Dayton does a series of six pops concerts a year for which they'll bring in a guest artist such as Carole King. And they'll send the instrumentation ahead of time, and say "Oh, gee, we need a guitar player." Then they have to go out and find somebody, and it's always a problem unless a contractor knows a player who can read. It's a continuous problem for them to find guitar players.

Many times a pops orchestra will use musicians who have theater music experience, because they combine rock and pop playing skills with the ability to read well and follow a conductor.

---

your college music program and feel that you didn't get the contacts or experience you wanted, you might want to consider going for a masters degree in as prestigious an institution as you can get into. This will give you yet another opportunity to improve your skills, make some contacts, and get your career moving in the right direction.

FINDING THE WORK

There are a number of methods you can employ to get work playing classical music. The most glamorous and direct way is to win one of the prestigious instrumental competitions as a soloist. You're then booked to play with big-time orchestras and, most likely, given a recording contract. Unfortunately, only the most supremely talented musical prodigies win these contests, while the vast majority of highly skilled players are left to find more conventional routes to success. Just as in other forms of music, networking plays a big role in getting work, but classical music also has an audition process, which is unique to the scene. The following sections will describe that process, as well as other common methods for finding employment in the classical world.

The Audition Process

Although there are other ways to get into an orchestra on a part-time basis, the most common method to get your own chair in a symphony is to audition. Because virtually all orchestra work is unionized, the methods for choosing players are heavily regulated. At face value, auditioning appears to be a fair way to choose players. The hopefuls all play behind screens so that only their playing, not their sex, race, or appearance, will affect the decision. As fair as this sounds, the audition process is in reality a very political one (more on that later). The following is a step-by-step examination of how the process works.

The applicants find out about auditions through ads in the American Federation of Musicians' monthly newspaper, *The International Musician* (see Appendix). They're instructed in the ads to send a résumé and sometimes an audition tape. The tape must contain examples of the musician playing excerpts of orchestral pieces in all the major styles of classical music: baroque, classical, romantic, and contemporary. The purpose of this is not only to show off his or her playing, but to demonstrate the ability to handle any type of composition that the orchestra might be asked to play. The résumés and tapes (if they're required) are then screened by a committee, which may consist of members of the orchestra, including the contractor. Those who are deemed qualified are invited to play in the preliminary round of the audition.

The contestants are expected to pick up their own expenses to get to the audition. This is an issue that gets brought up in almost every discussion of orchestra auditions, because unless a player limits him- or herself to orchestras within driving distance, he or she will have to spend quite a bit of money on airfare and lodging. Imagine the cost if the search for work required that someone fly to three, four, or more auditions. There has been some discussion in classical circles about establishing a regional audition period, which would enable players to attend multiple auditions in the same geographical area within a specified period of time, thus allowing them to maximize their auditioning prospects while keeping the expenses to a reasonable level. Unfortunately for the auditonees, these ideas have yet to become a reality.

There are usually two phases to the auditions: a preliminary and a final. These auditions are judged by a committee made up of players from the orchestra as well as the conductor. The winner of the final phase is then offered the chair. As you can see, it's not an easy process, and those auditioning face stiff competition from around the country. According to Bonnie Boss, who contracts orchestral work in the Los Angeles area:

> I think the mistaken impression that everyone gets is that you get the auditions out of the union paper, you go play them, and if you're good you're gonna win one and get a job. Well, that's not necessarily true, because there are far more qualified players than there are positions. And there are horror stories from here to eternity about how auditions go.

The horror stories that Boss refers to happen when the powers that be in the orchestra (the conductor, the contractor, or the section leader) know in advance who they want to hire to fill the opening. They can't just offer this person the job because they're obliged by union rules to go through with the audition process. So they go through the motions of having the auditions, knowing all along who's going to win. This kind of a charade is unfortunate for all applicants, especially those who come from far away at their own expense. The only positive in this kind of situation is that sometimes the other players who make it to the finals end up getting on the sub list for the orchestra. Certainly not all auditions are "fixed," but there's no question that it's not always the fair process it appears to be.

Despite the dubious reputation of the audition process, it's a good idea to apply for all the auditions *in your area* because you never know what's going to happen and it may help get your name out there. If you have to travel long distances and incur major expenses to get there, you should think long and hard before applying.

Getting Your Name Around

Short of winning an audition, the best way to get work is to make a reputation for yourself. This way you'll start getting recommended for work, which may lead to more opportunities. In order to maximize your networking, aim your publicity at the key, influential musicians who can do the most to help you get work. They are:

Contractors Making your name known to contractors is the most direct way to get freelance work. If you're a member, you can get a list of the contractors from the musicians union. If you haven't joined the union, you should, because virtually all orchestra work is unionized. Once you get the list, contact all the contractors on it. Bonnie Boss, a contractor herself, suggests this method:

> Call them up, be real polite, and say "I've just moved into town. . . . I want to introduce myself to you, and may I send you a résumé?" Just be super-polite about it. In my case, I want to know who everyone is. I always ask for a résumé because you can tell a lot about what they've played or whom they've played for. That is really how people do it: Join the union, go to the meetings and stuff, join whatever associations there are that are relative to what you want to do. Then show up and start networking with people.

Principal Players   Besides contractors, you'll also want to impress the principal players, or section leaders, of the orchestras in your area. The pecking order of an orchestra is structured as follows: After the conductor, the principal (or *first chair*) players are the top tier, and thus have a lot of influence. The highest-ranking principal player is the *concert master,* who is the first chair violinist. Principals are often on the audition committees, and are generally good people to know. According to Dale Stuckenbruck, "The contractor and conductor will rely on the principal player to add people to the section because they want him or her to be happy with it." Probably the easiest way to get the principals to hear you is at an audition, but that won't give you an opportunity to meet them and develop a rapport. You might try approaching them in order to arrange to play for them privately, but unless you know someone in common it's not too likely they'll agree to that. In any case, make an extra effort to meet principals on your instrument if the opportunity should arise.

Players of Your Instrument   The third group you should target for your networking efforts are the musicians who play the same instrument as you. Although in a sense they're your direct competition, they can also recommend you for work and help you out if they feel that you're worthy of it. You might even want to try getting the list of people who play your instrument from the union, then calling them to introduce yourself. It will almost certainly be an uncomfortable process, but it may land you some work leads.

Naturally, the best way to meet any of the above groups is in working situations, where they can not only hear you play but get to know your personality and work habits. Unfortunately, new players are in that familiar catch-22 predicament, where in order to get work they need recommendations, but in order to get recommendations they need people to hear them in working situations. It's not an easy spot to be in, but you need to persevere and constantly chip away until you've developed a name for yourself.

Another way you can help build your reputation is through self-promotion. One way to do that is to stage your own concerts. Depending on your budget, you can rent anything from a large recital hall to a small local church or library. You can not only choose what music to do, but you can hire the players you want—preferably those you would most like to meet and impress. Composer and violinist Dave Rimelis describes the process this way:

> You get a gig and you hire the best musicians you can. You try to get in with them, to make contact with them. You befriend them. And if they like you, they'll hire you if they're impressed with your work. If they aren't, well then, you're just hiring them and they won't do a thing for you. But what most people hope is that they get a gig, and they hire good musicians, and the musicians will think that they're good and then hire them. Once you get into that circle, it's just like a name pops up. "Oh, we need a violin." "How about Susan?" "Great." And then you're in.

To put on such a concert, you should only be spending money that you can afford to lose. Even if you promote the heck out of it, there's no guarantee you'll get your investment back. Then again, there's no guarantee you'll get the job when you buy a plane ticket and rent a hotel room in order to go to an audition. Nonetheless, in many situations the money you spend promoting yourself will be tax-deductible.

In any case, putting on your own concerts is an option that you may want to consider if your career isn't making the progress you'd like. Not only can you make contacts by doing it, you may even be able to get reviewed in the newspaper, which can help your résumé. Occasionally, someone can really launch their career that way. Dave Rimelis tells a story of a conductor he knew who did exactly that:

> She just took ten thousand dollars out of the bank, hired Symphony Space [a theater in Manhattan], put on a concert, and started her own orchestra. Now, eleven years later, her orchestra has a $600,000 budget and she's also the conductor for three other major orchestras. So I think that you can do that if you have the foresight. And if you have the money and the vision, the guts. Those are the people who can get something done.

DALE STUCKENBRUCK
VIOLINIST AND CONTRACTOR

Career Advice for Classical Musicians

Dale Stuckenbruck is a violinist who has played and contracted for many symphony orchestras, including the Brooklyn Philharmonic. He's also a Broadway musician and "in-house" contractor, and is one of the busier studio string players in New York.

Do the teachers from the music schools help students get work?
Today the pressure on teachers to help students . . . is much higher than it used to be. When I was at school, the main thing was to play as well as possible, and I never dreamed of asking my teacher for any help. But he did offer. It came from him, not from me, and it did open the door slightly. I got turned down by everyone in the recording business whom he had asked me to call, but it opened the door for an audition, to play for the contractor of the Brooklyn Philharmonic at that time. And I went and played for that person. The main thing is that when you're just out of school you can play everything, there's nothing you can't play, but nobody wants to listen to you. So just to be heard by somebody is the most important step, I think. Because you haven't proven yourself yet to your colleagues, or to anyone in the business as such, so to be heard is crucial.

For someone just starting out, is the route in to make as many contacts as possible so that you get recommended for things?
First of all, it's to be heard. [One way is] through auditions. We have people who nobody has ever heard of who play a wonderful audition and get hired. And people who've been in the business a long time and don't get hired. So that's one route to kind of jump forward, to do the audition process, as horrible as it is.

Are there a lot of auditions where the outcome is preordained?
Yes, I think the chances [of winning an audition] are slim, but if somebody is superior he or she will stand out. I contracted for the Brooklyn Philharmonic for three years, New York Virtuosi for five years or so, and I've been in-house contracting on Broadway for about five years, so I've had a little bit of experience in hearing people and I've done many auditions through the years and been on juries. It's very interesting. I remember hearing a tape of a violinist who didn't make it into the audition process. There was something

about the tape that I thought was very interesting and occasionally it was terrific. . . . I ended up going to the bottom of the list and trying out this person and this person turned out to be fantastic. . . . If you don't make it [at the audition], people think you have to get the job to get anywhere with it. Many people who do the auditions at City Opera or the ballet or something, get on the sub list just because they went through the process and at least got in the finals. . . . Even if you don't get in the finals sometimes you still get noticed. It is a process, it's a terrible process, it's not fair, but you've got to use every opportunity to at least be heard. The best thing is that people of the same instrument are going to help you the most. And then if you can play privately for any concert masters or principals of any string family member of orchestras in New York, just a private playing, that would be worth it, too.

How would you suggest that a new player get "heard"?
This is what I would recommend that a student do, it's a wonderful technique. If they do this with me, I'll come and listen to them: If a person called me up and said, "I just graduated, nobody knows me, I don't have a résumé but I think I studied the violin very hard and I'm very dedicated. I'd love very much to hear your comments about my playing. If nothing happens from this, that's completely fine, I'm just interested in your comments and trying to improve. . . . If you would be interested in coming to hear me play, I would be happy to rent a studio and have you come and listen to me." . . . I would think that this person is together, that he is trying to make it easy for me, pre-pared himself playing-wise, and rented a studio. That would be a very good technique.

Why is it so hard for so many talented classical players to make it?
The thing about this country is that there's no apprenticeship situa-tion. The apprenticeship ideal is crucial for survival in any part of this business. In other words, somebody's got to notice you. In Europe, when you get out of school you already know where you're going to go. They have apprenticeship programs in many of the orchestras. While you're in school you're already working at the phil-harmonic or subbing there. So you already have been groomed for a situation. I'm not saying that everybody will have a spot, but they can look toward at least being employed. In this country, once you've graduated, you're totally on the street unless somebody in the school has noticed you—a teacher who's willing to help you. Nowadays, people study with teachers who are politically very active that way, simply for that reason. Unfortunately, a lot of people are studying

with teachers for that reason, and are not getting the proper training with their instrument. They're putting the employment ahead of their own honest direction of their instrument.

Do people become extra players or subs in symphony situations because they know somebody, or is it because they did well in an audition but didn't win?
Sometimes people who got enough points in an audition will be included as possibles on the sub list. After a contractor goes though a recommended sub list that's put together either by committees or by principals, then he or she can go on their own. But these players generally come through recommendations of principal players or committees that are spelled out on the contract. Contractors these days are much more clerks than they are contractors in the old sense. They have to follow guidelines, and only when there is an emergency or they've gotten to the bottom of the list, because the calls were not made early enough or whatever, can they go on their own.

So there are preset steps that contractors have to follow?
That's right, and now the sub lists are pretty long these days.

Do orchestra musicians ever have subs in the Broadway sense?
Where the player determines the sub, no. In many orchestras, sub lists are put together at the beginning of the season or at the end of the previous season. A player in the orchestra may recommend someone to the contractor, or sometimes they fill out a form listing people they would recommend to be reviewed by the committee.

What would you say to people who are contemplating a career as a classical musician?
It's my firm belief that, if a person really loves what they're doing and is serious and honest and has the right attitude, in time nobody can refute good playing. In time, everybody will know who can play and who cannot. . . . If you're very good and you have the right attitude and you hang in, you cannot go unnoticed. I believe that you'll find your way. I think that people have to have other economic means to support the early years of making it. That's why their intelligence is important, and their ability to be flexible, their ability to do different things, is crucial.

PART THREE

❖

MAKING MONEY IN THE STUDIO

❖

CHAPTER 7 | **WORKING AS A STUDIO MUSICIAN**

❖

If your primary interest as a musician is in studio work, you've got a tough row to hoe. The pool of work for session players has diminished considerably since peaking in the 1960s and '70s. This is due in large part to technological developments in the music business, including MIDI and digital sampling/recording. These technologies have enabled individual musicians to "program in" the parts of entire bands or orchestras. As a result, many jobs have been lost. While it was never easy to get studio work, now everyone is fighting for a piece of a vastly shrunken pie.

The number of players who derive the bulk of their income from session work has dropped precipitously since the early 1980s. This can be attributed almost entirely to the new technologies. In fact, many of the players who once played sessions exclusively have had to move into other areas of the business such as private party work (see Chapter 4) and theater music (see Chapter 5).

Before you become utterly depressed by this information, you need to realize that, within the totality of the music industry, there are still plenty of studio musicians who are getting work. Yes, the numbers are significantly lower, but there's still work to be had. In order to get it, you need to be extremely talented, well-schooled, and aggressive. The studio scene is one of the more Darwinian segments of the business, and only the fittest will survive.

STUDIO WORK IN THE DIGITAL AGE

Although synthesizers and samplers have severely decreased opportunities for musical employment, certain areas of the recording business still rely primarily on live musicians rather than machines. In country music, for example, most of the tracks on commercially released CDs are recorded using real musicians rather than MIDI. Nashville has a very closed session scene, so the fact that a lot of live players are used there hasn't created a gold mine of opportunity for new musicians. Big-budget film scoring is another area of the recording industry that continues to use a large number of live players. In addition, the majority of rock recordings still include live rhythm sections. Since most of the bands are self-contained they generally don't have to call in outside players, except when specialty instruments are required.

R&B is another genre that once featured the sound of live musicians. The classic Motown and Stax recordings of the 1960s and '70s not only had great vocals and songwriting, but also outstanding performances by the studio musicians in the rhythm section. By contrast, today's R&B, as well as hip-hop, techno, and dance music, are completely dominated by sequenced instruments.

Musical situations that once primarily employed session musicians, such as commercials or records produced for vocalists, are those in which the use of session players has dropped most precipitously. Using live musicians for all instruments was once the reality for a producer or composer. If, for example, the sound of a flute was needed on a record or jingle, a flautist was hired. If timpani were called for, a percussionist was hired. Due to the rise of MIDI and digital sampling technology, the use of live players has now become more of a budget consideration. In many cases, producers have no choice but to use "virtual" instruments due to the cost savings that can be realized. For those instruments that are most easily approximated digitally, using actual players has, in many cases, become a luxury. Sadly, the sound of a real musician playing a real instrument has been relegated to the status of "flavor," used only occasionally to achieve a certain sound.

Another sector in which session work has declined is the area of preproduction. Songwriters, commercial composers, and producers once had no other option than to use studio players on their demos. Now, with the rise of home studios, much of the instrument sounds for demos are being programmed in via MIDI.

For those of you considering a career in session work, it may be helpful to examine how musicians on various instruments have fared in the digital age.

Bassists

Bassists have lost a great deal of work since the advent of MIDI. Once ubiquitous in the studio, they're now simply one option in a sea of synthesized and sampled bass sounds. In R&B and pop, live bassists are used only sporadically. The best opportunities for studio bass players are in jazz, rock and roll, country, and any roots-oriented music. Even in those fields, however, real basses are rarely used in the demo stages of projects anymore.

Drummers

The old joke goes something like this:

Q: How many drummers does it take to screw in a light bulb?

A: None. They have a machine that does it now.

Unfortunately, this is a sad reality for many drummers. Drums were once fixtures at practically every recording session, but that's no longer the case. Like bassists, live drummers are no longer used routinely in many areas of pop music. Live drums are rarely used on demos these days, for a number of reasons. First, it's cheaper to use programmed or looped drums. Second, many musical styles rely on drum sounds that can't be created easily on a live kit. Third (and most important), most home/project studios, where the bulk of demo production takes place, aren't equipped to record live drums.

Despite all the new technology and great sampled drum sounds, it's still not that easy to program drums to sound like they were played by a live musician. Because of their expertise, many drummers have now found that they can get work programming MIDI drums, or even playing parts into sequencers from MIDI drum kits. Although this doesn't come close to replacing the lost work, it at least compensates a little.

Guitarists

Luckily for guitarists, their instrument is one that can't be easily simulated in the MIDI environment. Consequently, guitar players haven't lost as much work as many other musicians. Nevertheless, their work has declined from the pre-MIDI days, when it was routine to have two or three guitar players at a session. Another advantage that guitarists have is that their instrument is relatively easy to record, and thus is often used to add some "life" to an otherwise all-MIDI arrangement.

Keyboard Players

There's no doubt that keyboard players rule in the MIDI world. The fact that a keyboard is the most efficient MIDI controller and is so versatile musically puts keyboardists in the catbird seat in this era of synthesizers and samplers. Nonetheless, they've probably benefited more in the areas of composing and arranging than they have as session players. Because so many composers are keyboard players and have the chops to play in most or all of a MIDI score, the demand for outside session keyboardists is generally limited to very specific parts; for example, such as a Dr. John–style piano solo or a Jimmy Smith–type organ sound.

String, Woodwind, and Brass Players

Although there is some work out there, primarily on movie sessions, MIDI has put a large dent in the amount of session work available. With the exception of solos, for which a live player is still a necessity, string, wind, and brass parts are generally played in via MIDI. The use of sequenced orchestral instruments may not be as good as the real thing, but it saves producers large sums of money and the bottom line is what it's all about. When budgets allow, there are some occasions when a small brass, wind, or string section is brought in to add realism to the sequenced parts, a practice known as *sweetening*. Nevertheless, most players of these instruments cannot depend on studio work to bring in large portions of their incomes anymore. Classical and jazz recordings still use live players almost exclusively, but they're not where the bulk of the session money can be found.

TAKING STOCK OF THE WORK THAT'S OUT THERE

Now that we've surveyed the field, let's examine the various sectors of the music business to see where studio musicians can still get work, and what that work is like.

Playing Commercials

The jingle business accounts for a good portion of the freelance studio work available today. Although MIDI has definitely taken away a huge chunk of the market, there are still many musicians who make good money from playing on commercials. In many cases, however, only the "first call," top-of-the-line players are working on a consistent basis. When the business was booming, these players often got multiple calls for the same time slot, and consequently had to turn down a lot of work. The calls they declined would go to the next in line, and so on. Today, the work has thinned out to the point where the topflight players are busy, but they're not busy enough to be turning down much work. Consequently, the next players in the chain are working much less, and the musicians below them are hardly working at all.

The lion's share of national commercials are produced in New York, Los Angeles, or Chicago. Ad agencies subcontract the music production to *music houses,* which hire most of the session players. This system differs from that of movie dates, for which contractors do all the hiring. For commercials, players are usually chosen by the composers or producers at the music house. When contractors do get used, it's often to hire orchestral musicians or to track down exotic instruments. John Miller, who contracts both for Broadway and the recording business, describes some of the more obscure players he's been asked to hire:

> The jingle thing has become a little more Third World–oriented. It's not like, "Well, we need a good funk drummer." The job description is, "We need an Egyptian chant singer." So a lot of people are interested in the real thing. "I don't want a studio guitar who can play a little bouzouki; I want the real Greek guys." So it often involves getting at the underbelly of some of the more esoteric scenes. And the other thing with jingles is that, more than anything, the turnaround time from getting the call to when the actual date happens is extremely

quick. Sometimes a job description is not hard to fill—a bass player, a drummer, and a guitar player. But sometimes it's five bagpipe players, or a Russian men's choir, and the turnaround time is very quick.

Turnaround time is the key phrase to remember in the jingle business, because the music is usually one of the last elements to be produced before a commercial is edited. As a result, most of the lead time is usually eaten up by the other elements of the production, and the music houses often have only two or three days to write and produce the tracks. Thus, the business is in a perpetual rush, and there's no time to waste on studio musicians who can't do the job quickly and well. The players who survive under these circumstances are the ones who can cover a wide variety of styles, think on their feet, and are not intimidated by the intense pressure to play well and do it fast.

On a jingle session, as opposed to a record date, there's rarely any time for experimenting and trying to find exactly the right sound. Instead, you're expected to go in, set up, run through the chart once or twice (while listening to the track, in the case of overdubbing), and nail it. To add to the pressure, there are often three or four agency people watching, in addition to the producer and the composer (who might be the same person) as well as the engineer.

The pay scales for jingles are decent, but not great. In New York, for example, a union musician nets about $90 (plus health and pension payments) for a session of one hour or less. More importantly, he or she is listed as a musician on the American Federation of Musicians contract and can make a lot more in residuals if the spot stays on the air for more than thirteen weeks or is reused. Basically, the initial session payment covers the first thirteen-week cycle, and a slightly smaller "reuse" fee is paid for every subsequent cycle in which the spot runs. The trick is to get on as many contracts as possible, because over time you can end up with a fairly steady stream of residual checks.

Sometimes you'll be called to play on a spot that's still in the demo phase. This occurs when one music house is competing with another (or more than one). Sometimes a music house has already been picked by the ad agency to do the music for the commercial, but is having an internal competition among its writers to see whose version the agency likes best. In many cases, if the demo you played on wins the competition and *goes final,* you'll be paid as if it had been a final session all along. If the spot you played on doesn't go final, you're often paid directly by the music house rather than through the union. This can be a real problem for musicians, because certain music houses aren't too enthusiastic about paying musicians for demos that didn't make it. Consequently, you end up having to hound them incessantly for your money. It can take months to get your $80 or $90 from a demo; in some cases, you may never get paid.

Jingles singers have a substantially better deal than musicians. They are represented by either the American Federation of Television and Radio Actors (AFTRA) or the Screen Actors Guild (SAG). They can make hundreds or even thousands of dollars for singing on a national spot (see "Jingle Writing" in Chapter 8). Unfortunately, studio singers are currently working much less than they used to because there are far fewer jingles being produced.

The majority of the union sessions for commercials take place in New York, Chicago, and Los Angeles. Outside of these areas there are many situations in which studio players and singers are asked to play on non-union spots, also known as *buyouts.* The initial payment for these jobs is usually in the same ballpark as for union spots, but there are no residuals and no health and pension payments. Another negative with respect to buyouts is that you have little or no recourse (other than your own persistence) if the music house refuses to pay you. When you play on a buyout, you're on your own.

Playing Movie and Television Dates

Playing for movie and television soundtracks is a desirable but demanding area of studio playing. It's desirable because, compared with jingles, the pay scale is much higher. In addition, TV dates can pay you residuals for years after you record them. It's also very prestigious work, and only the upper echelon of session players gets called for it. The bulk of the work is in Los Angeles, but there's quite a bit in New York as well. Contractors handle most of the hiring for this kind of work, and it's a closed circle that's difficult to break into. In Los Angeles, for instance, in order to get called to play on a soundtrack, you need to gain the good graces of at least one of a select group of contractors. One prominent L.A. music scene insider estimates that 85 percent of the movie work in L.A. is contracted by one person, and most of the rest is handled by three or four others.

Even more than in jingles, film and television sessions require heavy reading chops and the ability to follow a conductor. You're often recording live with an orchestra, and it's in the producer's financial interest to get the recording done as quickly as possible, with a minimum of mistakes, because the labor costs are extremely high. Los Angeles–based guitarist Al Vescovo, a veteran of numerous movie and TV dates, describes a typical session:

> Most of the time you can't be very creative. It's like playing a Broadway show. You've gotta play exactly what's written. . . . Typically, there'll be sixty to seventy musicians, and everything goes down live. Sometimes you're working with the click track, and other times you're following the conductor, who's watching the movie on the screen. . . . You rehearse it once and they look for any bad notes that might be in the copy. They'll correct those, and then the red light goes on. What makes it bad is if you've got a sixty-piece orchestra, you're down to the last thirty seconds, and somebody makes a bad clinker.

Vescovo says that *punching in* (re-recording a portion of your part from the middle on your own individual track) is usually not an option. The sheer number of players in a live orchestra make it impractical to mike each instrument individually. Instead, mics are set up to cover the various sections, such as strings, woodwind, and brass. This arrangement makes it almost impossible for a solitary musician to correct a mistake by punching in without erasing the parts of the other musicians in the section. Compounding the problem is the fact that the sounds made by one section are also picked up by the mics that are designated to record the other sections, a phenomenon known as *bleeding* or *leakage*.

Working as a Studio Musician

Jeff Mironov has been one of the top studio guitarists in New York for many years, playing on jingle, film, and record dates. He got his first big break playing on Gladys Knight & the Pips' early 1970s hit, "Midnight Train To Georgia," and has been busy ever since. He's recorded with such artists as Michael Jackson, James Taylor, Bonnie Raitt, Steely Dan, and Diana Ross.

How many sessions do you do in a typical week?
It varies. My barometer for a busy week is ten sessions a week—for a good week. I had that last week; I had more than that this week. However, the week before that I had very few sessions. I think I only had three or four. . . . The business, as it affects me now, as I perceive it, doesn't have the dependability, in terms of consistency, that it once had. It [comes] much more in waves. There'll be a flurry of activity for a week-and-a-half or two weeks, then all of a sudden the bottom will fall out and I'll have nothing for three days.

How did the downturn in the jingle scene affect you?
It's affected me; I think it's affected everyone who's still active in the scene. . . . The technology all of a sudden made it possible to do substantial demos without having to use a single live musician. In the old days, the way a jingle would be produced, the composer or writer, if he was a piano player, would just play his composition and have a singer there, singing it. That would be how they presented it to the client. If the client liked it, they would talk about arrangement and style, then actually book a session and hire musicians to come in and perform it. So, obviously, the drum machines and the sequencers and all the MIDI technology made it unnecessary to have to do that now. They can do really full-blown demo versions, without guitars, but with keyboard stuff and bass and strings and horns. So that definitely put a chink in everyone's workload. But strangely enough, one of the things that seemed to stay in place was the fact that a guitar player's addition to a MIDI arrangement made [it sound] a lot more believable. And that, I think, kept guitar players working when other musicians were not working so much.

Did your experience playing live help you develop the skills that you've used as a session player?

I've always had bands, ever since I was fifteen or sixteen years old and playing fraternity parties at colleges. When I got a little bit older, I started playing with a number of jazz players. So I was always performing on a certain level, and that, I think, was what allowed me to progress on musically, on a sensitivity and technical level, so that when the opportunity presented itself I could do something with it. . . . There's no way that anybody could become a vital, flexible, potent session player if he or she didn't have a lot of live performance experience. For obvious reasons, that's where you really learn how to play.

What is your basic studio rig?
It's an ever-changing set of circumstances. . . . I've got a number of old vintage amplifiers that I've acquired over the last three years. I don't use them that often, but when people want an actual amplifier and to mike a speaker cabinet, I use those because it's a great-sounding thing, but it requires more time to set up and acquire the sound. . . . But I also carry a small little Korg pedal board, which is a multi-effects processor that I use about fifty percent of the time, because most jingles are recorded in office space–type studios where they don't really have much room for an amplifier. It's also very fast, and you can get sounds that sound like the real thing fairly quickly. And in jingles, it's got to sound great but it has to sound great *fast.* The people don't want to mess around with it. The time frame is neurotically brief. They want you in and out; they don't want to have to think about it or hear it too many times, they just want you to sit down, plug in, and make it sound great right away. . . . I also have a little more elaborate rig, which is a tube preamp and a couple of effects processors. . . . It's heavier to carry and therefore not quite as mobile, but it's a little bit more real-sounding than the little pedal board. So basically I have three scenarios, three separate systems that I use: One is the live amp thing and the other two are "direct" setups.

Is it really important to be able to read well on a jingle session?
Well, you have to be able to nail it quickly, but the difference is that it's not so dependent as it once was on reading. It used to be that arrangers—the better arrangers—really thought about what they wanted you to do, and wrote out specific parts. There would actually be a part written for drums, and a bass part, and guitar parts. If there were two guitar players on the session, there'd be two different parts. And I think that years and years ago, before my time, arrangers were incredibly specific, where all they wanted you to play

was what they wrote. As time went on and the styles changed and became more creatively mobile and more improvisational, they would write that latitude into the arrangements. For instance, they'd give you a line to play in one section of the tune, but when it got to the next section there'd be some note about single-note improvisation, or rhythm ad-lib, or solo ad-lib, where they gave the musicians and the guitar players more and more room to improvise. Today it's a rarity to come upon a real arrangement in which someone has actually done something other than just sketched out the chord symbols on a piece of paper.

Do they at least write out rhythms with the chord symbols?
In this day and age, it's common to go into a session and there'll be no music at all. That has occurred in part due to the advent of the sequencer. There are a whole lot of people now who arrange in a sequencer. They play their parts into it and if they don't like it they rewrite it and play it again and again until they get it to where they like it. But they never have to think about what note it is, what rhythm it is. And so they'll flesh out a full-fledged arrangement for a tune without ever having to put a note on paper because they don't have to perform it. Then in comes the guitar player or the bass player who has to perform it, and unfortunately much of the time they [the composers/arrangers] don't want to be bothered with jotting down a chord chart. So you sort of have to suss it out while setting up and be very fast about learning this piece of music. More often than not, it's easy enough that you can learn it pretty quickly. Every now and then you run into something that's more involved and has odd bars or some irregularities and takes more time. I've been at sessions where people give you a piece of paper and a pencil and ask you to do it. I think it's pretty unfair, and it's part of the way the business has deteriorated. But that's just the way it is now. So reading today is not as crucial, at least from what I see. It's not as crucial a factor as having musical ears and a wide palette of styles to draw on so that you can hear something and immediately, or in a short period of time, start adding to it and contributing to it in your own unique way.

Are there times when you run up against a real tough reading chart?
The only time I could think of something like that is if you walked

in on a film date or something that involves a whole orchestra.

Do you have a specific routine that helps you perform better?
A big part of the job is being comfortable and confident enough to be able to think creatively and hear things. When you're overly nervous, you're not gonna perform very well, you're not gonna be overly flexible. . . . More often than not, you get to the session and just start listening. . . . And you're calculating and somehow thinking up ideas and things to try by the time your boxes are set up and you're plugged in and tuned up. The whole thing takes place in a short period of time. From doing it a long time and being successful at it, you get fast in determining what it is and how you're gonna relate to it musically, so that in a really short period of time you're playing something meaningful. Because really all you have is a short period of time. If you're really slow on the draw getting the right sound up and starting to play the right style, this business doesn't have the patience for that any longer. You might get through the session, but unless you played something extraordinary that would justify the time spent in getting it, the engineer, the producer, and the arranger probably would all agree: "Sounds good but takes too long—next." And that's unfortunate, but true.

What would be your advice to a new player (either young or new in town) trying to get on the scene?
I think playing live is probably the quickest way to get recognition. Play in as many high-profile or high-visibility circumstances as you can, because people in the business go to clubs. Very often, the singers or musicians who are performing may already be established in the recording scene, and the people they invite to come down are the people they work for. So by playing in those situations, you're gonna come in contact with people who hear you and are in a position to do something about it, to call you if you make an impression on them. That's a really important thing. . . . I suppose some people put together tapes of what they do, their best things, and try to get them out to people. In my experience, producers and arrangers who are in the business are so inundated with that sort of thing that I would be impressed if I found out that they ever listened to one. I'm sure that they do, but the odds are not high that you're gonna get discovered or get a lot of work from that.

Often on strict movie-scoring dates, they can't really punch it in because there's so much leakage. . . . So they usually start from the beginning again, but that really puts you in a bad situation because everyone's looking at you. If you make too many mistakes they don't call you back. So that's where the pressure comes in. And the budgets are really high when they're hiring sixty people. . . . Every minute extra is costing them money, so they don't tolerate too many mistakes.

To complicate things further, film composers work under unbelievably tight deadlines, and are often extremely stressed out by the time the project gets to the recording phase. All of these factors work together to create a pressure-cooker atmosphere in which the contractors use and reuse the same musicians because they know that they'll come through with a minimum of mistakes. Consequently, the openings for new musicians are few and far between.

The musicians who do get the work not only have to be great readers but must have the ability to play authentically in many different styles. Los Angeles–based trumpet player Gary Grant has appeared on close to four thousand albums, as well as on numerous film soundtracks, including *Forrest Gump, The First Wives Club,* and *The Long Kiss Goodnight.* He had this to say about the requirements for film musicians on his instrument:

A guy could be a virtuoso trumpet player and still wouldn't necessarily be right for this kind of work because it's pretty versatile. . . . it's pretty rangy. You have to play in the upper register without overpowering the orchestra, and then you've also got to be symphonic. You need to be classically trained. You can't go in there and play like you're playing out on a big band and have that kind of sound and approach. You've gotta blend with a hundred-piece orchestra . . . and they're mixing it right there. So you have to balance, and it takes real musicians to do it. And even if you are a virtuoso player, it doesn't mean that you can do it. You may play incredible stuff, but you may not be able to play stylistically with the other guys. However, if you could do all those kind of things, you certainly would have more of a chance to do this kind of work.

On a typical film date, there are usually several distinct pieces of music, or *cues,* to play on. There is often an opening and closing theme, as well as many permutations of it for a variety of scenes. In addition, there are likely to be plenty of other cues that are completely different musically. Some will be very short *bumpers* (short pieces of transition music that move from one scene to another), and other long pieces. Usually the orchestra plays everything live, but occasionally certain instruments will do overdubs as well.

Playing Record Dates

Like other forms of studio work, freelance session work on commercially produced CDs (still referred to by musicians as "record dates") has diminished notably in recent years. As mentioned earlier, technology is the major reason for this decline. Also, given the nature of current pop styles, there just isn't the call for freelance studio musicians that there once was. Although it appears to be changing somewhat, the most recent pop music has been centered around alternative rock as well as rap and dance music, and the production of these styles doesn't necessitate the extensive use of freelance studio musicians.

Buddy Collette, a sax player in the Los Angeles area who experienced the record business during the boom of the 1960s and '70s, has seen the amount of session work drop significantly: "Compared with before, it's probably less than half. . . . Let's say if there were three thousand or four thousand [musicians] doing the record dates before, there may be a thousand doing them now, and they're no longer doing ten, fifteen dates a week. They're lucky if they're doing three or four."

For the sessions that do occur, the hiring is usually handled by the producer, although contractors may be brought in for sessions involving large groups or orchestras. Producers generally have a cadre of musicians with whom they work regularly and who are their first choices for most projects. On some occasions the artists themselves have an impact on who gets hired to play.

On most major-label records, the musicians are well-established, high-caliber session players. Unless you've got a one-in-a-million talent, it's likely to take years to build your talent and reputation to the point where you might get called for this kind of session.

If you do end up playing on a record date, the basic union scale for a three-hour session is (at the time of this writing) $271.72 plus pension. For each additional instrument you play (known as a *double*), the scale increases. In many recording sessions, the musicians end up playing a lot longer than three hours, so the money can add up. In addition, there's a special payments fund that pays royalties for five years from the CD's release date to the musicians who appear on commercially released records.

The major labels are no longer the only game in town, however. The growth of independent labels in recent years has led to the production of an increasing number of CDs. Also, many artists release their own CDs today without being signed by a label at all. Although many of these releases are by self-contained groups, there are still plenty of sessions going on for which freelance studio musicians are required. This is an area where less established musicians have a better chance of breaking in, especially if they've made a reputation, through club work, with the singers and groups who are recording.

The problem with these kinds of sessions is that they're mostly non-union and low-paying. The American Federation of Musicians has made an effort to encourage the unionization of lower-end projects by establishing the "Low-Budget Phonograph Recording Scale," which applies to albums whose total budget is $85,000 or less. While this has helped somewhat, the great majority of the lower-end CDs are not union-affiliated and the players get only a session fee.

There's no way to say definitively what a typical record session is like, because each production is fairly unique. As a studio player, your situation will vary a lot, depending on whether you're part of the rhythm section cutting the basic tracks, or coming in to overdub. If you're a drummer, bassist, guitarist, or pianist and you're playing on the basics, you'll often be working for a number of days. You may even get a chance to rehearse before going in to cut the tracks. Unlike jingles or movies, musicians on record dates are often given somewhat more of an opportunity to experiment and develop their parts. Nevertheless, as a freelance session player you're viewed as a "hired gun," and expected to come up with good parts quickly.

Playing for Song Demos and Independent CDs

The easiest avenue into session work is via the song demo. Anyone who's trying to make it as an artist or songwriter has to have demo material. In many cases, this provides opportunities for studio musicians to play on the sessions. Because they've become so inexpensive to produce, many songwriters release their demos in the form of a CD. Most of the recording for this kind of project takes place in home studios rather than commercial facilities.

There are a number of advantages to this sort of session work. First, you don't have to be in New York, Los Angeles, or Nashville; in fact, you can find it just about anywhere in the country. Second, you don't have to be on some contractor's "A" list to get asked to play on demos. Most of the hiring results from a musician's reputation as a live player as well as from recommendations and word of mouth. Third, the pressure is much less intense and the competition is much less cutthroat than for traditional record dates.

There are also a number of disadvantages. For instance, playing on song demos doesn't usually pay as well as other types of recording, and almost never falls under the auspices of the union. There's no such thing as typical pay for demo sessions, because each is negotiated separately. In the New York area, a player can make anywhere from $50 to $150 per song. The more "in demand" a player is, the more money he or she can make, whereas those newer to the scene have to pretty much take what they can get.

Another problem inherent with demos is that they're harder to get on a steady basis, because many of the people you work for won't be hiring musicians regularly throughout the course of a year. If you're lucky, you can get yourself hooked up with a producer who's got a steady clientele of songwriters.

Reading is not usually as important in song demo situations as it is in other types of session work. I've played many demo sessions for which the only written music was a lyric sheet with the chords added in. Despite the low-key nature of these sessions, you're still expected to play a great-sounding part, quickly.

One city where demo work is on a higher level is Nashville. It's a town full of songwriters, musicians, and studios, which has led to a thriving demo scene. Unfortunately, because there are so many great players who are starving for any kind of studio work, the competition for these sessions is more intense than in most places. On the bright side, having so many good players around means you have a better chance of working with top-shelf musicians and enhancing your contacts.

PREPARING YOURSELF TO BE A STUDIO PLAYER

Playing in the studio can be one of the most stressful activities in the music business. Performing live is much more forgiving because mistakes are fleeting, and unless they're monumental they're usually forgotten by the next measure. In the studio, every screwup is captured for eternity (or at least until the next take) on the multitrack. There are few things more embarrassing than being at a session and not being able, for whatever reason, to cut the part. You struggle and struggle to get it right, and you know all along that the people who hired you will never do so again. You only hope that you haven't damaged your reputation with others as well.

When you're in a session, especially a high-level one like a jingle or a movie date, the clock is ticking and everyone expects you to nail your part almost immediately and to play great. It takes a great deal of confidence to be able to do this, especially when you know that if you fail there are plenty of other good players in line to take your place. Although it's nearly impossible to avoid being a little tense, but you must not let your fear overwhelm you. When you get overly nervous in the studio, your ability to play with creativity and emotion can go right out the window. You've got to strive to be confident at all times. You've got to get past the point where you're just trying to survive the session and move to a level where you're really contributing musically.

One of the toughest things to get used to is the amount of scrutiny, especially in an overdubbing situation. Everyone in the room— the producer, the client, other musicians, and even the engineer—is listening critically to every note you play. It takes a lot of self-assurance to be able to handle this and not let it affect your playing.

Being prepared is the best way to avoid being overwhelmed. This begins with being confident in your abilities, and the best way to build that is through experience. The more comfortable you are in the studio, the less nervous you'll be and the better you'll play.

A mediocre player with a good attitude can get by as a live player, but in the studio you've got to be a great player.

Knowing Your Role

As a session musician, you're usually hired to execute the musical ideas of the producer, composer, arranger, or songwriter. Although there will be sessions where you'll be allowed a lot of creative input, remember that it's always a good idea to defer musically to those who hired you. There may be times when you feel comfortable enough with the people you're working for to make suggestions counter to what they're asking, but for the most part it's best to play it the way they want you to.

The person you really need to listen to in the studio is the producer. A record producer and a movie director have analogous roles because they both have ultimate control over the creative direction of a project. In the same way that good directors get the most out of actors, accomplished producers know how to maximize the talents of session musicians. In addition, the producer's demeanor often sets the tone for the entire session: If he or she is tense, the session is tense, but if he or she is relaxed, everyone's much more at ease and probably plays better. If you do end up working for a producer with a bad attitude, try not to let it elevate your tension level to the point where it affects your playing.

Understanding the Importance of Reading

Reading music is an essential skill in the studio. Just about anyone who hires you for a session will assume that you can read fairly well. If you're a classical or jazz player, chances are you're probably already a good reader. If, on the other hand, you're coming out of a rock, blues, or country background, you may not have a lot of sight-reading experience. This can be a major problem. Reading wasn't one of my strong points when I first started doing sessions, and I often found it difficult to follow the charts. Even when the music was simple, I discovered (to my dismay) that my reading ability diminished considerably due to nervousness when I got to a session. The only way to avoid this kind of problem is to have done enough reading in other areas of your musical career in order to be able to go into a studio situation with utter confidence in your abilities.

Although you may play a lot of sessions for which you simply need to read a chord chart, you've got to be prepared for occasions when you're hit with something more complex. Richard Crooks, a veteran session drummer who's played on countless jingles, film scores, and albums, puts it this way:

> There's going to be that one time when you walk in and have to pull out every stop. You're going to have every note, expression, everything written out on a piece of paper. . . . You're going to get called on that one time for something that's not what you're used to doing, and it'll all be written out and you're going to have to interpret it.

If you're not ready to handle a complex chart, you run the risk of having a disastrous session and damaging your reputation. Improve your reading skills as much as possible to avoid being put in this position (see "Improving Your Reading Skills" in Chapter 2).

Handling the Variety
One of the more difficult aspects of studio playing is that you will be expected to handle a wide cross section of musical styles. Some players enjoy this challenge. Richard Crooks remembers when he first started doing a lot of session work:

> The thing that impressed me the most was the variety. Especially in jingles, but in everything, really. Obviously, for records you get called for what you're best suited for, more or less. You can't be a jack of all trades. . . . But the commercial aspect of it [jingles] was so intriguing because you never knew what you were going to walk into. It could be reading, or they'd hand you this blank sheet of paper. It could be a country date, a pop date, or a little jazz thing.

Even if you're considered a specialist and only get called to do sessions of a particular style, there are many subgenres within each style that you've got to be familiar with. For instance, if you're called for sessions as a country guitar player, you not only need to be familiar with straightforward country playing, but with rockabilly, bluegrass, and even some western swing. Producers generally assume that you'll know all of the subtleties of your genre. In addition, you'll sometimes be asked to play in the style of a particular musician, so it really helps to know your stuff. You've not only got to keep up with the current styles, but with the older ones as well.

Getting Comfortable in the Studio

As mentioned earlier, it's very important to feel comfortable and confident in recording situations so that you can relax and be musical. The best way to achieve this is to get as much experience as you can. In this era of home studios, most musicians have had at least some exposure to recording and recording equipment. If your ultimate goal is to be a session player, take all opportunities to get involved with recording and all its facets. Even familiarizing yourself with basic audio engineering principles will be beneficial, because it will help you better understand what's going on during a session. It will also improve communication with any of the engineers you'll have to deal with. It's especially important that you understand the best techniques for recording your instrument, whether it's miked or taken *direct* (plugged directly into the recording console).

Working with a Click In a jingle, film, or television session, or any situation in which the timing of the piece must be regulated, you'll have to play with a *click track*. It sounds simple enough—a metronome clicking along as you play—but in reality it takes some getting used to. This is especially true for drummers who are used to working live rather than in the studio. In live situations, drummers are in control of the tempo, while with a click, the tempo controls the drummer. Players of other instruments often have trouble playing with a click as well. The problem is that a human being's sense of rhythm is not nearly as regular as a metronome's. If you analyzed the tempos of a grooving live band, you'd see many minute fluctuations in the speed of the piece. With a click, the beat is completely regular, so it can be hard to play along with while keeping your groove feeling natural.

This is one area where you can prepare yourself pretty thoroughly at home by practicing regularly with a metronome. If you have home studio equipment, try recording some parts with a click. If you have a sequencer, program a click with some tempo changes, write a chart that reflects where these changes occur, and then play along with it. The reason for this is that occasionally you'll be faced with tempo changes, which can throw you if you're not used to them. The more you familiarize yourself with playing to a click (whether at a static tempo or a changing one) the better prepared you'll be when you get into a session situation.

Working with a Conductor In sessions that involve an orchestra (usually film and TV dates), you'll be working with a conductor. While this is second nature for orchestral musicians, rhythm-section players may find it difficult if they haven't done it before. Guitarists, bass players, and drummers especially need to get some experience following a conductor before sitting in on any sessions that feature one (see "Learning How To Follow a Conductor" in Chapter 5).

Getting Your Gear in Shape

It's extremely important to use good-quality instruments and equipment in the studio. You want to make it easy for the engineer to get a good sound on you as quickly as possible. If you have an inferior "axe" (whatever instrument you play), it's going to take a longer time to get it sounding right, and you can bet that the producer will hear about it.

If you're a woodwind, brass, or string player, make sure that you're using a good-quality instrument and that you bring with you any requisite accessories (such as mutes) or spare parts (reeds or strings) that you might need. If you're a rhythm-section player, there can be additional considerations.

Guitar If you're called for electric guitar these days, you need to be prepared for direct recording. Unless you're at a full-blown commercial studio, many of the sites you'll be recording at won't have a good guitar amp—or even the facilities to record one that you bring yourself. Even if they're well-equipped, you may still be asked to go direct because some other instrument is being recorded in their isolation booth. To be prepared for this, you need a multi-effects box with a speaker simulator in it. You'll need to program the box with good-sounding *patches* (sound combinations) that cover a variety of contemporary sounds, both clean and distorted. In addition, you should also know your box well enough to be able to quickly tweak a patch if needed. You might want to consider owning a tube preamp as well, to help warm up your sound. (There are many products on the market that contain both a tube preamp and a multi-effects processor.) If you're using multiple pieces of gear, they should be rack-mounted and precabled so that your set up and break down are easy and quick. Make especially sure that any gear you buy is quiet. Guitar effects are notoriously noisy, so beware. You don't want to make the engineer jump through hoops trying to get a quiet sound from your rig.

While on the subject of noise, you're much better off having a guitar with hum-bucking pickups for recording. Single-coil pickups may sound great, but they're incredibly noisy in the studio. If you're addicted to a single-coil sound, there are many hum-buckers available that are designed to sound like single-coil pickups. You don't want to be in the position of having to aim your guitar in a specific direction to keep it from humming while you try to read a chart and concentrate during a session.

Whether you have an acoustic or electric guitar, make sure the intonation on it is accurate so that you can play in tune all over the neck. Tuning is critical in the studio, and it'll make you look bad if you can't play your parts in tune. You can help the tuning situation by going no longer than four weeks between string changes. Old strings make for dull tone and bad intonation, so change them even more often if you can. Just one caveat: Don't put on a fresh set of strings the night before or the same day as a session. They won't yet be broken in and may slip out of tune when you're trying to record. Finally, make sure you have a good tuner and bring an ample supply of spare strings, picks, and cables.

Bass Most of my advice for guitar applies to bass as well. You want a quality instrument that's quiet and plays in tune. Steer clear of basses that don't put out a "Fender"-type sound, because that's the standard for electric bass. You probably won't need effects, but you may have a box you like to use for getting a good direct sound.

Keyboards Although there will times when you can use an acoustic piano that's in the studio, you'll probably want to have a keyboard setup that includes a full-sized controller with weighted action, and some rack-mounted MIDI sound modules. Besides having good piano and organ sounds, you'll also want to have a good variety of synth sounds at your fingertips. Try to have your sound banks arranged in such a way that you can easily access particular instrument sounds without doing a lot of hunting around. You don't want to have to be scrolling through banks and banks of sounds saying, "I know it's here somewhere. Just give me another minute" while the clock is ticking.

Drums   Chances are that any studio that's going to record live drums will already have a kit set up. For the sake of comfort, though, you may want to bring your own snare or even your own bass drum pedal. Always bring a pair of brushes as well as plenty of extra sticks.

If you're looking to get work as a MIDI drummer/programmer, you'll need a good set of triggers and a quality drum machine, or preferably a sampler with an extensive library of sounds. Make sure to troubleshoot your setup so that it consistently works correctly, without needing a lot of tweaking.

GETTING THE WORK

There's no easy way to become a big-time studio player. Most successful session musicians begin their careers in bars and clubs, where they develop their skills and contacts. If they're good enough, they eventually get calls for studio work based on reputation and the recommendations of other musicians. Word of mouth is the best kind of publicity for anyone trying to get session work, and unless you're the second coming on your instrument, it will take time to develop a good buzz about yourself. With that said, there are things you can do to help move the process along and put yourself in a better position to start getting some sessions. Here are some ideas.

Taking Stock of Your Contacts

If you're lucky, you already know some people who can help you in your quest for studio work. Think about musicians you know, teachers you've studied with, and any friends or relatives who are involved with the recording business or know someone who is. Through them, you might be able to get a recommendation that will land you a session. As I've stressed throughout the book, the best contacts are fellow musicians who've worked with you and have a good idea of your abilities. If you do get work from a contact, it's up to you to put forth a good effort on the session and try to parlay it into more work. However, I advise strongly against using your contacts until you feel absolutely sure you're ready to handle the gig. Although much of your learning as a session player comes from experience, you don't want to leave a trail of burned bridges in your path. If you have some really plum contacts, you might want to hold off on using them until you've gained some experience and confidence.

Studying with the Players

One potentially fast way to develop high-level contacts is to study with someone who's active on the session scene. The idea is to find a successful player who teaches and hope that you can make enough of an impression during the course of your lessons that he or she will recommend you for some work—or at least give you some names to call. The hard part is finding someone who's busy in the scene, yet still interested in taking on students. If you know the names of session players in your area, you can find their numbers through the union directory. If you don't know any names, try asking around at the union.

Doing the Hang

Just about all the studio musicians I've interviewed for this book suggest that players who are new in town or new on the scene should help get themselves known by hanging out at the clubs frequented by session players and others from the recording business. Besides the musicians, it's also a good idea to get to know producers, contractors, studio owners, engineers, and anyone else involved with the session scene.

In New York as well as in other cities, there are clubs where top studio musicians play out to keep their live chops up. All kinds of bigwigs in the recording and advertising businesses tend to frequent these "industry haunts" because it's hip to be "seen" at such places, and the music's usually top-shelf. Identify these clubs and start hanging out at them. If you're friendly and outgoing, you should be able to meet some of the industry people and start making

---

PROFILE **LARRY CAMPBELL**
SESSION MUSICIAN

Working as a Multi-Instrumentalist

The ingredients for a successful studio career include abundant talent, the ability to make contacts, hard work, and being able find to a niche for yourself, and New York–based session player Larry Campbell has used all of them to propel himself to success. His story also illustrates that you can build a successful studio career from the contacts and reputation made as a live player.

Campbell plays a variety of stringed instruments, including guitar, pedal steel, fiddle, and banjo. He's recorded and/or toured with artists such as Bob Dylan, Cyndi Lauper, Tracy Chapman, Roseanne Cash, and k. d. lang and played on numerous jingles, television shows, and sound-tracks. He started playing guitar at the age of eleven, and knew when he graduated from high school that he wanted to be a professional musician.

> At that time, anyway, I was really heavily into country music, and I didn't see that it would go anywhere in New York. My heroes were the Burrito Brothers and Gram Parsons and that whole scene out in L.A., so I packed everything up, got in a car with two friends, and just drove out there and starved for about eight months.

Larry's ability and versatility eventually landed him a gig with a touring country show band that played the hotel circuit. He stayed with that band for four years, and also spent some time in Nashville and Austin, Texas.

> There was this vibe in Austin in the seventies, that if you didn't have any money or any food you'd always find somebody willing to feed you or give you some money. . . . [There were] always places to play, events to play at, things where you could make a couple of bucks. It was as close to a paradise as I'd ever been in.

Despite all that, he felt that it wasn't leading anywhere careerwise. "It was bad for the ambition down there. I knew I had to get back to New York, [to do] something that would kick my ass a little."

Back in New York, he started playing with singer John Herald, whom he had met in those early, starving days in L.A. That gig led to a stint in The Woodstock Mountain Review, a band featuring such notables as Happy and Artie Traum, Bill Keith, John Sebastian, Paul Butterfield, and Eric Anderson. Campbell also began playing at the Lone Star Cafe, where he made contacts that helped kick his career into high gear.

Eventually, a couple of other musicians and I became sort of like a house band at that place. If anybody was coming into town and needed a band, it was pretty common that we would back them up. And playing at the Lone Star and meeting all these people started leading to session playing and things like that. It just sort of snowballed, and it's still continuing to snowball.

Another contact led him into the world of playing jingles.

I had met Eric Weissberg in Woodstock, and he was doing most of that [jingle] stuff then. But he needed a sub every now and then, so I went in and subbed for him, and then that thing really flew. You start getting a reputation. People call you back, and then other people call them for recommendations and they hand out names.

Larry was well positioned as one of the few people in New York who could play the variety of instruments that he did. That niche, combined with the fact that he played them all so well, helped him solidify his position in the New York session scene. A position so solid, in fact, that he hasn't been hurt by the downturn in studio work that's occurred since the mid-1980s. "Where most people I know have been bitchin' about getting less and less studio work," he says, "it's only been going up for me. . . . Fortunately, the instruments that I play don't work as synth parts."

Campbell suggests that the best way for new players to get hooked in the scene is to network.

Play clubs, hang, and be a good guy. The personality thing has a lot to do with it. . . . The thing to keep in mind is that there's room for everybody, including yourself. Try to stay out of the competition head as much as possible. I've just seen people do sleazy things; otherwise, they would be working now. They're really talented, but because of this sleazy part of them, people don't want to deal with it. You can really screw yourself that way. The advice I would give somebody just moving to town is go to the clubs, . . . or wherever they're playing music, and be friendly. Because most musicians in this town are friendly; that's really true. Meet people, talk to people, fit in where you can. You never know who's gonna hear you. As trite as that sounds, it's really true. Once the right set of ears is listening to you, then it starts to grow from there. Keep your personality together and keep practicing. The degree of success you'll have corresponds with the degree of talent, and talent is really just passion and hard work. There are lucky breaks, but I can't say that my career's gone that way. Everything I've done has been a result of work.

contacts. If you can befriend one of the musicians, there's always a possibility that you could sit in with the band and get your skills known that way.

One way to find out where recording types hang out is to look in the entertainment listings of your local paper for clubs that list studio players among their performers. At the time of this writing, two of the session hangouts in New York are Triad (Dark Star Lounge) and Bell's Cafe. In Nashville, you might try The Station Inn, Douglas Corner, and The Bluebird Cafe (The Bluebird is known primarily as a songwriter's hangout, but you'll often find musicians in there as well). In the L.A. area, Chadney's in Burbank is a good place to hang out. Bear in mind, however, that the club scene changes constantly, and some of these places may not be in vogue by the time you read this.

Developing Your Niche

One approach that can get you noticed in a crowded studio scene is to stake out a niche that sets you apart from the competition. If you can show that you have something unique to offer, like playing an unusual instrument, or playing a common one in a rare and distinctive style, you can put yourself in a much better position to be recognized.

Let's say, for example, that you're trying to get sessions as a rock guitarist. Even if you've impressed the heck out of a producer, it's likely that there will be quite a few other players who've been doing it longer and will get called ahead of you. Of course, the reason that there are so many really good rock guitarists is because it's such a popular style to play. If, however, you present yourself instead as someone specializing in a less common style, such as acoustic slide guitar, you may be able to get closer to the top of the list because there's a lot less competition. With a little luck you might get some calls, and if you prove yourself you'll be in a much better position to get work in other styles. It could be argued that this strategy could limit your opportunities, because there are far fewer sessions requiring acoustic slide than electric rock guitar. I'd counter that by saying that your odds will still be better, because you'll be competing against far fewer guitarists. The advantage of this kind of "niche" marketing is that it creates an identity that can help you stand out from the multitudes. The disadvantage is that you can be pigeonholed as someone who can only do one type of session.

The key is to get a sense for the session scene in your area and try to figure out which of your instruments or skills is most in demand. You can then decide how to market yourself in the most advantageous way.

Putting Together a Demo Tape

Another thing you can do to help improve your visibility with producers, contractors, and other musicians is to send or bring around a demo tape of your playing (also known as your *reel*). Although this sounds like a direct route to get yourself heard by the people who can hire you, it can often be pretty difficult to get anyone to listen. The problem is that the people whose attention you want to get are often very busy and deluged with other tapes like yours. Even if you do get them to listen, it's unlikely that they'll hire you unless they've also gotten a recommendation from another player. Nevertheless, it's a way to get your name out there, and you never know where it could lead.

Your tape should consist of short-length examples of your playing, edited tightly together so that one piece runs into the next. Marshall Grantham, one of the cofounders of Russo/Grantham Productions, a very busy New York music house (see "Q&A/Marshall Grantham, Creative Director, Russo/Grantham Productions: A Music House's Perspective on Freelance Composers" in Chapter 9), has this to say about musicians' demo reels:

> I like a good four-, five-minute tape. You don't need to let a whole song play to show how you play drums or guitar. [Give me] thirty seconds, then move on to something else. Show another side of your talent, whether you're diverse, and what you do best.

While you should master your demo in a digital format (DAT, preferably), you'll probably want to make your copies on cassette. I wouldn't advise using any noise reduction on your cassette copies because they may be played back on machines that don't have your format or aren't calibrated the same as yours. It's best just to make your copies (if you're making them yourself) with as hot a level as possible without distortion.

When figuring out what material to use and in what order, here are a few things to keep in mind:

• Always put your best material at the front of the tape. Your listeners may not have time to listen to the entire tape, so it's important that they at least hear your strongest pieces.

• Make sure that the total length of your tape is no more than five minutes. You want it to be fast-paced, short, and sweet.

• If you're trying to position yourself as a player whose strength is in a certain style (see "Developing Your Niche," earlier in this chapter), make sure to load the tape with that kind of material.

• If possible, use pieces from real projects. It's much more impressive to show that you have experience playing in professional studio situations.

In addition, be sure to package your tape nicely. Handwritten labels will make you look inept. At the very least, use a computer labeling program to print up cassette labels and *j-cards* (the paper inserts that go in the cassette boxes). You don't need a picture of yourself or a super-fancy design, but you want the package to look clean, neat, and professional. Make sure your name is printed on the spine of the j-card so that it's visible when your tape is on a shelf or in a pile of other tapes. Print your name and phone number on both the j-card and the cassette label. You want to do everything you can to make it easy to contact you. If you've gathered your material from previous sessions, you might also want to print a list of pieces (along with brief descriptions) on the j-card.

Contacting the Right People

If you live in or around a major city, you should first send your reel to music production houses. It's likely that they'll be hiring session players for jingle work in your area. You'll find them listed in annual publications such as *The Shoot Directory* (see Appendix). Some of these directories have listings for the entire country. Your union local might also have a list of music houses and contractors who hire for sessions. You can also call commercial recording stu-

---

SESSION PLAYER'S SURVIVAL GUIDE

• When sending out reels, keep them short, and don't claim to be able to play styles you're not strong in.

• When doing a session, always arrive at least fifteen minutes before the scheduled start (also known as the *downbeat* or the *hit*) of the session so that you can set up and, with luck, have a chance to check out the chart.

• If there are difficult passages on your part, try to work out how you're going to play them before the start of the session.

• Go along creatively with what the producer asks. You can tactfully make suggestions, but don't get into an argument or you won't get hired back.

• Be sure your equipment is not only quiet but functional. You don't want to hold up a session due to a malfunction. If you play a guitar, make sure you have relatively fresh strings on it to minimize tuning and breakage problems.

• Always introduce yourself and try to schmooze with the other players on the date (hand out your business cards). If they like you, they may be willing to give you a recommendation.

• Try to do more than just survive the session. Relax and let your musicality come through.

---

dios, because they'll sometimes recommend studio musicians to their clients.

Another suggestion (especially for those who play instruments other than guitar and keyboard) is to call the owners of small project studios who advertise their services as demo producers because they may need players on your instrument from time to time.

Call all of the above-mentioned places and try to at least get them to agree to listen to your tape. Ideally, you'll set up appointments to play your tape for them, but most likely they'll just tell you to send it in. Give them a week or two to listen to your tape, then make a follow-up call. If you're able to reach the person to whom you sent the tape, get their reaction to it and inquire about getting future sessions. They're likely to tell you they've put it "on file," which in some cases is the truth, and in others a euphemism for the garbage. In any case, make a follow-up call every month or so to try to develop a rapport and keep yourself visible. You'll find that many of the people you're trying to call are very hard to reach, or are perpetually "in session" (another euphemism). If you are able to reach people, you can also use the opportunity to invite them to any gigs that you're doing around town. You might even want to send out postcards announcing your upcoming gigs.

It's unlikely that you'll get a lot of immediate work from sending your tape around. Most of the studio players I talked to agreed that it's not a tactic that will directly result in a lot of session calls. Nevertheless, it can be valuable in laying the groundwork for future work, and perhaps even developing some contacts. The hope is that the name recognition you've gained from sending your tapes will dovetail with a recommendation from another musician, and the result will be a session. According to Marshall Grantham, "You have to be persistent. It's a tough business to get into. . . . If you can deliver and get in there and do a good job, then you can definitely crack in—but it takes time."

CHAPTER 8 | **PREPARING TO BE A COMMERCIAL MUSIC COMPOSER**

❖

Although the record business is by far the most glamorous part of the music industry, there are also many opportunities in the commercial end of the business: writing music for ads, television shows, industrials, stock music, and even multimedia.

To be successful in the commercial sector, you must be willing to put up with far more creative constraints than you would as a recording artist. You've got to become what amounts to a "composer for hire," whose ultimate creative direction comes not from within, but is instead based on the whims of those who hire you. If you can handle that kind of limitation, as well as heavy deadline pressure and intense competition, then read on. This chapter is for you.

WHERE THE WORK IS

Let's take a look the major areas that encompass the commercial music business. (We won't deal with movie scoring because it's beyond the scope of this book.)

Composing Jingles and Underscores for Television and Radio

The advertising music scene has changed a great deal since the 1960s, '70s, and early '80s. Those were the glory days, when many ad campaigns had jingles, most ad agencies had music departments, and just about everyone working in the ad music field was extremely busy. Ad agencies would either write their music in-house or farm it out to a (relatively) small number of music production companies (also known as *music houses*).

In many ways, a composer's life was simpler then. MIDI had yet to be invented and, unlike today, demos were not expected to be fully orchestrated. In fact, much of the time a piano-vocal treatment was all that was necessary. When a more full-blown version was required, the instruments, which were played by studio musicians, were recorded live. Composers whose jingles were picked would make a lot of money from singing a part in the group vocals that appeared on virtually every jingle. While singing on a jingle is still one of the most lucrative activities a composer can partake in, it's a much rarer occurrence these days. Much of the music you hear on the air now is instrumental music that's written to fit the picture (or the dialogue, in the case of radio spots). This is what's known as *underscoring* or *postscoring*.

Around the mid- to late 1980s, jingles became passé in the eyes of the advertising community. For both financial and aesthetic reasons, music that sounded like pop became the vogue, displacing the generic, big-group jingle sound. To some extent, this was caused by the advent of MIDI, digital sampling, and the affordable personal computer. These technological advancements engendered an incredible explosion of small (often home-based) studios capable of producing great-sounding instrumental music. This, in turn, created a lot more music production houses whose strength was underscoring rather than jingles. At the same time, a recession in the ad business and a consequent rash of mergers created a cost-cutting climate that was hostile to big-budget jingles and enamored of the lowered costs of the new music technology. This trend has continued to the point where the jingle, in its classic form, now makes only an occasional appearance in nationally broadcast advertisements. There are plenty of ads with vocals, but the big-group sound has, for the most part, been relegated to the cheesy world of local ads.

Today, the new technology has brought about a "democratization" of the ad music production business, often allowing a single composer with a home studio to compete for a national spot against large music companies. The revolution in digital recording has advanced this trend even further. Because it's gotten so much easier to produce good-sounding tracks, a large number of new music houses have sprung up and begun competing for the work. One of the results of this heightened competition is that today's composers must write and produce demos that are of "final" quality in order to compete successfully: If they don't go all out on the demo, they don't stand much of a chance of winning the account. Consequently, composers and music companies are forced to do the bulk of the work for a project while it's still in the demo stage—the least lucrative phase of the process. Agencies generally pay music companies demo fees, but they're very small in comparison to the sums paid for spots that go final.

Despite the difficulties, writing music for ads remains an extremely exciting field. With the amazing palette of sonic tools available you can produce some really cool tracks, even with the creative limitations that are often imposed on you. It's a unique thrill to turn on the TV or radio and hear the music you've created. What's more, the growth of audio and video on the World Wide Web means that opportunities for advertising music may be expanding in the near future.

There are three basic ways to get work as a composer of advertising music. The most lucrative approach is to establish your own music company so that you can get jobs directly from ad agencies. You can then pocket 100 percent of the creative, production, and arranging fees (after expenses) that ad agencies typically pay to music producers. The total amount paid for a spot can range anywhere from a couple of thousand to just under $20,000. It depends on what market you're in, whether the spot is national or local, and your reputation (or that of your company). You can also make money for singing and playing on the spot, and if it's produced under the auspices of the American Federation of Musicians, SAG (Screen Actors Guild, for vocals on TV spots), or AFTRA (American Federation of Television and Radio Artists, for vocals on radio spots), you're eligible to receive residual payments, depending on how long the spot runs. For singers especially, this can be extremely lucrative (see "Jingle Writing," later in this chapter). When the spot is a *buyout*, however, it's not produced subject to union rules, and the talent gets paid only for the actual session and not for any subsequent use. It's always better to do a union spot because you get on the vocal and/or musician's contracts and stand to make a lot more money.

The second way to get composing work is as a staff writer for a music house. You won't get to keep the creative fee, but you'll get both a steady salary (or sometimes an advance against the money you bring in) and be listed on the performance contracts for the spots you do, and often for whatever spots your company does. This is an ideal situation, because you'll be making steady money and accumulating a great deal of experience as well as material for a future demo reel, should you want to strike out on your own. In some situations, the music house won't actually put the writer on staff, but instead will offer him or her what's known as an *exclusive.* This arrangement keeps the writer from working for any other companies in exchange for a promise of a specified amount of work. In many instances, music company staff jobs start out as nonwriting, lower-level, production positions, where one has to work his or her way up to being a writer.

The third method is how many new composers have to start, and that's as a freelance writer for other music houses. Most music companies won't put writers on staff unless they're so good that the company wants to keep them from working for other houses. Usually, they prefer to hire their composers on a per-job basis. Generally, the writer will get paid a small fee to write and produce the demo, and if the spot goes final he or she will typically receive between 30 and 40 percent of the creative fee. In addition, the composer will be listed on the performance contracts as well. Although freelancing is probably the simplest way to get involved in the business, you've got to become extremely busy in order to make a decent living from it.

Writing Music for Television
A composer can also get work writing for television. Composing themes and incidental music for dramatic shows, documentaries, news programs, and cable systems can be lucrative as well as exciting. This kind of work can be obtained either freelance through a music company, or directly from the production company or director of the show.

Composing the score for a major network show is something that usually only goes to composers with strong reputations and backgrounds. However, a couple of notches below the glamorous work is the nuts-and-bolts TV scoring work, such as local news themes and *bumpers* (pieces of transition music) for cable channels. Even getting these kinds of jobs is very competitive, but as a new composer you at least have a shot at this type of work if you have contacts.

Scoring Industrial Videos

Composers can also find work composing and scoring for industrial videos, which range from corporate training films to video trade show presentations. Scoring for industrials is not nearly as sexy as scoring for commercials, and the subject matter can be downright dull. I once scored a ten-minute video on how to clean and operate a pizza dough machine.

Exciting or not, it's composing work and it does pay. Keep in mind, though, that the creative fees are generally a lot lower than for commercials and there are no residuals. You'll have to negotiate your own deal with the company hiring you, so beware of getting ripped off. This kind of work can be obtained from a variety of sources, including clients (the companies for whom a video is being produced), ad agencies, PR firms, video production companies, and sometimes music houses. In many situations, the composer of an industrial is also responsible for providing any necessary sound effects.

Writing Stock Music

Stock music, which is also known as *production music* or *library music,* consists of preproduced tracks that are used in commercials and industrials when budgets don't allow for original music. Stock music is typically produced on CDs, each of which usually features one musical style. You can find stock music in just about any genre you can imagine, from heavy metal to traditional Irish folk. There are quite a few companies that produce stock libraries, and the quality varies greatly. Stock producers are constantly updating their libraries to keep up with the changes in popular music and have to regularly call in composers to write and produce new tracks for them.

The payment arrangements vary from company to company. Some will offer you an advance against royalties while others will try to negotiate a buyout. As it is used in reference to stock music, the term *buyout* means that the library buys all rights to your music for an up-front fee, and can use it as much as they want without compensating you further. Others will offer to license your music without paying you up front, but will concede a cut of any future royalties. As with any contractual situation, tread carefully and get legal advice if you can afford it. In most cases, composing stock music is much less lucrative than doing commercials. You have to view it as a supplement rather than as a centerpiece of your musical income.

One of the nice things about stock music is that you tend to have more creative freedom when composing it, and many of the pieces are three to four minutes long. On a typical stock CD there will be a full-length version of a piece, as well as five-, ten-, thirty-, and sixty-second versions. These short takes usually consist of edits from the full-length version. Sometimes the music company that hired you takes care of the edits, and sometimes you are expected to provide them. In any case, keep the short versions in mind when composing the full-length piece.

You'll often be asked to deliver a fully mixed master of the piece (or pieces) that you've been hired for. This means you've got to have good-quality equipment and good engineering chops in order to be able to handle the work (see "The Equipment You Need" and "Engineering," both later in this chapter). Stock music may not always be wonderful musically, but the recording quality is expected to be pristine.

Composing for Multimedia

A decade ago, the term "multimedia" evoked the thought of a guy with a slide projector and portable tape player. Today, multimedia is a cutting-edge business involving CD-ROMs, video games, the Internet, and lots of potential opportunity. As was touched on earlier, the World Wide Web is an area in which there's a great deal of promise for composers. This is true not only because so many sites are starting to use music, but because the Web has such a heavy advertising presence. As audio becomes increasingly prevalent in cyberspace, the possibilities for composers will continue to grow.

Along with these new opportunities have come new complexities. Writing music for an interactive project isn't as straightforward as just composing, scoring, recording, and mixing a piece of music. You might have to write a score that's entirely General MIDI, one that's all digital audio, or a combination of the two. (Also referred to as GM, *General MIDI* is an extension of MIDI that standardizes the types and locations of various instrument sounds to allow complete cross-compatibility between any two GM systems.) You've got to consider the delivery platform and make sure that what you're writing will sound good on it. It's an evolving field and there are many different formats, protocols, and platforms that you have to be familiar with in order to compete.

The bottom line is that you need to have technical chops as well as musical ones in order to be a successful multimedia composer. In addition, you've got to have a great deal of business savvy, because this field is so new that the standards and structures have yet to fully develop. There's also no established amount or method of payment, so you'll have to negotiate each deal individually, which opens you up to a great deal of potential risk. The watchwords are "be careful."

If you think you might be interested in this field, do as much reading as you can, and talk to anyone you know who's involved in it. Remember that this is budding area with some pretty hefty upside potential, so it's worth putting in some time learning about it.

WHAT YOU'RE IN FOR

As exciting as it may sound, commercial composing (especially advertising music) is a unique field that will present you with a lot of unexpected difficulties. Here's a brief look at some of the hurdles you'll encounter.

Deadlines

In many instances, music is added to a commercial or other project after the picture has already been shot. This is why underscoring is often referred to as postscoring. The agency people, video producers, and others responsible for producing the nonmusical elements of a commercial usually use up most of the production time. By the time they get around to commissioning the music, there's rarely more than a few days left to compose, arrange, produce, and mix. As a result, you can expect an incredibly short turnaround time on just about every project you work on. Working under this kind of pressure takes some getting used to and leaves precious little room for error.

Changes

Besides having to work fast, you often have to deal with the ad agency changing the picture at the last moment. It's pretty standard procedure to have to compose to a *rough cut* (a working version of the picture), which is often changed one or more times before a final version is settled on. This can wreak havoc on the music; by its very nature, scoring requires that music be composed to accentuate various visual events (see "Scoring to Picture," later in this chapter). When they reedit the picture, these events end up falling in different places and you're forced to adjust your music to compensate. Today's digital editing tools make those adjustments a lot easier than they used to be, but they're still a pain.

Sometimes the changes you'll be asked to make have more to do with aesthetic considerations than technical ones. These can be the toughest to take, because they're often coming from people who have only a layman's understanding of music. After you've put your heart and soul into a track, it can be maddening to hear an agency creative say, "This doesn't sound peppy enough," or "I think it needs to feel more uplifting."

According to Doug Hall, co-owner of MessHall Music and Sound Design, a New York–area music company, you have to learn not to let it bother you.

> You really have to start to develop a kind of a Zen approach to your music, and by that I mean kind of a nonattachment to it. Because you can do something that you think is the greatest piece of music in the world, and it just gets shot down and you have to try something else. You have to be able to roll with those kind of punches. I've seen a lot of guys who really get so upset about that, or upset with nonmusicians suggesting [that they] do something different, that it makes it impossible for them to enjoy working in this area. And I was like that at first, too. I remember my first couple of jobs, where I

was having to sort of adjust things that I didn't feel needed adjustment and being kind of upset about it. I had to learn very quickly that you do your best work and you put it out there and then you can't be overly attached to it. And if somebody wants it changed then you've got to be willing to change and do it cheerfully.

Competitions and Multiple Approvals

It's now a common practice in the ad business to hire two or more music companies to compete for the privilege of writing the music for a given commercial. Each music house submits four, five, or more versions, which results in the agency and client having ten or fifteen versions to choose from. Depending on how close it is to the airdate of the spot and how far along the picture is, the composers will write these demos either with the picture, or from a storyboard or animatic (See "Scoring to Storyboards, Animatics, and Voice-Overs," later in this chapter). Having all these versions to choose from is great for the client but hell for the composers, because they're always competing against ten to fifteen other versions. Even when there's only one music house involved, four or five writers are usually called in to compete for the job.

Even if your version does get picked by the creative team at the agency (the producer, creative director, copywriter, and art director working on the spot), you're not out of the woods yet. It can still get shot down at one of several points along the way. Higher-ups in the agency or the client can still veto it or ask for changes. I've learned not to get too excited when someone from the music house tells me, "The agency picked your version; now they're sending it to the client."

DEVELOPING THE SKILLS YOU NEED

To succeed in today's technological age, you need to possess more skills than simply the ability to write music. In contrast to twenty years ago, when a composer could put all of his or her energies into composing, one now must be an accomplished arranger, engineer, producer, and sound designer as well. A composer also needs to be a computer power user, and must stay abreast of the racing tide of technology to avoid being left in the dust.

It's a daunting amount of knowledge to have to absorb, but it's also very exciting to wear so many hats. This section will give you some basic information to help you get started.

Composing

I'll assume that most people reading this have either studied composition, or have at least had enough experience writing music to consider themselves composers. For those who are unsure of their abilities, let's take a look at the minimum skills you'll need in order to start looking for work. Because it's beyond the scope of this book to teach you how to compose music, if your skills aren't close to or above the levels described in this section, you should consider furthering your education in order to bring your abilities up to a professional working level.

Reading and Writing Music To start down the road to success as a commercial composer, you must have at least a rudimentary ability to write and read music. You need to be able to write out charts for musicians you hire, read music given to you (such as a melody for an already existing tag line in an ad campaign), and, most importantly, keep track of your own compositions. While I've heard of a few successful composers who were not musically literate, it puts you at a great disadvantage. If you need to brush up on your reading skills, now's the time to do so.

Basic Compositional Skills You also need to have the capacity to write melodies at will. Just about any composing assignment will call for some type of melodic line. In addition, you've got to have a working knowledge of music theory to be able to harmonize those melodies in appropriate and interesting ways.

In creating music for advertising, you frequently get directions such as "That needs to be more happy sounding," or "Make that trumpet line less humorous." In order to respond to such comments you've got to be able to write music that fits a specific mood. This is a basic compositional skill that you'll often use when writing music for commercials.

Arranging

Today's new technology has given composers access to an incredibly extensive palette of sounds. Just about any instrument can be reproduced with varying degrees of success via digital sampling and MIDI. To make the most out of this technological windfall, you have to know how to arrange for at least the most commonly used instruments in pop music. You also need, at minimum, a rudimentary knowledge of arranging orchestral instruments. If you don't have these skills, composing music digitally is like owning a garage full of vintage cars and not knowing how to drive.

Obviously, it's easiest to arrange for an instrument that you play: You know the range, the tonal possibilities, and what types of parts are and aren't possible. This kind of information is not only important if you're writing for a live player, it's also very helpful in a MIDI context. Granted, in the MIDI realm you can go far above or below the range of an actual instrument, but it's not going to sound realistic if you do. In some situations that won't matter. One of the coolest things about MIDI is making instruments do things they can't do in the real world. Nevertheless, you need to know what the real-life parameters of a given instrument are so that when you exceed them, you do so intentionally. If you haven't studied arranging and have no feel for it, you might consider taking some classes or lessons, or at least doing a lot of reading on the subject. A thorough book on arranging that lists all the instruments and their ranges and capabilities is a good reference to have around (see Appendix for some suggested titles). The following are some tips and general advice for arranging some of the more common instruments.

Drums You should have a good idea of what a drum part consists of and be able to break it down into its component parts (such as kick, snare, high hat, and so on). Since the majority of home studios aren't equipped to record live drums, most of you are going to have to program MIDI drum tracks. You should develop your programming skills with the aim of constructing parts that really groove and don't sound like a machine. Unless you're a drummer, this takes a lot of practice. If your budget permits it and you know a drummer with a MIDI drum kit, by all means hire him or her to play on your project; it'll make a huge difference. Unfortunately, that probably won't be an option in most situations, so follwing are some tips on programming your own drum parts.

- Be minimalistic. When you try to put in too many fills (especially tom fills), your parts end up sounding like a cheap drum machine. Also, beware of using too much percussion. Use it for color, but be careful or your tracks will sound like they're being played by a bad salsa band.

- Don't overquantize your drums. (When a MIDI sequencer *quantizes* a part, it moves the notes closer to the exact beat locations by a user-specified amount.) A real drummer doesn't play everything exactly on the beat, so your sequence shouldn't either. A trick you can use to avoid having to quantize too much is to slow down your sequence when you're playing in your drum parts. This allows you to be more accurate and thus lessens the need for quantization. Be careful, however, because if you slow it down too much it'll be impossible to play with any kind of groove. A lot of sequencers have *groove quantize* functions, which can also help inject more of a human feel.

- There are certain musical styles, especially techno and dance music, for which it is desirable for your drums to sound like a drum machine. In these cases, feel free to quantize to your heart's content.

If you have difficulty with drum programming, consider purchasing a collection of preprogrammed MIDI drum parts. There are a number of them available that give you sequences in a wide variety of styles played in by real drummers using MIDI drum kits. Although these can be very helpful, they don't eliminate the need to program, since you'll invariably have to customize these parts to meet the needs of your project. Nonetheless, they can be a very helpful tool.

More and more composers are using sampled *drum loops* (recordings of a real drummer playing short phrases at specific tempos) on their projects. You can now purchase CDs and CD-ROMs that have numerous loops in a wide variety of styles. These collections typically contain enough fills, hits, and endings to construct an entire, authentic-sounding drum part. On the minus side, though, you don't have as much mixing flexibility with loops because all the drum sounds are already mixed together in the stereo field. A lot of people use a combination of loops and MIDI to assemble their drum parts.

Bass If you can bring in a live bass player, don't worry too much about arranging the bass part. Just write out a chart with the chord changes and let the player interpret it. (This approach works well with a live player on just about any instrument. Nine out of ten times, he or she will come up with a more interesting part than you can.) In most cases it's unnecessary to write out an entire part note for note; give the bassist at least some room to use his or her creativity and expertise. For those (probably frequent) times when you can't bring in a live bass player, here are some tips for programming MIDI bass parts.

• No matter what musical style you're composing in, it's essential have a good idea of what bass players typically do in that genre. Having inappropriate parts makes your music sound unprofessional. If your job calls for you to work in a style that you're unfamiliar with, do a lot of listening before you start working and try to pattern your arrangement after something you've heard.

• Like programmed drums, programmed bass should err mainly on the side of simplicity. Generally speaking, the more intricate you make the part, the more "programmed" it will sound. If you err too far on the side of simplicity, however, your parts can sound lifeless.

• Make sure that the bass is pretty closely locked in with the kick (bass) drum. As a general rule (although there are exceptions), you don't want to have a lot of beats where the kick is sounding and the bass isn't. You don't want them to sound robotlike either, so on beats where they sound together it's a good idea to have them a few sequencer ticks apart.

• When you're choosing a bass sound, pick one that's true to the genre you're working in. It's okay to be creative, but in most cases you won't want a synth bass sound on a country track or an acoustic bass sample on a techno tune.

• Be careful not to overquantize your bass parts and keep the *attack velocities* somewhat variable. (Attack velocity is a MIDI parameter that measures how hard you attack a note, and it has a direct correlation to the volume of that note.) Unless you're playing a style that's supposed to sound programmed, you'll want to retain the subtle variations to help give the part a human feel.

• Finally, something you can do that'll help to "humanize" any instrument you're programming is to "play" in the part (on your keyboard or other controller) from start to finish. That way you've got a complete performance, rather than a few measures cut and pasted together to construct a composite track. Playing from beginning to end is particularly easy when you're working on a commercial because you're dealing (for the most part) in thirty- and sixty-second lengths.

Keyboards Since a large majority of composers are keyboard players, I'll assume that they won't have great difficulty arranging for piano, organ, and synth. For those of you who are non-keyboard players (like me), here's some arranging advice.

It's actually relatively easy to arrange *pads* (long, sustaining chords that typically hold until the next chord change) and melody lines for synths. You can use your knowledge of melody and harmony to create good-sounding parts, and you can often play them in yourself without much trouble. However, when it comes to piano and organ parts (piano especially), you're usually better off either leaving them out, calling in a keyboard player, or making them incredibly simple. The reason for this is that there are so many nuances and idiosyncrasies in a piano or organ performance that it's next to impossible for a non-keyboardist to recreate them. Knowing what voicings to use, what to do with the left hand, and when to use the sustain pedal (in the case of piano) are just a few examples.

When you're dealing with synth parts, do a lot of experimenting if time permits (which it usually doesn't). Some of the most interesting parts I've ever arranged came when I accidentally had the wrong sound assigned to a part. One of the great things about MIDI is the ability to map any sound to any part.

Guitar It's very difficult to program realistic guitar parts, so whenever possible use a real player. You'll find that adding a live guitarist can "humanize" a MIDI arrangement and move it to a whole new level. If you are able to bring someone in, don't overarrange his or her part. Generically speaking, guitarists are not the best readers, so having a lot of notes written out will simply slow them down in many cases. Of course, if there's a specific melody line you need played, by all means write it out. Otherwise, a simple chord chart and an explanation of what you're looking for is probably the quickest way to achieve good results.

If circumstances don't permit using a live player, there are some things to keep in mind when doing MIDI guitar arrangements. Arpeggiated, single-note parts are the most convincing. This is true whether you're using an acoustic or electric sample (or synth patch). Conversely, parts that are supposed to sound strummed rarely do.

If you do come up with a nice, arpeggiated line, it often sounds cool to double it and detune one of the doubled parts. Then pan one hard-left and the other hard-right to achieve a fat, *chorused* sound.

Strings   You can bet there'll be situations where you'll need to be able to program realistic-sounding string pads and melody lines. Although it's relatively easy to find good string sounds, programming them correctly is not so simple. If you had unlimited time and unlimited tracks, you'd probably be best off constructing a MIDI version of an actual orchestra string section using layered, individual string sounds. Unfortunately, that's extremely time consuming and difficult, so the more practical approach is to use string section or ensemble patches from your synth or sampler.

When you're programming pads, try to use good *voice-leading* so that the motion from chord to chord is fluid and natural. Strive to write your string arrangement so that if you were to extract individual parts from those moving chords, each line would sound good on its own. The most important thing to remember is that if you keep your string part as simple and as sparse as possible, it will stand a much better chance of sounding realistic.

Horns   As an arranger of pop music, there are probably going to be times when you need to add horn parts to your piece. If you're fortunate enough to be able to use real players, you want to make sure you have a solid arrangement so that you don't waste their services. If you don't have experience writing for horns and the part you need is a section part, talk to the players you're going to hire about the arrangement. They may be able to help you write it (for extra money, of course) or they can turn you on to an arranger whose services you can contract.

In most cases, you'll probably have to program your horn parts, which you'll find are even more difficult than strings to make sound realistic. There are many nuances in a horn section arrangement that are very hard to achieve via MIDI. I've found that "less is more" is the best approach for programming horns. Unless you're doing *stabs* (short staccato horn hits), it often sounds more convincing to use octaves rather than full chords. Obviously, there'll be some occasions where the musical style will call for fuller harmonies, but try to stay away from them when you can. In the MIDI environment, fully harmonized horn parts often sound cheesy. If you must use more complicated chords, the rules about voice-leading and individual lines that pertain to strings are also applicable here.

Some woodwinds, such as oboes, clarinets, and flutes, are fairly easy to reproduce convincingly via MIDI. Saxes, on the other hand, are not. Even if you have a good sax sound, you often have to spend a lot of time adding grace notes and other small nuances in order to make it sound more convincing.

Scoring to Picture

If you want to be a commercial composer, you're going to have to learn how to score to picture (also known as "underscoring"). This is the ability to compose music that supports a video or film by setting a mood and *hitting* (accentuating) certain key points. Scoring is a real art but it's not impossible to learn, and the best way to get good at it is through experience.

For those of you who've never scored to picture, let's go through the basics so that you'll be able to handle an assignment or at least begin practicing on some mock assignments. You can treat the information in this section as "Scoring 101."

Locking to SMPTE The first thing you need to do on a scoring job is to make sure your sequencer is able to *lock up* (synchronize) to the SMPTE *time code* (see "SMPTE Basics," below) that's recorded on one of the audio tracks of the video. This allows your sequencer to start playing at a user-specified point on the video and makes the process of scoring much easier.

Whoever is hiring you for the job (ad agency, music house, or individual client) will give you a video containing the picture you'll be scoring. Especially in the jingle business, the industry standard is 3/4-inch video, but if you ask you can usually get a copy on VHS. If you're going to be working with VHS, make sure to request your copy in VHS Hi-Fi format. Ask them to record the SMPTE time code on one track and the audio for the spot on the other. The time code must be completely separate from the audio for the spot or you won't be able to lock up with it. Also request that the time code numbers get *burned in* to the picture. This *window burn,* which is also referred to as an *SMPTE Burn Window,* allows you to see the actual SMPTE numbers of each video frame as it goes along (some people refer to these numbers as *visual time code).* These numbers correspond exactly to the audio time code that's recorded on the tape. This audio code, which represents elapsed time from an arbitrary starting point, provides a standard reference for various pieces of gear so that they can be synchronized together.

SMPTE Basics Time code is an incredibly tedious subject, but you need to have a basic understanding of it in order to score to picture. Consequently, I'll try to keep this explanation as brief as possible.

In case you're wondering, SMPTE stands for the Society of Motion Picture and Television Engineers, the organization that developed the time code format. A typical SMPTE display looks like this:

00:00:00:00

From left to right, this represents hours, minutes, seconds, and frames. Occasionally you'll come across a piece of gear or software that displays yet another two-digit column of numbers on the extreme right, which represents "subframes," but the standard display doesn't usually have that.

Let's say you hit stop on your video deck and your burn window displays this number:

01:00:21:15

This means that one hour, zero minutes, twenty-one seconds, and fifteen frames have elapsed from zero. This doesn't necessarily mean, however, that you're at a point that's an hour, twenty-one seconds, and fifteen frames into your video. This is because SMPTE time code is usually *striped* (recorded) onto the video so that *the start of picture* (the first frame of the commercial, industrial, or whatever it is you're scoring) occurs at an arbitrarily chosen round number, typically 01:00:00:00. Therefore (to continue with our hypothetical example), if the start of picture occurred at 01:00:00:00, then the point at which you stopped (01:00:21:15) would represent an elapsed time of twenty-one seconds and fifteen frames from that starting point. You can determine the SMPTE location of the first frame of picture by observing the "burned in" number at the frame location where the commercial starts to fade up from *black*.

The reason that the time code at the start of picture doesn't begin at zero is that it takes some gear fifteen or twenty seconds to lock up to it. As a result, there must be plenty of code recorded on the video prior to the actual start of the commercial (or whatever you might be scoring) so that the various pieces of gear can comfortably get locked. The time code that elapses before the start is know as *pre-roll*. There's also video information that needs to be displayed prior to the start of the commercial, such as the name of the spot, the name of the editing house, and most important, the countdown.

Those Darn Frame Rates Without a doubt, the most confusing aspect of SMPTE time code is the issue of *frame rates;* in other words, how many frames are in one second of video. In the days before color video, the standard frame rate was 30 frames per second *(FPS)*. When color was introduced, it was decided that the standard should be changed to 29.97 FPS. (This was done in order to make room for the color signal information while leaving the black-and-white signal intact, thus assuring reverse compatibility.) The result of this adjustment was that the SMPTE code was no longer completely accurate when compared to actual elapsed time—it was off by close to two frames per minute. The Society of Motion Picture and Television Engineers came up with the *drop frame* format to address the discrepancy. In 29.97 drop, the time code is adjusted by roughly two frames per minute to alleviate the problem. For the most part, however, the videos you work on when scoring commercials will be in 29.97 non-drop format.

How does this affect you as a composer? Usually not a whole lot, but it's important to find out what the frame rate is on the video you're working on so that you can set your sequencer accordingly. Fortunately, because most TV commercials are thirty seconds or shorter, the discrepancy in 29.97 non-drop isn't very significant. If you find that events are not happening exactly where the visual display says they should when you're locked to picture, slide the event back and forth by a few frames till you find the correct hit point. Trust your eyes, not the numbers, and you'll always be OK.

Now that you're completely confused, let's deal with some of the more clear-cut technical issues related to scoring.

The "Two-Beep" When the countdown occurs prior to the start of the picture, there's usually a beep or click on the audio track of the video that occurs at exactly two seconds prior to the start of picture. This *two-beep,* as it's called, can be a helpful reference when you're scoring. You'll probably hear it referred to a lot, so it's a good thing to know about. Sometimes when you're doing your final mix you'll be asked to include the two-beep on your *DAT* (digital audio tape— the format you'll usually be mixing to) in real time with the mix. This way, the person doing the *lay-back* (combining your music and the video) will have a reference point at which to line up your mix with the video so that everything hits the way you intended.

Dealing with Lockup Problems As mentioned earlier, the first thing to do when you get your video from the music house or agency is to make sure your sequencer will lock to it. Listen to the audio portion of it to determine which side the time code is on and which side the audio program is on. Patch the time code into the input of your SMPTE reader (usually your computer's MIDI interface doubles as a SMPTE reader/writer). Set your sequencer so that it's paused to receive time code (different sequencers may use different terms for this) and hit play on the video deck. It's important to remember that in this setup, the video deck is the *master* and the sequencer is the *slave.* This means that the sequencer will follow the commands of the video deck.

Once you hit play on the video deck, the sequencer should spring into action and start moving ahead. If nothing happens, check your connections to make sure that things are patched correctly. If nothing happens again, you may have a situation in which the SMPTE was striped at too low a level to register on your SMPTE reader. The level at which the SMPTE time code is recorded is somewhat of a touchy issue, because if it's recorded too loud (in the neighborhood of 0 db [decibels]) it can bleed into the other track and mess up the audio. Conversely, if it's recorded too soft, you may have lockup problems.

If you have such a problem, here's what you should do. First, make sure that there isn't something wrong with your equipment. One way to check this is to try locking up to an older video you've successfully used in the past. If you don't have one, stripe thirty seconds or so of code onto a blank video (DON'T use the video with your current project on it!) at a healthy level (around -4 db) and see if you can lock to that. If that works, the problem most likely lies with the time code you were given.

One quick-fix solution that sometimes works is to patch the time code through a preamp or some sort of signal processor (such as a compressor with the compression turned all the way off) that can boost the level of the signal to the point where your SMPTE interface can read it. With luck, that'll take care of the problem for you.

Once you do get locked up, play the video from the beginning to the end of the piece to make sure that it stays locked up the whole time. Sometimes SMPTE code have dropouts that can interrupt your lockup. Some SMPTE readers can compensate for these by continuing to output time code at the same rate that it was coming in prior to the dropout. This feature is usually referred to as *jam syncing*.

If you're completely unable to achieve a successful lockup and you don't have time to get another copy from the music house or agency (which will be true in most cases), don't worry—you're not out of luck yet. If you have a second video deck you can make a copy of the tape and let your SMPTE box regenerate the code at the proper level, with any dropouts compensated for by jam syncing. If this doesn't work, you can make a copy while generating a completely fresh time code. The problem with this, however, is that there's no way to make the time code correspond exactly with the visual numbers "burned" on the video. Set the start time for your SMPTE generator so that it will be as close as possible to the visual code; later, you'll have to figure out the approximate difference between the visual code and the actual time code that you striped onto one side of the audio track as you were making your copy. This difference, which is known as an *offset,* will have to be taken into account when you're scoring.

What To Do When There's No Time Code Sometimes you'll be put in the unenviable position of receiving a video with no time code at all. The easiest way to deal with it is to make a copy of it onto another video and stripe it with time code as you go. You won't have any "window burn," but at least you'll be able to lock up. When you don't have visual time code (or an accurate visual time code), the best way to deal with it is to lock your sequencer up to the video and record a short percussion sound at each obvious hit point on the video. It's hard to be totally accurate, so edit these percussion notes until they're as close as possible to the visual hits. Your sequencer will display what the SMPTE times are for these notes, and you'll have a reference from which to score.

If you've got no way of making a copy of the video and can't get a replacement, you can, as a last resort, work without locking up. Set your sequence to start with two seconds of silence. As the video counts down to the two-beep (you can reasonably expect that it will have a count and a two-beep), ready yourself and hit start just as the two-beep sounds. This "pseudo lockup" will probably be off by a frame or two, but at least you'll be in the ballpark.

"Spotting" the Spot Assuming you don't have any unmanageable time code problems, you should now be ready to start *spotting* the tape (a film music term for watching the tape from top to bottom, writing down the time code numbers of the important hit points), and starting to get an sense of what your overall approach is going to be. A hit point, or *hit,* is a visual event that requires a musical accent or a sound effect to give it more impact. One example of a hit would be a visual showing a tennis racquet striking a ball. The moment the racquet connects with the ball would be the hit point, and the impact on the viewers can be seriously exaggerated if it occurs on a significant musical beat, especially when it's the first beat of a measure.

When first searching for hit points, you'll probably have a tendency to write down too many of them. The events that are usually important enough to notate are cuts from one scene to another, dissolves (note the beginning and end of the dissolve), and shots of the product and/or its logo, which typically appear at the end of the spot. When the logo appears, it's often referred to as the *super* (a reference to its being superimposed on the picture). For the most part, the agency or music house will give you a sense of what parts of the spot need to be hit. Any other hits are up to you, unless you're instructed not to hit too much. It used to be more in fashion to try and score things really tightly so that the music hit almost all potential points in a given spot. Now that's become somewhat passé, except in the case of *sound design* spots, which generally place a heavier emphasis on effects than on music (see "Sound Designing," later in this chapter). On more "music"-oriented spots, there may be one or two important hits to make and the rest of your job will just be a matter of making the track "feel good" with the picture.

When I do find a hit point on the picture that I want to mark, I input the time code reading of it as a *marker* on my sequencer. The good thing about time code markers is that, because they're expressed as SMPTE locations, they refer to elapsed time and always stay at the same location no matter what you do to the tempo of the song. For example, a hit at 01:00:10:05 will always occur at that time code location, regardless of where you set the tempo and start point of your sequence. The location as expressed in bars/beats/units will change when those variables are adjusted (for example, bars go by faster at quicker tempos), but the elapsed time at which the hit occurs will always remain constant. This is very important to understand when you're trying to figure out a good "click" (see "Finding a Click," below).

When you're writing down or entering in hit points, give each one a descriptive name such as "cut to bird flying" or "dissolve to product shot." It's also useful to number the hit points so that you can easily refer to them on your music paper when you're writing your chart (more on this later). You should also have markers that correspond with the first frame of your commercial (or whatever your project is) and the first frame after it ends. Label these "picture in" and "picture out," respectively.

Finding a Click In order to score to picture, you need to find both a tempo and a *start point* (the SMPTE number at which your sequence begins to play) for your music. In many instances the music house or agency provides you with reference music, also known as *temp* (short for "temporary") *music* or *temp tracks,* which will give you a rough tempo. If you aren't given any reference, come up with a tempo that fits in with the type of music you've envisioned for the spot.

The next thing to do is to input your approximate tempo idea into the sequencer. Once you've done that, make sure the sequencer is set to receive time code and its metronome is turned on and set to quarter notes. Hit play on your sequencer (most sequencers will pause while waiting for time code) and start your video deck, and the metronome will click along with the picture. Watch the picture and see how the metronome clicks are working with the hit points. Optimally, each of your important hit points will coincide with a metronome click, meaning that the hits will occur "on the beat." In the real world, however, you'll probably have to do some tweaking to get the metronome beats to line up with the hits. This is known as *finding a click.*

As mentioned previously, there are two variables you've got to work with when trying to find a click that fits the picture: The first is the tempo, and the second is the start point of the sequence. One thing to keep in mind about start points is that your music can never begin at the first frame of picture. You need to begin your sequence at least three or four frames in, because otherwise the music will be starting as the picture is fading up and it will seem as though the music is coming in early. Bearing in mind that a frame is only about a thirtieth of a second, you can even wait as long as ten frames in (about a third of a second) before starting your music. Therefore, you have the latitude to set your sequence start between three and ten frames in (from the first frame of picture). Experiment with small variations of your BPM (beats per minute) setting as well as your start time.

By slipping and sliding the start point and tempo around, you can (in most cases) find a click that feels good with the picture, and makes at least some of your significant hits. It's interesting to note that if you put almost any random piece of music to a video, you'll always find some parts of the music that hit with events in the picture. The problem will be that other parts will hit in the wrong place, or at least be early or late. Keeping this in mind, your goal when finding a click is to get one that makes as many of your hits as possible, but, more importantly, feels good with the video. There are usually ways of fudging hits to make them work (more on this later), but if the click is fighting against the picture you'll never get it right.

Here's a very important point: Don't ever start looking for a good click before you've decided on a musical style and an approximate BPM setting. You want to make your music fit the picture, but you don't ever want the picture to dictate what your groove or style will be. It's very tempting when you first start scoring to find a click that makes all the hits and then write your music to fit it. In 90 percent of all cases, that's an ass-backwards approach that will undermine your project. My most successful scoring jobs have been the ones where I had a style and an approximate tempo figured out in advance.

Writing a Sketch Once you've got a click that works, the next thing to do is to get a piece of music paper, sit down at your instrument, and start composing. You want to come up with a rough sketch of the spot, after which you can start working on the finer points of the arrangement and orchestration.

I find it very helpful to write down the important hit points in music notation as rhythmic figures, so that while you're composing you can see where the hits are in a musical context. Your sequencer can convert SMPTE times into bars, beats, and units, thus giving you the information you need. (Units are also known as *pulses;* most sequencers have a *resolution* of 480 pulses per quarter note, or *PPQ*—although some have 960 PPQ and others 240.) Let's say for the sake of argument that a sequence starts at the SMPTE time of 01:00:00:05 with a tempo of 110 BPM. Let's also say that the first hit you need to make occurs at 01:00:08:10 (one hour,

0 minutes, eight seconds, ten frames). If you check your sequencer, you'll see that the corresponding time in bars, beats, and units is 4-3-467 (bar 4, beat 3, 467 units, based on a 480 PPQ sequencer). On your music paper you can write in an accent or a note to indicate that there's a hit at the fourth beat of bar four. Even though it's not right on the beat, it's close enough to make it work.

If you do a little basic math, you can see how the "units" measurement gets subdivided. Let's continue using the 480 PPQ sequencer as our example. If your sequencer uses a different resolution, simply divide or multiply the numbers given here, depending on what that resolution is.

- The duration of each quarter note is 480 units.

- The duration of each eighth note is 240 units.

- The duration of each sixteenth note is 120 units.

To put this in context, a hit occurring at 1-2-220 would be the first measure, second beat, plus 220 units, which is practically another eighth note.

HIT LIST FOR "BOTTLED WATER :30"

Bar	Beat	Unit	SMPTE	Description
			01:00:00:00	Picture starts
1	1	0	01:00:00:07	Music in (sequence starts)
5	1	30	01:00:08:12	Water splashes across
10	1	71	01:00:18:05	Water drip
10	6	367	01:00:21:05	Bottle spins
13	2	130	01:00:26:10	Product shot
14	4	450	01:00:29:27	Picture out

These are the major events and hits from the spot "Bottled Water :30." In addition to the hits that need to be made, information such as when the picture starts and stops and the beginning of the sequence is also noted.

This is the chart that I ended up with when I scored this spot. Having the hits written in on music paper helps give you a framework for composing your piece.

Massaging the Hits You're never going to find a tempo at which the hit points all fall exactly on the beat. Fortunately, you have enough leeway so that the actual beat can fall between one and two frames before or after the hit point on the video and still probably look okay. As a rule of thumb, it usually works better to hit late rather than early. The best judges of whether a hit works are your eyes and ears, so let them be the final decision-makers rather than a bunch of numbers.

Many times you'll get the hit on or near a beat, but it will be something other than the *downbeat* (first beat) of a measure. If the event that you're hitting is important and requires strong musical support, it might work a lot better to have it occur on a downbeat. In that case, one approach is to change the meter of the sequence at that point. If your hit is on the fourth quarter note of a 4/4 measure, for example, you could make that measure a 3/4 bar, and your hit will then be on the downbeat of the next measure. The problem is that odd bars (such as the measure of 3/4 you hypothetically just added) can sound very unnatural, so you must use them judiciously.

Another method you can use to hit something better is to change tempo at some point after the beginning of the spot. If, for instance, everything in the first twenty seconds of the commercial is laying really nicely, but an important hit at the end is falling in an awkward place, you can experiment with subtly changing the tempo in the middle. Sometimes, by adding or subtracting one beat per minute to the tempo at an appropriate point, you can cause that hit near the end to be in a better musical location. You have to go through a lot of trial and error to find exactly where to apply the tempo change (or changes). You want to make sure that the viewer doesn't perceive the change, so make sure it's not too abrupt.

Almost inevitably, some of the hits will fall on highly syncopated beats that aren't easy to accent naturally. An example of this would be a beat that falls on a sixteenth note rather than a quarter or eighth note. Unless your piece is full of syncopations, an accent on that beat will sound out of place. In a case like this (especially if the piece is at a relatively fast tempo), you may be able to get away with putting your accent a sixteenth note late (at the downbeat of the next measure, in this example), and it may work. If this doesn't work, perhaps a musical figure or a drum fill that includes the syncopated beat but has a lot of notes around it might help mask the problem. Again, let your eyes and ears be the judge.

No matter how much massaging of the hits you do, there'll sometimes be one that you can't get to work musically no matter what you do. Perhaps you'll have found a click that sits really well with the picture and makes all the hits except for that one. In this kind of situation, you can sometimes use a musical effect to accent that pesky hit point. A cymbal roll that swells up to it can sometimes be used (depending on the nature of the picture), or a high gliss played by a synth set to a harp or vibe (or similar) patch. The problem is that it has to fit in with the rest of the track and not sound like it's coming out of left field.

Structuring Your Spot In many cases, music for a commercial will have a dramatic structure that follows the picture closely. The music will usually have a distinct beginning, middle, and end. Although there are certainly plenty of exceptions, many underscores begin with a *setup,* which might be a V chord or a suspended chord of some sort that gives the effect of a buildup. At this point, the commercial itself is often in its setup phase, where the problem being described will eventually be solved by the product. In this type of spot, the product is subsequently introduced, and at that point the music resolves harmonically and kicks into high gear. It usually continues until the very end, when the product's logo appears. This is also known as the "super." Frequently, the ending accentuates the super in some way, either by stopping the tempo or suspending harmonically, or both. When the logo appears there's some sort of resolution and the music either rings out or continues on until it fades at the end.

The majority of the TV spots on which you'll work will be thirty seconds in length or less. The only time you're likely to have to work on a sixty-second TV spot is for local or cable television. On radio it's much more common to have sixty-second spots, but on network TV today it's almost unheard of.

Scoring to Storyboards, Animatics, and Voice-Overs

Sometimes you'll get called in to do a demo when a spot is in a very preliminary phase and there isn't a finished picture. In such cases, you'll often be asked to write your music using *storyboards* (also referred to as *boards*) as your only reference. If you've never seen a storyboard, it's usually an 8¹/₂-by-11-inch horizontally oriented sheet of paper with six to eight little boxes that contain simple drawings of a scene, an event, or an action in the commercial. Below each box is a description, or a line of dialogue or voice-over. The agency frequently faxes storyboards to a composer; in the process, they can become almost totally illegible.

In one sense, scoring to boards is easier than scoring to picture because you only have rough timings (if any) to go by, so you're less constrained by the need to make the hits work. In another sense, however, it's harder because you don't have the picture to make the whole thing come alive, and it takes much more imagination on the part of the agency (or music house) to "get" what you're trying to do.

In some cases, composers work with storyboards because there isn't a final picture yet; in others, they are *prescoring,* which means that the agency will cut the picture to fit the final approved piece of music. This is a rare but ideal situation because you don't have to worry about making everything hit right (they'll do it for you) and you can concentrate more on the musical elements.

Animatics are crude, low-budget animations that agencies do of spots when they're still in the preliminary phases and awaiting final approval. Although it can be easier to get your ideas across using animatics because you're actually working with picture, you'll probably have to do another version at some point (assuming your version is picked) because the real picture will almost certainly have different timings.

There will also be times when you're asked to write to a voice-over (also known as a *VO).* This is usually the case with a radio spot. Scoring to a voice-over is similar to scoring to picture in that a composer has finite timings to work with. The major difference, of course, is that the music is supporting aural rather than visual events. Because there are no visual elements, the hit points are usually far more flexible than for scoring to picture.

Sound Designing
Commercials that place a strong emphasis on sound effects (which is abbreviated as *sfx* or *efx)* are known as *sound design* spots. Such

commercials sometimes have effects only and no music; more frequently, there's a combination of the two. When I first got into writing commercial music, I was surprised to learn that very few of the action sounds (such as door slams, footsteps, and dog barks) recorded during the shoot are used in the final version. Most of them get replaced, and many times it's the composer or the music house that does the replacing.

One of the definitions of the term "sound design" is the creation of sounds and effects from various sources, including synthesis and digital audio. In order to be a successful sound designer, you not only need a great deal of creativity, but you should also have abilities as a synth programmer and an audio engineer.

Commercials requiring a great deal of sound design are, by their nature, heavily scored. Coming up with a good click for such spots isn't as difficult as you might expect given the number of hits involved, because many are being made by sound effects that don't necessarily have to be on a beat. If the effect isn't a musical one (cymbal crashes and harp glisses are examples of musical effects), the viewer/listener won't perceive it as part of the music track, so it can be inserted wherever it fits the picture.

There are two basic types of effects. The first, *literal sound effects,* are recordings of actual sounds of the same type that occur in the video. Let's go back to the tennis racquet striking the ball as an example. If you wanted a literal effect for it, you would search your sound-effects library, find the sound of a racquet striking a ball, and place it at the exact point in the video that the event occurs. This might work fine in many cases. However, if you wanted to heighten the impact of that moment, you could design a nonliteral, "larger-than-life" effect, either by creating a synthesized sound (such as an ambient, percussive noise) or by substituting the real sound with another one; for instance, the sound of a small explosion, or of metal impacting a hard surface. This would add quite a bit more drama than a literal sound would. When you're dealing with a television spot, the effects are more like icing on the top of the visuals. The picture tells the viewer what's happening, so the effect doesn't have to. On a radio spot, there are no visuals, so the effects are more likely to be literal.

When you're designing sound effects, the possibilities are endless. You can combine sounds, slow them down, speed them up, reverse them, and add ambiance to them. What you need to be successful, in addition to a great deal of skill, is a good collection of sound effects CDs, a sampler, some synths, a versatile effects unit, and preferably a computer-based, digital audio recorder/editor.

Even if you're not expecting to do a great deal of sound design, it's a good idea to have at least a small library of sound effects on hand because you're likely to need them at some point. Such libraries are available on CDs and often on CD-ROM as well. Most well-established sound designers also record many of their own sounds rather than relying exclusively on libraries.

Jingle Writing

Although the number of commercials featuring vocals has declined a great deal in the last ten years or so, it's still important for a composer to be able to write and arrange for vocalists should the opportunity arise. One of the more lucrative facets of the commercial music business is getting on the vocal contract of a jingle, and it's been a long-standing practice in the commercial music business for the jingle writer to be included on the vocal contract as one of the singers. In fact, there are plenty of stories of writers who were lousy singers, standing with the other singers in the vocal booth and pretending to sing the words to the jingle so that they could legitimize their place on the contract.

Unlike the musicians union, whose recording contract is relatively weak, SAG and AFTRA (the unions that represent jingle singers) have very good contracts. If you sing on a spot that runs on a network, you get your session fee plus a payment each time the spot runs. Contrast this with jingle musicians, who get a smaller session fee and only a single (smaller) residual payment for every *thirteen weeks* that a spot stays on the air.

In the past, jingle singers were able to make tremendous amounts of money from just one spot. It was not unheard of for a single spot to earn a singer $10,000 to $20,000 over the course of a year due to repeated plays on the networks. Singers make less for spots that run on independent stations (known as *wild spots*) and on cable, for which they get flat residual fees based on thirteen-week cycles.

Writing Jingles

Mike Kenny has been a freelance composer in the advertising music business for fifteen years. Based in the New York area, Kenny has developed a steady clientele of music houses that gives him regular jingle and underscoring assignments. At the time of this interview he had spots running on the air for Kool Aid, Diet Coke, Sprite, A-1 Steak Sauce, and Mercedes Benz.

How did you get started in the jingle business?
No one grows up wanting to be a jingle writer; although I remember being in high school driving around with my friend in a convertible and hearing some great 7 UP jingle . . . and it actually flashed through my mind that it would be a cool thing to do to write this spot. But I didn't know anything about it. It's such a bizarre, behind-the-scenes sort of industry. . . . Basically, everyone grows up wanting to write hit songs. I think the jingle thing is something that you really fall into. I did all sorts of things. I was in a band and then I made an album by myself on a small label distributed by RCA. This was back in 1975 to 1976. It was sort of pop-rock, but a little bit more in the MOR ["middle-of-the-road"] vein. I got some airplay but nothing really happened from it. Then the label folded and I got a singles deal on another label called Private Stock Records, and nothing happened with that. At that point, I didn't really know what I was going to do; I was playing a lot of piano bar. A friend of mine who was an engineer told me, "You know, you ought to try writing some jingles to make some money." I didn't know anything about it. . . . And then another engineer friend of mine said, "You ought to send some tapes around to jingle houses to try to get a job as a writer because you're a good writer." And that's what I did. I got a job with a small house that did mostly scoring. They were older guys, not the hippest guys in the world, and I kind of filled a need for them, writing pop jingles. And I stayed with them for a few years.

Were you building a reputation at your first staff job?
Yeah, because the other singers come around and they all talk and word gets around. When I went freelance, singers told me about other jingle houses and I would bring my tape to them.

Currently, how many demos a week do you compose on average?
Three; two to three. It used to be that I could do five spots a week, but

that was only if I was doing it with a band [of studio players hired by the music house, as opposed to doing MIDI demos]. When I first went freelance, [I was working] mostly with bands . . . on five, six spots a week; it was amazing. But a lot of times you'd spend a whole week and not make any money. You wouldn't win anything. With the way it is now, I spend a lot of time on spots. I'm not the fastest sequencer. I know guys who don't spend that much time on it. They just churn them out and they're really good technically. It takes me longer; I'm more of an obsessor.

Describe your equipment setup.
I'm a believer in low overhead—that's why I'm a freelance writer. I work for guys who have a studio in the city and people on salary. And they may make a lot more money than I do, but they have four times the overhead—so maybe we're making a lot closer to the same amount of money because I don't have the overhead. . . . I have a couple of little Mackie boards with the Mixer Mixer, the 1604 Mackies; they work fine. I've done national jingles in my own little studio at home. I use an M1 as a controller, but I hardly ever use the sounds from it. I have a Roland 760 sampler with 32 megs and a lot of sounds, and I have a JV-1080 and a JV-880—and that's it; that's all I use. I've got a [Macintosh] Quadra 650 computer and I have one Alesis ADAT.

What's your general routine when you get a video in for a spot?
I look at it a lot. And I ask for whatever musical reference there might be. A lot of times they don't have musical references. So you look at the spot and try to picture what type of music you think would really fit. And you try to get as much out of them as possible. If they can't give you musical references then you try to get feelings from them and some kind of style—what *isn't* this? You've got to pare it down some way, 'cause a lot of times they just go, "Just make it up." You know the clichés: "We want it upbeat and fun." . . . You try to get as much creative information from them in terms of the style of music as possible. A lot of times you take records and play them against the film [video] to see if that feel would work. Not to rip off the song or anything, but to see what ballpark would kind of work with the film. Needle drops can really help determine where you'll go.

Do you do a lot of scoring to picture?
This week I did a couple of things. It comes and goes.

Do you sometimes have to write to storyboards?
Most of the time that's really where it's at. Unless they have the film. If they give you the film you get real excited because you know it's a

real commercial and if you win you know it's going to go on the air—
usually. Yesterday I got a [film] for a new Dentine gum, Dentine Ice.
. . . You don't even know who you're competing against. You don't even
bother to ask, you just do it. And you hope you get a shot at it.

So usually there are few houses competing?
I think the norm is two to three houses.

And each of them has four or five writers doing versions?
Depending on the philosophy of the jingle house. Some jingle houses
have two main guys, or they'll assign it to one guy and they'll feel that's
the way to go.

And then they can pocket all the demo money?
That's right.

What do you get paid for demos?
Around $200 or $250; that's what I usually ask for. But if I'm working
for someone that I work with all the time, if they don't have any money
I'll still take it because I know where my bread is buttered.

If you win, what percentage of the creative fee do you get?
I get forty percent of the creative fee. I ask for a certain amount of lines
on the musician's contract.

*What advice would you give to somebody new in town who's trying to get
into the business?*
You have to make a tape. Don't make it too long. People most of the
time won't even listen to the tape; that's the reality. They just don't

A number of factors have cut into the incomes of jingle singers
(and jingle writers) in recent years. For one thing, styles have
changed and the big-group vocal sound is out. As a result there are
fewer jingles to write, and when you do write one, it's less likely
that there will be a group vocal for you to sing on and make your
SAG or AFTRA residuals. In addition, even if a writer does get on
a contract, advertisers are not nearly as free with the network buys
as they once were, so there's not as much money to be made in
residuals. Composer/vocalist Mike Kenny (see "Q&A/Mike Kenny,
Freelance Composer: Writing Jingles," pages 218–221) makes this
observation:

It seems that ad agencies and clients have become cost-con-
scious over the years. . . . Now they buy a lot of cable time and

have time, they don't care. People are creatures of habit, so they use the same people all the time. There are a few people out there who'll give you a break. Get in the door anyway you can, whether it be by writing, singing, or playing. . . . Keep trying, that's the thing; you just gotta keep hackin' away at it. Somebody'll give you an opportunity. When you get that opportunity, try not to screw it up. Don't let your ego get in the way. You're probably gonna get taken advantage of in the beginning somehow. Try to make the most of whatever break you can. . . . Another thing I think is important: Don't tell somebody you can do something when you can't do it. That's the thing that can really kill you. Because if you really do bluegrass great and somebody wants you to do a heavy metal thing, and you can't do it but you're dying for the gig and say you can, and they're disappointed in it, then you're not doing them or yourself a favor. . . You gotta find out what you can do. You really do. I'm at the point in my life where I know. If they're looking for really great sound design and I needed the job, I might take it from somebody I know really well with the caveat, "Hey, this is not my thing but I'll give it a shot." . . . But you gotta let people know what you can do. Your first impression is so important.

Do you think you should go for a niche?
I think niches are pretty good. You hate to be labeled as one thing, but people want to label. They want to get you into a niche. I mean you can be niched as a guy who can do a lot of things; that would be great. I'm kind of niched as a guy who can do a lot of different things, but it's a certain area of a lot: a lot of things within pop music. I can do R&B, I can do rock, I can do MOR. But it's within a defined area.

you get paid maybe $300 or $400 for a thirteen-week cable run. They'll also buy a lot of wild spots, and specific network times; they're very careful about that. There rarely are spots that make a lot of money.

These days, jingles are often nothing more than underscores with a sung tag at the end, or maybe a solo vocalist singing a few lines of lyrics. As previously stated, the big-group jingle is pretty much a thing of the past on network TV. The ones that can still be found on local commercials are primarily buyouts, so the singers aren't making any residuals on top of their session fees. On national spots, however, the lure of the vocal contract is strong enough to inspire jingle composers to come up with ingenious ways to get their voices on the track. The term *vocal textures* describes the practice of using voices in ways other than straight-forward singing. I've heard of spots featuring "walls of whispering," or vocals processed through a distortion box, or even vocals doing sound effects. Although there are certainly aesthetic reasons for this kind of voice track, you can bet that the thought of lucrative residuals has had some impact on the arranging decisions.

The bottom line is that, despite their decline, jingles can still make you a lot of money. Therefore, if you're not strong at vocal arranging and lyric writing, you may want to take steps to improve yourself in those areas. Vocal arranging is particularly important, because if you don't know what you're doing, you're liable to write something that's unsingable. Just as you need to know the range and capabilities of a particular instrument in order to be able to arrange for it, you need to possess the same information for vocals.

If you end up writing a spot that features a group vocal, it's often better not to write out the harmony parts but to let the singers figure them out instead. Unless you've had a lot of group vocal experience, it's usually better to leave it to the experts.

Engineering

Today's composer has to wear many hats, not the least of which is that of an audio engineer. If you're going to compete successfully with other composers, you must be able to track, mix, and edit audio cleanly so that your compositions will hold their own sonically with the competition. Even if you've written a great piece, you can easily lose out to an inferior composer with a slicker-sounding spot.

If you've had audio engineering training and experience, you'll be that much better off. If you haven't, take classes, read books and magazines, and, most importantly, get a lot of experience with your equipment. The following is a brief overview of the skills you'll need to master.

Tracking The term *tracking* refers to the act of recording audio of any type (voices, instruments, or sounds) into your multitrack. The ability to do this cleanly, at the correct level, and without added noise, is a very important skill to master. The basic rule of thumb is that you want your levels to be as hot as possible without distortion. In the old days, when everything was analog, you could get away with overly hot levels; in fact, sometimes they even sounded better. When you're dealing with digital, however, it's a completely different story. Recording past zero will cause nasty-sounding distortion on digital machines, so you must be careful to keep your levels below the line. You can't record them too low, though, or you'll compromise the sound quality.

It's helpful to also know a good bit about microphone placement. Even if you're a keyboard player and you're planning to use mostly MIDI tracks for your projects, there will be times when you have to add voices or a live instrument such as guitar or saxophone. In such cases, you want to be able to get as good a sound as possible, so it's important to have some idea of how to mike voices and various instruments. There's plenty of literature available on this subject, as well as information on the Internet (see Appendix).

Mixing Your proficiency as a mixer can have a big impact on the success of your demos. There are a number of areas in which you need to be proficient, including:

• *Equalization.* You need a basic understanding of when to use EQ, what the various types of equalizers are (parametric and graphic), and how to use them.

• *Dynamics processing.* A thorough understanding of the theory and practical application of compression and limiting are particularly important skills to have. Optimally, all the elements in a mix will be "in your face" without seeming too loud.

• *Effects processing.* In order to make a mix come alive, you've got to know how to use (but not overuse) reverb, delay, and pitch-based effects such as chorusing. It's very helpful to listen to CDs in the genre in which you'll be mixing and note how the producers and engineers utilize these kinds of effects. The better understanding you have of the genre that you're mixing in, the more successful your mix will be. You'll have a better sense of how to set your levels, and you'll also be better able to place the various elements in the stereo field.

As a commercial composer, mixing under the gun is likely to be routine. Therefore, you not only have to learn how to mix well, but you also have to learn to do it fast. This is one of the most difficult parts of the job, because when you're rushing to complete an assignment it's easy to screw up your mix. Mixing is a process in which you've got to be deliberate, and that can be tough to do when you're rushing. In order to come up with good mixes under these circumstances, you need to utilize routines, mental checklists, and other methods to help keep yourself organized and focused. If you don't, it's very easy to have a mix that includes such problems as one element being too loud (especially true with bass) or noise getting into the mix. You'll help yourself out immensely not only by being organized but by being disciplined when you mix.

Editing   In the age of digital audio, editing has become a much simpler skill to master. When everything was analog, editing was done with a razor blade and was tedious, difficult, and tense. Edits were often performed on a two-track master tape, and an error could wreck the song. On the other hand, digital editing is generally *nondestructive,* which means that no matter how many edits and changes you make, your original remains intact. In addition, today's digital editors allow a visual as well as an aural edit by providing a scaleable display of the waveform. Most editing software also offers a palette of crossfades that go a long way toward smoothing out the transitions between edited sections.

You might be wondering why you would need to be able to edit, and the answer is that in order to get work in the commercial music field, you're going to have to put together and constantly edit a demo reel (see "Putting Together a Reel for Composing Work," in Chapter 9). The prevailing style for such reels is to tightly edit them with virtually no space between the segments. Plus, if you do any work composing stock music, you're likely to need to edit full-length pieces down to sixty-, thirty-, fifteen-, and even ten-second segments. It's not that hard to learn to edit digitally on a computer. If you apply yourself you can achieve a high level of proficiency rather quickly.

The more you know about engineering, the faster you'll work and the better your projects will sound. For this reason it's crucial to develop your skills in this area.

KEEPING UP WITH THE EVER-CHANGING EQUIPMENT MARKET

Like computer gear, musical equipment practically becomes out-dated the minute you walk out of the store with it. Because there's always a newer and better version or upgrade to be purchased, it's difficult to stay on the cutting edge, especially as computers become more and more central to the recording process. As a home studio owner, you're faced with the unenviable task of keeping your studio reasonably up-to-date by selling older gear and buying new stuff. The trick is to hold on to a piece of equipment long enough to get your money's worth out of it, but not so long that it loses a large share of its resale value due to obsolescence. This is the hardest call to make, and it's inevitable that you'll end up with a few pieces of gear that were once the latest rage but are now useful only as doorstops and paperweights. (Some people have actually turned their old Mac Pluses into fish tanks.)

Anticipating the equipment market is almost as difficult as timing the stock market. Your only defense against creeping obsolescence is to stay as informed as possible by talking to people and reading the trade magazines. You also have to be willing to sell something at a loss with the realization that if you don't, you won't be able to sell it at all in a year or so. Although you're never going to be able to be totally up-to-date (unless you're independently wealthy), you can keep up reasonably well without spending your life savings.

Speaking of which, the subject of equipment lust deserves a bit of space at this point. There's something quite seductive about synthesizers and recording gear that makes us musicians want to run into the nearest music store, slam our credit cards down on the counter, and shout, "I'll take one of everything!" We'd all go broke very quickly if we didn't temper that urge. With the easy availability of credit these days, you've got take steps to curb your equipment "jones" so it doesn't lead to financial distress. As a freelance musician/composer, you're essentially running a small business, so you'd be wise to make your equipment purchasing decisions in as businesslike a manner as possible. Buy stuff that will help you get and maintain work without causing your debt level to become unmanageable.

One thing to keep in mind is that, depending on your tax status, you may be able to depreciate the cost of the gear, deducting it from your taxes gradually over a number of years. Check with your tax advisor for more precise details.

The Equipment You Need

In today's commercial music scene, you're going to need your own studio (or unlimited access to someone else's) in order to compete. If you don't already own the equipment, you're going to have to make a pretty sizable investment. The good news is that prices have fallen with each new advance in digital technology, so an awful lot of sonic power can now be had for a relatively small amount of money.

If you're starting your studio from scratch, you can figure on investing around $10,000 in order to set up a bare-bones but functional studio. This estimate is based on buying new gear, and assumes you don't have to sink money into the physical aspects of your studio, such as soundproofing or erecting walls. If you want a more full-blown, high-end setup, you're looking at a budget of $15,000 to $25,000 or more. Some of the gear you'll need for your studio is reviewed below.

Mixing Console　Mixers have come down considerably in price in recent years and have a much better price/performance ratio than they used to. Because MIDI gear has so many outputs, you're probably best off getting at least a twenty-four channel board, if not a thirty-two. You might be able to get away with a sixteen for a while, but you'll eventually expand out of it. As a result, it's best to get as many inputs as you can afford right away.

You also want to get a mixer that's clean and quiet. More important than all the bells and whistles is the sonic performance. Every note of your music will be going in and out of that mixer, so the more transparent it is, the better the sound of your final product. This said, there are certain features that are very useful. The ability to solo and mute each channel is extremely helpful in both recording and mixing situations, and a good EQ section can be a godsend. In addition, having at least three (if not more) effects sends will greatly facilitate your ability to produce a good mix.

If you can afford it, it's advisable get an *eight-bus console,* which allows a great deal of flexibility in routing signals to a multitrack. You can get away with a four-bus model or even a two-bus, but you're likely to have to replace it in the future if you expand your studio.

By the time you read this, there will be a number of affordable digital mixers on the market. You might want to seriously consider purchasing one. There are numerous advantages to a digital mixer if your primary multitrack is digital as well. For most applications, digital mixers allow you to keep your signal in the digital domain, which can greatly enhance sound quality. In addition, they have sophisticated automation and recall options that can make your studio much more efficient and enable you to easily reconstruct a mix at a later date. Further, most digital mixers come with built-in effects processors.

With mixers, as with all equipment, you need to do a lot of research in order to decide which one to buy. Don't rely solely on the advice of the salesperson at your music dealer. Not only do they not know everything, but they'll often also have hidden reasons for pushing one piece of gear over another that have more to do with their inventory than what's best for you. Look for reviews in music magazines, post questions on Internet news groups, and talk to your friends and colleagues. If you know someone who owns the particular model that you're interested in, ask him or her to give you the lowdown on it. Perhaps he or she will even let you try it out.

Computer It's no longer a question of whether you need a computer for your studio, it's a matter of which platform and model. Having a powerful computer is even more important now, as hard disk recording increasingly becomes the standard multitrack format.

If you don't already have a computer, the question is: PC or Macintosh? The Mac has been and still is the computer of choice for the majority of music professionals. However, the PC is making large inroads and now is supported by many professional-level recording and sequencing packages.

I've always been partial to Macs and find them to be much more intuitive and easy to use than PCs, even since the advent of Windows 95. In addition, the Mac has now drawn almost even when it comes to price/performance ratio. Nevertheless, I'd be hard-pressed to make a strong argument against buying a Windows machine to someone who was strongly inclined to do so. There are plenty of music professionals who use them, so it really comes down to a matter of personal choice.

Once you've decided on a platform, you've got to choose a model. Here you'll run into another quandary. Because computers obsolesce so fast, it's wise to purchase as up-to-date and fast a model as you can afford. This is an area where trying to save money on a lesser model can definitely be penny-wise and pound foolish. I'll never forget when I bought a Mac Plus many years ago, the salesman assured me that it would be a solid computer for years. Shortly thereafter Apple introduced the Mac II, and my Plus instantly became a dinosaur.

When you're budgeting money for your computer, don't forget that you'll have to spend a little extra to get more *RAM* (Random Access Memory), which is the memory that your computer uses to run its open applications and system software. RAM should not be confused with hard disk space, which is where your files and programs are stored. For today's applications, you should have at least 24 megabytes (megs) of RAM, and probably more. Depending on how much RAM your computer has to start with, you're probably looking at spending an extra few hundred dollars to get the RAM you need. RAM used to be extremely pricey, but as of this writing it's a relative bargain. Shop around when buying RAM, because the prices vary considerably. If you look in the back of computer magazines, you'll find ads for companies that sell RAM at cheaper prices than the big computer catalog retailers. Just make sure to make your purchase with a credit card so that you have some leverage if you're shipped defective goods, or shipped nothing at all.

Multitracks Even if you're planning on doing only MIDI scoring, you're going to need a multitrack. There will be occasions when you have to record a real instrument, and it's possible that some of your spots will have vocal tags. If you're primarily a keyboard player, you'll be fine with a sequencer that records four tracks of digital audio. If you use a lot of guitars or other "live" instruments, you might want to consider an eight-track.

Modular Digital Multitracks (MDMs) such as the ADAT or the DA-88 are excellent units, but they use tape technology and therefore aren't nearly as convenient to use as hard disk systems, also known as *Digital Audio Workstations* (DAWs). Two of the primary advantages of DAWs are that they offer incredible editing flexibility and they can access your data instantly without any rewinding or fast-forwarding. They're also much easier to use when locking up to video. Certain MDM models need an external sync box, and it's often necessary to figure out complicated offsets and wait five or ten seconds as the machine locks up to the SMPTE from your video. With a DAW, however, locking up is simple and instantaneous. Moreover, many DAWs can do all kinds of *digital signal processing* (DSP) "tricks," such as changing the tempo of the audio without changing the key. This gives you a lot of flexibility to make changes, a quality that can be very useful when dealing with ad agencies.

There are some advantages to using MDMs, and the biggest is stability. Because they record on tape, the digital information is much more stable on an MDM and there's no need to constantly back it up, unlike when you're dealing with a hard disk. It's a good idea to back up your MDM data (to guard against dropouts and accidental erasure), but it's imperative with a DAW. Given the constant danger of a hard disk crash, DAW owners must have a systematic method for backing up their data. A removable drive is a good option for backup, but buying one will add additional cost to your setup.

Another advantage to MDMs is that a lot of studios and music houses have them. This means you can record tracks at home and bring them in for mixing or adding vocals or instruments (assuming their machine is the same format as yours). Ideally you'd have both—a DAW for recording and an MDM for backing up the data and transporting it if necessary. Financial concerns might make that difficult, however, so if you have to choose, I'd suggest getting a DAW, because of its flexibility and editing features.

Samplers Although samplers aren't absolutely essential, you'll almost never see a composer's studio without one. Samplers are like the Swiss Army knives of the studio: They come in handy in all kinds of situations. At their basic level, you can use them to play back samples of instruments and synths via MIDI. There's an ever-growing number of commercially available sample CDs and CD-ROMs (as well as floppy disks) that offer an incredibly wide variety of sounds for loading into your sampler. You have much more flexibility here than with a synth, because you're in control of the sounds you buy. You can also buy CDs of drum and instrument loops to add the sound of real instruments being played by real players to your spots. Though using loops is not a simple process, and it works better for certain types of music (dance music, for example), it's still a really cool option.

Samplers can also be used to *fly-in* vocals or lead instrument parts when you're out of tracks on your multitrack. If, for example, you have background vocals using up two of the four tracks on your hard disk recorder, you can sample them in stereo on your sampler and trigger them at the correct time via MIDI. Once you get them lined up correctly (which isn't difficult), you can use those two tracks of the multitrack to record something else. Just make sure the original tracks are saved in some form.

Yet another use for samplers involves sound designing. Because a sampler can map its samples over the entire keyboard at different pitches, you can easily slow down or speed up a sound effect, which allows you to readily create new sounds. Some samplers have built-in effects that can aid in the sound-designing process.

While there are many brands of samplers available, the common thread for all of them is that you need to expand their RAM. On a sampler, RAM is used to store the sounds that are in the sampler's memory while it's turned on. To save sounds, on the other hand, you have to store them on a hard drive. For example, if you had a 16-meg grand piano on your hard drive, you'd have to load it into your sampler in order to hear it and use it. If your sampler only had 8 megs of RAM, you couldn't load the sound in at all. You'd either have to find a smaller piano sample or expand your RAM to 16 megs or more. Most pro samplers can be expanded up to 32 megs of RAM. The price of RAM fluctuates a lot, but as of this writing you can max out a 32-meg sampler for $200 or $300.

In addition to RAM, there are other hidden costs to owning a sampler. For instance, you'll need a hard drive to store your library of samples. A removable drive, such as a Jaz, Zip, or SyQuest, is the best option, because it allows you infinite expansion of your library by simply purchasing more cartridges or disks. You'll also need a CD-ROM drive so that you can access all the cool sounds that are available. A sampler is a big investment, but if you're composing a lot you'll be glad you have one.

A new and exciting development in sampler technology that is just starting to surface (at the time of this writing) is the capacity to read samples directly off hard disks in real time, obviating the need for RAM. If this technology is effective and takes hold, it will eliminate the RAM constraints that have hindered samplers until now, and offer the user a dizzying and instantly available array of sounds. In addition, because sound developers won't be constrained by the limits of RAM, they can devote much more memory to each instrument or sound, thereby increasing their realism significantly. Stay tuned; this could be something really cool.

Synths Deciding which synths to use is pretty much a matter of taste and money. Be aware, however, that periodically there are certain synths whose technological advances define a new sound and become "hip" for a period of time. Over the brief history of MIDI, some of these defining instruments have included the Yamaha DX7, the Roland D-50, the Korg M1 and O1W, and the Roland JV-1080. Because you may be expected to produce sounds from whatever the "in" synth is at any given time, it's advisable to keep up with what's hot and what's not. Even if you can't buy one, you can always purchase CD-ROMs or disks with some of their signature sounds for your sampler.

Trade magazines such as *Keyboard* and *Electronic Musician* are good ways to keep up with the ins and outs of the synth world. The latest buzz in synth design is about "physical modeling" synths that are supposed to more closely emulate actual sounds than a sample-based synth. The synths of this type that are available (as this is being written) haven't yet realized the full potential of this technology, but by the time you read this there will probably be some cool models on the market.

One thing you'll definitely need for your studio is a keyboard controller. If you're a piano player, you may want to get one with weighted-action keys so that it feels more like a real piano. The problem with weighted-action controllers is that they are generally separate units and usually only have a handful of onboard sounds, if any. If you don't mind the artificial-feeling "synth-action" keys, you can buy one of the cutting-edge synths and use its keyboard as your controller. Either way, you really only need one keyboard, and the rest of your sounds can be synth modules (keyboardless synths). It's much more space efficient to have a single keyboard and a bunch of modules than multiple keyboards.

Signal Processors Although many synths, samplers, and hard disk recording systems feature built-in effects processors, it's also a good idea to own some outboard gear (separate stand-alone units) as well. A good multieffects processor that includes reverb, delay, and pitch effects will always be of use. You probably want one that's particularly strong in the reverb department so you can dedicate it as your primary reverb, and another that you can use for delay and other effects. The prices of digital effects have come down so much over the years that you can get some very cool units in the $300 to $500 range.

It's also essential to have a stereo compressor on hand. When recording live instruments, compression is almost always needed to keep the dynamic range under control. A two-channel unit gives you the option to compress something recorded in stereo, such as an acoustic guitar, background vocals, or even the entire mix. Many compressors have gates built in as well, which can come in very handy when tracking or mixing.

Another handy tool that you'll use constantly is a tube mic-preamp. There are some very inexpensive tube preamps on the market that are of amazingly high quality. These units can add warmth to harsh digital signals. If the unit has *phantom power* (a power supply needed by most condenser mics), you can plug a mic into it and record directly into your multitrack without having to go through the board. By doing so you can improve the quality of the signal going to tape because it doesn't have to go through all the circuitry of the mixer, where it can degrade and pick up noise.

Patch Bays Although it's one of the least sexy parts of a studio, a patch bay can help you keep from drowning in a sea of cables. If the inputs and outputs of all your gear are wired to patch bays, you'll save a lot of time and effort when you have to connect one piece of gear to another (which is something you do constantly in a studio). Tempting as it might be to sink the money into another synth instead, you'll be happier in the long run if you spend it on developing an efficient patching system.

Power Amps Another of the less exciting pieces of gear in your studio, a power amp is nonetheless an essential piece of equipment. If at all possible, use a power amp that's designed for studio monitoring applications. When you're mixing, it's essential to get as accurate a sound as possible, and having the correct amplification is part of the way you achieve that accuracy. You don't want to use an amp from a home stereo system, which is designed to make things sound good, rather than flat, and may accentuate the bottom or top end in a way that will fool you when you're mixing. There are some good-quality studio power amps in the $300 range, so you don't have to spend a fortune.

Monitors As with power amps, your goal with studio monitors is to achieve as flat a sound as possible. Most studios use *near-field monitors,* which are relatively small speakers designed to be listened to from no more than a few feet away. The theory is that by listening at close range, you minimize the affect that the room's characteristics have on the sound. The de facto standard in near-field monitors is the Yamaha NS-10 M. They're not the best-sounding speakers, nor the flattest, but they're used in a huge percentage of studios around the country. If you want your mixes to sound good when they're played in other studios (for instance, when you send your mix to a music house), NS-10s are a good, relatively inexpensive choice.

If at all possible, you also want to have an alternate set of monitors to check your mixes on. Most studios, in addition to their regular monitors, have a small pair, such as Auratones or Radio Shack Minimus-7s. Especially when mixing for television, it's good to have small speakers whose frequency responses are closer to that of TV speakers. As a general rule, it's always a good idea listen to your mixes in a way that's similar to how they'll be listened to in the real world. If you're doing a TV mix you want to check it at low volumes on small speakers, whereas you'll probably want to listen to a rock-and-roll mix at a very loud volume on larger speakers.

No matter what type of music you're mixing, it's always sound practice (no pun intended) to check your mix on as many pairs of speakers as possible, in accordance with the theory that if it sounds good everywhere, it's usually a good mix. That's another reason why it's practical to have an alternate pair in your studio. If you don't, you'll constantly have to leave your studio to listen to the mix in another room or in your car.

Mixdown Deck Over roughly the last five years, the DAT machine has become the universal choice as a mixdown deck. If you're going to work in the commercial music field, you absolutely must have a DAT recorder. The prices for professional DAT machines have dropped somewhat and there are now plenty of good models to choose from, with prices typically in the $800 to $1,500 range. Panasonic, Sony, and Tascam are the major players in the pro-DAT market, and they all make good-quality machines. If you're planning to make digital transfers from your DAT to your computer and back, check with the makers of your sound card and recording software to make sure that the DAT you're planning to buy is compatible with their products.

There are also DATs available that allow you to record SMPTE time code to a discrete third channel. This way, if you're scoring to picture you can record SMPTE from your video onto the DAT as you're mixing, and whatever post-production facility you're sending your tape to will be able to sync it up exactly. Unfortunately, time code DAT machines are about four times as expensive as standard models. Luckily, you really don't need them for most advertising jobs. You can record the two-beep from the video on to a standard DAT, and most places can line up your audio to the picture that way. My advice is that unless you're sure that you're going to have a lot of use for a time code DAT, it's better just to rent one on those rare occasions where it's required. At the beginning of a job, make sure that you ask whoever's hiring you what format they want the mix to be on. If a time code DAT is necessary you'll know it from the beginning, which will give you time to arrange a rental.

This brings up a very important point: If you're doing a composing job, don't ever assume that you know which format your employers want the final mix on. Although DATs are the industry standard there can be exceptions, so you should always ask. I learned that lesson the hard way a number of years ago, when I did an industrial for a small video production company in New Jersey. I assumed the final would be on a standard DAT, but when I got to the video mixing session, they didn't have a DAT machine. They'd expected me to bring it on four-track analog reel-to-reel. The studio owner had to go out and borrow a DAT machine while the video producer (who was paying the studio by the hour) sat there and fumed at me. It was kind of ridiculous that the studio didn't have a DAT, but it was still my fault for not asking.

Besides being a mixdown deck, your DAT machine can often do double duty as a backup medium for your digital audio. Many DAWs allow you to make real-time backups to DAT. This is important because hard disk space gets eaten up quickly by digital audio, so you'll need to free up room on your drive more often than you'd expect. Nevertheless, these kinds of backups are not foolproof, so you may want to consider copying the audio files to a removable drive as well.

Video Deck In the advertising music business, the video format of choice is 3/4 inch (U-Matic). These are great machines to have—that is, if you can afford one. Because this isn't a consumer format, the prices for 3/4-inch decks are quite high and you'll need to spend at least a couple of thousand dollars to get one. Many composers are able to get by with VHS decks, also known as 1/2-inch. As mentioned in the scoring section of this chapter, a VHS Hi-Fi Stereo deck is a reasonable alternative to a 3/4-inch machine; just make sure that you remember to tell whoever's sending you a tape to work on that you need a 1/2-inch copy. Otherwise, they're likely to assume that you have a 3/4-inch machine and will send you the wrong format.

If you're shopping for a VHS deck, you'll need a model that allows you to advance the tape one frame at a time, both backward and forward. This is essential when going through a tape and writing down hit points. In addition, you should go for a deck that has audio metering and input controls. There may be times when you have to restripe SMPTE onto a video, so you'll need to be able to see and control the input level. Before you plunk down too much money on an analog video deck, remember that computer-based video technology is advancing rapidly. In the not-too-distant future, it's likely that the video an agency gives you to score will be in the form of a computer file rather than an analog tape.

Microphones All studios should have at least one decent, all-around mic for recording vocals and instruments. There are some good all-purpose condenser mics out there that will do a decent job and only set you back a few hundred dollars. If you plan on doing a lot of vocal recording, you may want to consider an even higher-quality mic with adjustable pickup patterns. When recording a group vocal, it's helpful to be able to switch your mic to *omni* so that it picks up sound uniformly from all directions. For this kind of mic, you'll be spending between $600 and $1,000, and even more for the really nice models.

Having Your Equipment Ready

Once you've got all your equipment in place and you're up and running, concentrate some energy into getting your studio as organized and prepared as you can. When a job comes in, you won't have time to spend wading through huge libraries of sounds and samples and learning how to operate your gear. Develop systems that enable you to work as quickly and efficiently as possible.

One way to help yourself out is to have template patches for all your synths, samplers, and drum machines that provide you basic starting points from which to build your arrangements. It also helps to use the same MIDI channels for the same instruments on every project. The less searching, scrolling, loading sounds, and hunting through floppy disks you have to do, the faster you'll be able to work, and the more mental energy you can devote to creating good music.

If you're using a sampler and have some CD-ROMs of sounds that you like to use, it's wise to save some of your favorites to disk so that they're ready and easily accessible. You'll find that when you're working on a jingle or underscore, you just can't afford the time it takes to be searching through and mapping out countless sounds. If you have a patch librarian on your computer, consider organizing your synth patches by instrument so that you can quickly find what you need if you do have to hunt for sounds.

CHAPTER 9 | GETTING COMPOSING WORK

❖

"Recommendations are so powerful, so, so powerful," says Leland Bond, Los Angeles–based composer for advertising, television, and feature films. "Most of the jobs I've gotten are through recommendations. In fact, ninety percent of them, now that I think of it."

Like any other area of the music industry, getting work as a composer is much easier if you know people in the business. This seems to be especially true in the world of music for advertising. Many of the people working in it jealously guard their turf and are rarely receptive to outsiders. I remember contacting a well-known music house in New York and being told that unless I was recommended by one of their composers, they wouldn't even listen to my demo tape. With this in mind, you should take a moment to consider anyone you might know who's associated with the commercial music business.

Any kind of entrée can help get your foot in the door for composing work. If you've been working in another sector of the industry, think about whether any of the people you used to work with are now doing composing work. Many players who were once exclusively doing sessions have branched into composing in order to compensate for the loss of studio work to technology.

Unless you get a staff job where you're handed assignments (an unlikely scenario for a newcomer), chances are that you're going to have to spend a good bit of time selling yourself as a composer. Although it's not an easy thing to do and can be quite discouraging, it's a necessary evil in this end of the business. When it comes to selling yourself, the best tool you'll have is your demo tape, which is referred to as your *reel*.

PUTTING TOGETHER A REEL FOR COMPOSING WORK

Reels come in various formats, including video, audio, and even CD-ROM. Ultimately, they all have the same goal: to show off the talents of the composer in the best light possible. A successful reel not only sounds good, it moves along quickly and never lags. Your reel must be edited with the listener in mind—an individual with a hair-trigger finger on the stop button. The cold, hard reality is that the people who have the ability to hire you are usually inundated with composer's tapes, and even if they do listen to yours it's difficult to hold their interest.

I remember once getting an appointment, through a contact, to meet with a producer at a large music company about the possibility of a staff position (the ultimate goal for aspiring ad music composers). I sat down in this guy's office, handed him my reel, and watched with horror as he proceeded to have a conversation with an associate while my tape was playing. This kind of rudeness is, unfortunately, very common in the world of music for advertising, so you have to learn not to take it personally.

You've also got to learn that the opinions of people who work in the business tend to be based more on subjective criteria than any industrywide standards. I remember going to one appointment at a music house and having the person there tell me I should move one of the spots from the back of my reel to the front because it was "by far the strongest." Imagine my surprise when, at another appointment, I was told that same spot shouldn't appear on my reel at all. How, I wondered, could two successful music producers have such divergent opinions about the same piece of music? The answer is that, for the most part, what people think of your reel is derived purely from personal taste. Naturally, if there's a consensus that a particular spot (or your entire tape, for that matter) is lacking, then you ought to take that as a sign you're doing something wrong. Conversely, if everyone (or a majority) agrees that a certain spot is your strongest, then you ought to move it to the front of the reel. In any case, when you do receive criticism, take it in a constructive way and try to learn from it instead of letting it crush you.

Giving Your Reel an Identity

Before you begin putting your reel together, think about your strengths as well as how you plan to market yourself. Ask yourself whether you want to get jingle work or underscoring or both, as well as which musical styles you're strongest in. Based on your answers, you can attempt to tailor your reel to fit your needs. Whatever you do, don't try to be all things to all people. You don't want to end up as the musical equivalent of a jack-of-all-trades, master of none. It's better to find an area in which you excel, then aim yourself in that direction. By giving yourself a musical identity, you provide your potential employers with a frame of reference in which to view you. It's much easier to build a reputation via the specialist route than it is by being a generalist. If, for instance, you're particularly good at writing rock and roll, think about emphasizing that by putting rock pieces at the front of your reel.

You do have to be careful not to paint yourself into too small a corner or you'll end up missing out on work because people won't think you're appropriate for most types of music. There's a fine line between a niche and a pigeonhole, so tread carefully. Ultimately, though, the decision as to how to market yourself will be dictated to a large degree by your talents. One important caveat that many people in the business have stressed is that you should *never claim to be able to do something that you can't do.* If you do get work under those circumstances, you'll end up doing a bad job, you won't get hired back, and you'll most likely hurt your career.

Another consideration is making your reel stand out from all the others. There's an enormous amount of competition for commercial composing work, and you'll be just one of many trying to get the attention of the agency, music house, production company, stock music producer, or whatever entity you're hoping to get work from. One way to grab their attention is to do something unusual in the packaging of your reel; for example, you could include an illustration or cartoon on the cover to attract interest. This can spark a little name recognition that leads to their remembering you the next time you call. The best way to make people remember you, however, is simply to have a great-sounding reel.

Assembling an Audio Reel

For someone new to the business, the easiest kind of reel to put together is an audio one. An audio reel shows off your composing skills, is relatively cheap to produce, and can incorporate some of your existing, nonadvertising material. It's an especially good choice if you're a songwriter trying to push for work writing jingles.

Your audio reel should run no longer than five minutes and consist of roughly seven to ten thirty-second (or shorter) pieces. If you've got any actual spots or demos for spots that you've already written, you'll want to have those at the top of the reel, assuming that they sound good and fit with your self-marketing concept. As was mentioned earlier, you can also use edited portions of songs you've written or pieces of music that you've composed for something other than commercials, as long as they sound good. If you don't have enough of these two categories to fill a reel, you need to write some *mock spots,* which are pieces written specifically for the reel. The advantage to writing mock spots is that you can write in the styles that you're strongest in without deadline pressure and other constraints you'd face in a real situation. Given these advantages, you have the opportunity to come up with some dynamite-sounding material. Filling out your reel this way won't help you prepare for the stresses of actually working in the advertising music field, but it will help you put together a good-sounding tape, which is crucial for getting any work.

Try to make these pieces run thirty seconds or less. You don't want to have anything longer, in view of the short attention spans of the people who'll be listening. What's most important is that the music sounds great.

When you're writing your material, try to make it fit the standard formats that you hear on commercials. If it's supposed to sound like an underscore, think about giving it a setup and a payoff or conclusion (see "Structuring Your Spot" in Chapter 8). If it's a jingle, make sure the vocals on it sound great. If you can afford it, I'd highly recommend hiring two or three professional jingle singers to sing on your reel. Even if you're singing the leads, they'll make the *group vocals* (background vocals) sound much more like a real spot.

On some of your pieces, you may want add some sound effects to help the spots feel more realistic. This also gives you a chance to show off your sound design. Don't overdo it, though, and don't put effects on every spot unless you're trying to push yourself primarily as a sound designer.

On the cassette jacket (also known as a *j-card*) or CD label, some people assign real product names to the "mock" spots they've written. Because so many demos don't make it to air, people who listen to the tape don't really have any way of knowing whether the spots were demos for those products or not. Having actual spot names can help add credibility to a reel. If you feel uncomfortable using this approach, give your spots generic names like "Beer :30" or "Tacos :15." Another option is to dispense with listing the spots altogether and let the music stand on its own.

Editing an Audio Reel

In the advertising music business in particular, reels are expected to be very tightly edited, with little or no space between spots. As a result, you should choose the order of your pieces in such a way that you keep the reel as fast-paced as possible. These days, anyone with a computer has access to audio editing tools that would make the razor blade–wielding audio engineers of the analog era green with envy. Thus, there's no longer an excuse for a poorly edited reel. I can't stress enough that you always have to keep in mind that hypothetical listener with the hair-trigger attention span. Because he or she is ready to hit the stop button at the slightest dwindling of interest, it's imperative that you to place your strongest material at the beginning to make sure it gets heard.

Once you've decided on what spots should go where, you'll probably want to load the spots into a digital editor in the order you've worked out. Listen to the whole thing, see how the pacing feels, and then ask yourself some questions: Does spot one feel okay going into spot two? How does two seem going into three? How does the ending of spot four work with the beginning of spot five? Are there too many spots in a row in the same key? Does the spot at the end leave the listener with a good last impression? The answers to these questions will determine whether the order needs further revisions.

If any of your spots feels like it's dragging on too long (even a thirty-second spot can feel long if it's very static), you may want to consider shortening it. If you have two spots at a similar tempo, it can be effective to chop off a section at the end of one and edit it right into the next as if they were part of the same piece. If there's a drum fill or pause in the first piece, you can use that as a good transition point. Fool around and see what you come up with. The great thing about most digital editing is that it's nondestructive, allowing you to try things many different ways without altering the source material.

Once you're satisfied with the order and the flow between the pieces, it's time to do some fine-tuning. If you haven't already done so, edit out all the silence between the spots. You want each piece to butt up against the next. This can sometimes cause harsh transitions, but there is a good solution for that: *crossfading.* Most digital editing software will allow you to *crossfade* between two pieces, so that the ending of piece A and the beginning of piece B will overlap slightly. Usually, there are a number of different crossfade types that govern what happens to the sound during this overlap (which is user-specified but generally lasts only a fraction of a second). You can choose whether each piece will fade up, down, or not at all during the crossfade. Typically, you have to experiment a little with both the crossfade type and duration until you find a combination that feels right.

Once you've got the order and the transitions done, you need to check that the volumes are consistent, both between each spot and for the reel as a whole. It's not uncommon to adjust the volume of each piece to match that of the one before and after, only to discover that the piece at the beginning of the reel is at a noticeably different level than the one at the end. This problem can force listeners to adjust their volume control in the middle of the reel, which can break their concentration, annoy them, or prompt them to turn off your tape.

After you successfully adjust the volumes, you're ready to master your reel onto a DAT. The best way to do this is to transfer the audio digitally between your computer and your DAT machine. However, if you're equipment doesn't allow that, an *analog-to-digital* transfer will be sufficient. (In this process, the analog signal from the computer is reconverted to digital as it gets recorded by the DAT.)

Since you probably won't want to leave all the audio from your reel on your hard drive (it's bound to take up a great deal of space), make a backup copy onto another DAT tape. If your software allows, you might also want to make a backup to DAT that preserves all the editing regions and crossfades so that you can easily reedit or update your reel when you get new material.

When it comes to distributing an audio reel, the medium of choice for years has been the good old cassette. That's changing now, though, as many music houses are putting their reels on CD. The obvious advantages of CDs are that they're impressive-looking and have far superior sound quality. The problem is that the cost is quite high. If you're trying to get work directly from agencies, think seriously about doing your reel on CD. If you're only trying to get freelance work from music houses, you'll probably be okay with just a cassette, although it's likely you'll be competing more and more with writers who have their reels on CD.

No matter how much effort you put into getting your reel to sound great, all your hard work can go down the drain if it's listened to on a lousy system. While you might assume that when a reel is listened to at an agency or music house the equipment used will be of good quality, this is not always the case. I've been in situations where I went to an appointment only to have my reel played on some cheap little system. At one music house, it was played on a boom box. At another, their cassette machine was running about 30 percent slower than normal, and they didn't even notice it until I pointed it out. After all the effort you put into recording and editing your material, such situations can be very frustrating and disheartening, and are yet another reason you're better off with a CD. Even the cheapest CD player runs at the right speed and usually sounds decent.

Assembling a Video Reel
When it comes to getting advertising work, video reels are the most impressive because they show, or purport to show, actual work

done for the most glamorous part of the ad business: television advertising. A video reel also demonstrates your ability to score to picture, which is not something you can show with audio only.

Putting together a video reel, however, is much more difficult. The first hurdle is getting material together. If you're new to the business and don't have any TV spots or other video that you've scored, you can use the "mock" approach by taping actual commercials and then adding your own music. This approach can also be a useful if you've already had some experience but need a few more pieces to fill out the reel. Nevertheless, there are a number of inherent problems with this method. First, there are quality considerations. If you tape a spot off the air, make a copy when you *lay-back* your mix on it (add the music to the video), make another copy for your master, and make a third copy on your duplicates to send around, you're reducing the quality by four generations. This can result in a noticeable loss of video quality, which can make your reel look less than professional. If you have access to a digital video editor, such as an Avid system, you can avoid some of this generational loss.

Second, if a spot you want to use already has music on it, you'll have to get rid of the entire audio track of the commercial, including the voice-over and/or dialogue unless they don't overlap the music at any point (which is pretty unlikely). If a spot shows someone actually talking, obviously you won't be able to use it if you have to remove the dialogue. Unless you get real lucky, you'll have to use spots that can work with just music and picture and don't really need voice-overs or dialogue.

This discussion of video reel material brings to mind one very important point. If and when you do get actual work writing music for a TV commercial, make sure that you get a 3/4-inch or *Beta* (another professional video format) copy as soon as you can after completing the job. If you wait with the expectation that you'll be able to get a copy later on when you need it, you may be in for a rude awakening. You need the cooperation of someone at the agency to get copies, and because of the high turnover in agency personnel the person with whom you worked may not even be there a year or two down the road. Whoever replaced them might not want to go through the trouble of finding and copying your commercial, in which case you're out of luck. Do yourself a favor and strike while the iron is hot to make sure you get your video copies. They can be very important for your career.

Editing a Video Reel

Although many musicians own high-quality audio editing gear, not many own professional-level video editing equipment, so chances are very good that you'll have to go to an outside facility to edit a video reel. You can do it on the cheap by editing it yourself from one VHS deck to another that has a *flying erase head* (which allows for smooth transitions between edits), but it's a tedious job because if you make a mistake you often have to start over. Furthermore, the quality won't be nearly as good, so I'd only recommend this approach as a last resort.

If you do choose to go to a video editing facility, make sure they're clear about their pricing structure and get an estimate from them as to how long they think it'll take. Be very diligent about making sure that the audio gets recorded correctly. Some video facilities aren't well equipped or knowledgeable when it comes to audio, and thus can mess up the sound quality of your reel if you don't keep close tabs on them. Make sure to stress to them that the finished product must be in stereo and to watch that the levels are hot enough but without distortion. When you go in to pick up your copies and before you've paid for them, I'd suggest that you randomly check a couple to make sure that both the audio and video have been transferred correctly.

When editing a video reel, your goals are similar to those for editing an audio reel: You want a fast pace, with as little transition time between spots as possible. You also have to consider which spots have the most compelling video. Although the reel is designed to show off your composition, arranging, and scoring abilities, the video quality is going to affect the viewer's perception of the different pieces. If you have a spot that has great-sounding music but the picture is boring, you might not want to put it as close to the front as you would have on an audio reel.

Many music houses and composers start off their video reels with a title sequence that displays their name. If you're ambitious, you can ask whether the video editing facility can provide you with a brief opening title sequence that has some motion to it. If so, take a copy of it home, score it, and you'll have a cool opener for your reel.

When you get the reel done, get copies made in both 3/4-inch and VHS. The 3/4-inch copies are going to be quite a bit more expensive (around $12 to $15 apiece), but some agencies and music houses will request that you send your reel in this format. If you're trying to get work from ad agencies, a 3/4-inch reel is essential for your image.

Assembling Reels for Other Composing Work

Up to this point, we've been discussing reels designed to get advertising work. If you're looking for other types of composing work, the material on your reel may need to be different. You may even need to prepare several reels, each of which is used for a different purpose.

Stock Music Reels When constructing an audio reel for obtaining stock music work (see Chapter 8, "Writing Stock Music"), you face a bit of a dilemma. You want it to be fast-paced and exhibit a variety of your material, yet you've got to be able to demonstrate the ability to write three-minute-plus pieces, which are the staple of many stock libraries.

I remember sending my commercial underscoring reel to a number of stock music producers (music libraries) and receiving an almost identical response from each one: "We like it, but we need to hear how you handle full-length stuff." As someone who's accustomed to the rapid-pace, impatient world of advertising music, it went against my grain to put three-minute pieces on a reel because I was afraid that listeners would shut it off in the middle of the first song. Casting my fears to the wind, I went ahead and included the longer pieces, and was pleased to discover that I got a much better response.

Although stock music is used mostly for commercials, its producers prefer longer-length pieces that can be used for films, industrials, and other contexts in which something more than thirty or sixty seconds is needed. They usually want instrumental music that states and restates a melodic theme as the arrangement develops over the course of the piece. Stock music differs from much instrumental music in that it's generally not written as a framework for soloing. Think of it instead as a song with instruments taking the place of the vocals.

There's a secondary benefit to writing pieces specifically for a stock music reel: If the music library you've send it to indicates that they like your work, you can let them know that some of the pieces on the reel are available. You may be able to interest them in buying some of this preexisting work, which is always better than having to write and produce new material.

Multimedia Reels It's hard to say definitively what should go on a multimedia reel because there are so many different types of music, in so many different formats, being used for interactive media. Obviously, if you've already written something for a CD-ROM, video game, or Web site, you'll want to include it on the reel. Otherwise, you should just demonstrate your composing abilities. You should consider composing and producing some General MIDI (GM) compositions and labeling them as such. This would show that you can write cool-sounding GM tracks, which is a very important skill in the interactive arena because many games and even some Web sites utilize them.

The question of which format your reel should be in is an interesting one. Just because you have a cassette or CD reel doesn't prove that you have the requisite understanding of sample rates, audio formats, and MIDI, all of which you might need on an interactive project. You'll enhance your status with potential employers if your reel in some way demonstrates your ability to understand these issues. One way to go is to create a Web site with a reel that can be downloaded, or a perhaps a GM reel that can be listened to directly from your site.

Although you can usually get by with a standard audio reel when looking for multimedia work, you'll make yourself a more attractive commodity if you try to do something interactive.

GETTING JINGLE AND UNDERSCORING WORK
DIRECTLY FROM AD AGENCIES AND CLIENTS

If you have both a strong reel and some contacts in the advertising business, you may want to go into business for yourself. You're your own boss, and the potential is there to earn substantially more money than you could as a freelancer. Keep in mind, though, that it's extremely competitive. If you have little or no experience you're going to be out of your depth. Without a very impressive reel (with lots of actual work on it), it's going to be difficult to get taken seriously for any high-level work. Consequently, unless you're extremely confident in your contacts and their ability to throw work your way, I'd be very wary of this approach. You're far more likely to succeed by working for an established music company at the start. If, however, your local market has little or no freelance scene, and you've tried and been unable to get a staff position at a music house, going direct may be your only option.

When you're starting out, it's easier to get work in smaller markets or from local clients than it is to land any national accounts. You can't expect to walk into ad agencies in New York, Los Angeles, or Chicago and immediately get a Coke jingle or a Nike spot. It just doesn't work that way. To get the big accounts you're going to have to spend some years establishing your reputation and contacts. As in other areas of the music business, networking plays a key role. Because there's a big turnover in creative personnel at ad agencies, you've got to hope that a copywriter or creative director you've been cultivating at a small agency ends up working for one of the major national agencies. If this happens, you have an instant high-level contact.

This propensity for job-changing among agency personnel can also work against you, such as when a prime contact suddenly leaves or is let go from an agency. This is almost inevitable, not only because agency people move around a lot, but because a lot of their jobs are predicated on whether the agency has a certain account. If the client from that account drops the agency, many of the creatives who worked on it are likely to get laid off.

When I was new in the business, I had first-hand experience with agency turnover. An old friend became a producer at a medium-sized, Midwestern ad agency, and was able to involve me in writing the music for some pretty decent accounts. Despite my neophyte status, I took the jobs, handled them, and was expecting to get a lot more work. Then my friend left her job for family reasons, and it was as if I'd never worked for the agency. I contacted the other creatives there but they basically ignored me, probably because they had their own friends they were throwing work to.

There's also the story of the music company that had a successful first year based primarily on one very large account that generated an incredible amount of work. At the end of the year, the client decided to suspend its advertising in that area, and suddenly the music house had virtually no work.

The moral of these stories is that a music company cannot base its business on one contact or account. If you have a contact somewhere, you've got to find a way to schmooze with other creatives at that agency so that if your person leaves you still have an in. You've also got to try to diversify your work so that it's not dependent on one source.

Forming Your Own Music Company

The first thing you need to do before trying to obtain work is to create a company name. You'll sound a lot more impressive if you seem to be a company rather than an individual. (I know a composer who changed his answering machine message to make it sound like the caller had reached an office rather than his apartment.) You might also consider incorporating, but that's something to be left up to you and your attorney.

As a music company, you need to have an audio reel on CD as well as a video reel. In addition, your letterhead, envelopes, business cards, and tape labels should feature a professionally designed logo that suits the image you want your company to project. You might also consider creating a Web site, since many of your competitors will already have them. Obviously, you're going to have to commit a sizable amount of cash toward publicity. The good news, though, is that the majority of business expenses are tax-deductible.

Researching Your Market

While you're getting your company's publicity together, it's a good time to do some research. Find a directory of ad agencies in your area that has an up-to-date listing of creatives. *The Shoot Directory* has listings of agencies and some of their personnel from all over the country. You can also find sites on the Internet that provide agency information (see Appendix). If you can't find a *Shoot Directory*, you can go to the library and look up agencies in your area in

The Red Book, which is a directory of all the ad agencies in the country. This directory doesn't list personnel, however, so you'll have to call around to the agencies you'll be targeting to see if they'll send you a list of creative and broadcast personnel. Even if you have access to *The Shoot Directory* you may want to call for these lists anyway, because they're much more up-to-date.

Making the Calls

Without a doubt, your best chance at getting work will come from your personal contacts at agencies or area businesses. Beyond that, you're going to have to go through the tedious process of contacting as many other agency and business people as you can in order to try to drum up work.

Contacting Agencies

Your goal should be to contact as many of the agency creatives (in order of importance: producers, creative directors, copywriters, and art directors) as you can in an attempt to set up appointments to play your reel. There are many ways to go about this. One effective approach is to systematically make phone calls, introduce yourself, and try to set up appointments. You might have more success sending out a postcard mailing that extols the virtues of your music company first, then following up about ten days later with phone calls.

Don't expect it to be easy; it'll be anything but that. You'll probably have a lot of trouble even reaching anyone on the phone. Since most of your calls will result in your leaving messages on their voicemail, you should prepare what you want to say beforehand. If you leave a stammering, nervous-sounding voicemail message, you're not going to enhance your chances of being taken seriously. Keep in mind that, if you're lucky, you'll eventually speak with about one-third to one-half of the people you call. Although there's no hard-and-fast rule as to what is a good time to reach someone, I've found that I've had more luck calling between nine and ten in the morning, when people are just getting in and have yet to really focus on their work.

When you do reach someone, you need to have a short pitch worked out to introduce yourself. It could go something like this:

Hi, this is John Doe from High-Energy Music. We're a small, boutique music house that specializes in underscoring. I'd be happy to set up an appointment at your convenience to meet you and show you our latest reel [or "play you our latest reel" if you don't have a video].

Expect that only a tiny fraction of the people you're able to reach by telephone will be willing to meet with you. Most will tell you to send in your reel, but chances are good that they'll never listen to it. You've got to remember that these are very busy people who often have heavy deadlines and are inundated with calls and tapes from music companies (and lots of other kinds of companies, for that matter). If you're able to reach someone on the phone, you've got to somehow convince them that it's worth his or her time to meet with you. You've got to sound confident and experienced.

It helps to be super-organized when conducting your publicity campaign. Keep a database of all the names and numbers you've called, and make sure to write down when you called and when you should make a follow-up call. By the way, after leaving a message on someone's voicemail as your initial contact, don't call them back again for four or five days, assuming that they haven't returned your call (which is a pretty good assumption). You want to be persistent but not annoying. After a meeting, send your contact a thank-you letter, then call him or her back every six weeks or so to remind them of your existence. If you do any jobs in the meantime, you might send a postcard saying something like, "High-Energy Music is proud to announce that it's just completed the music for the latest campaign of Ultra-Thin Diet Drink," or whatever the product is. This will bring your name to mind in a positive way, with the hope being that at some point they'll think of you when they need to hire music and give you a shot to at least do a demo.

Now that you've heard all this, you're probably thinking, "I'm a musician, not a salesman; I'll never pull this off. And even if I'm able to make the calls, I'll be spending so much time doing sales work that I won't have time to do any music." This is one of the many dilemmas you'll face when trying to contact agencies directly. There's so much phone-calling and paperwork involved that you'll be doing little else for a long time. It can be very discouraging. You've got to remember that what you're essentially doing is throwing as much stuff against the wall as you can in the hope that some of it sticks. If only a few out of the hundreds of people you contact give you work, you'll be doing well. You've always got to keep the big picture in mind.

Contacting Businesses

When watching or listening to local ads on TV or radio, the viewer can see immediately what a step down they are from national commercials: The acting is poor, the writing is lousy, the video quality is substandard, and the music is rarely anything to write home about. Most of the time, local spots use stock music because it's much cheaper for them than commissioning a track from a music house. When original music is used, it's usually a cheesy jingle that sounds like it was produced in the 1970s.

Some local ads are done through agencies, while others are produced by cable TV companies and radio stations. Besides trying to get those entities to employ your services, your best bet for getting in on this market is to try and convince a business person to use your music. With luck, you'll have a friend or relative involved in a local business who can introduce you to the right person. If not, you've got to do the contact thing. Do some serious TV-watching and radio-listening to get a sense of which local businesses do a lot of advertising. Make a list and use it as a starting point for your search. You can also contact competitors of the companies on your list, figuring that they might be running ads as well, or that they may be contemplating it if their rivals are.

Unlike ad agencies, local businesses aren't as used to getting solicited by a music company. As a result, it's harder to predict their reaction. You're going to have some serious convincing to do to persuade them that they need original music in their advertising. You're also going to have to work pretty cheap because the budgets will not be big.

Finding a Rep

If you feel that you absolutely can't handle all the sales work, you can find a *rep* to do it for you. Believe it or not, there are actually people who enjoy this kind of work and may be willing to do it on a commission basis in order to be involved with the music business. If you can find a willing person it can free you up to concentrate more on the musical end of things. You might also want to consider forming a partnership with someone who has a strong business sense. Many successful music companies have been formed by two people: one with creative abilities and another with business smarts.

"Handling" the Agency Creatives on a Job

As an independent music producer, getting the work is only the first hurdle you have to surmount. You've then got to successfully manage the work itself, which can be pretty dicey at times. For one thing, composers traditionally resent having to take direction from agency people, who generally have little or no formal music knowledge. As annoying as these ad folks can be at times, it's extremely important to get along with them and understand not only the type of music they're looking for, but the role the music will play in the commercial. It's not an easy situation for either side, because the ad people are trying to tell you what they want but frequently have trouble putting it in musical terms. One of the best ways to overcome this problem is to use reference music (also known as *temp tracks* or *temp music*).

Agency people will often bring or play a CD of an artist whose music they want your track to sound like. They'll sometimes even put this temp track up against the picture (if there is a picture). Occasionally they'll want you to do a knock-off of that track, but more often than not they'll just want something in the same ballpark. Temp tracks are great for agency types because it gives them a vehicle for communicating what they want for the music without having to get too musically technical. Chip Jenkins, who's composed numerous spots for Elias Associates in Los Angeles, has this to say on the subject.

> Sometimes they'll come with that [a temp track], and we'll still sit down with them and say, "Is there any way we can enhance that? Here are some other ideas, and we'll see if we can do it one better." And we'll sit down with some needle drops and see if we can . . . talk about music in nonmusical terms. . . . It's not like saying it's gonna sound like this track;

DOUG HALL

From Staff Composer
to Music House Owner

After working for ten years at Elias Associates, one of New York's premiere scoring houses, Doug Hall cofounded and is the chief composer for his own music company, MessHall Music.

Hall got his start in the ad music field through, of all things, a classified ad. "A friend of mine alerted me to an ad that was running in the *Village Voice* for a studio assistant with synthesizer knowledge and classical training." A keyboard player by trade, Hall's music degree and synthesizer experience gave him the requisite experience to get the job. "[It] turned out to be the gig at Elias. . . . They were like a young, hip, boutique-type place. I ended up staying there for ten years. Very soon after starting there, I was writing spots, writing for orchestras and for smaller groups, working with synths, and doing arranging."

In his ten-year stint at Elias, Hall estimates that he composed or arranged for close to a thousand commercials. "Probably mostly finals," he adds, "because we didn't do too many demos there." Having been in the business since just before MIDI came into being, he understands the impact technology has had on everyone involved.

I think these days, if I had to choose between having a lot of experience with live instruments or having a lot of experience with technology, I'd have to say that technology is more important. But having said that, the more music experience that you bring to your music, the better it's going to be. Like for me, I think it was really important that I sang in choirs and I played in bands and played trombone in a symphonic band. All of my music experience has come to bear very directly on what I'm able to do now. So I really encourage people to learn to read music, but also to get as much musical training as they can.

Hall has had a lot of dealings with agency people, and he feels that they respond more to music that pushes the boundaries a bit.

People are looking for stuff to be really cutting-edge and creative. It's like a cliché almost, but you have to push yourself real hard all the time to just do great music because "good" music isn't good enough. . . . I think it's more of a mistake to be too conservative, and I think I've been guilty of this myself in the past, of maybe not taking enough chances all the time. Ad people love it if you're out there. You can always tone it down, but it's harder to "tone it up," if you know what I mean. In order to distinguish yourself from everybody else, everything has to sound great. They're used to everything sounding great because people can do amazing things just out of their bedrooms. You're up against so many different people that it just has to be really high quality all the time—if you want to make a mark at all.

One of the ways in which Hall distinguishes his work from the competition by using a lot of live musicians.

I like to use live players because there are so many great session players in New York, and I feel that they always really add something. And drums is one area where most of the time you can always improve just by having a well-recorded live kit—and have the drummer actually addressing the piece of music that you're doing, as opposed to just playing a loop. Typically, I'll have a group of musicians that might include drums, percussion, bass, and guitar to augment whatever I've prerecorded.

Hall has this advice to give to new composers trying to get into writing ad music:

I think the way to get into the business is to hook up with somebody who's already doing it, because if you don't have a reel together you can't approach the agencies. You could, I guess, approach music companies and try to freelance. Or try to work there and learn whatever you can learn by observing. You could do what I did and go for a studio assistant job and hope that it pans out into more than that. I think I was very lucky in a sense, because I just happened to land at a place that was growing by leaps and bounds, which gave me an opportunity to do things right away.

If you're interested in hearing some of Doug Hall's music, you can check out the MessHall Web site at *http://www.messhall.com.*

it's like, what in this track are we responding to? Is this making you feel the right amount of sadness or excitement or energy?

If the agency people don't have a piece of temp music, you can come up with your own ideas to play for them. According to composer Doug Hall (see "Profile/Doug Hall: From Staff Composer to Music House Owner," pages 254–255), that can be a good way to get a musical dialogue going:

> Sometimes I put together a concept reel—which is simply pieces of music that I've either done before or that just came from a CD—that they can play up to picture and say, "That's a good tempo," or "We like this instrumentation," or "We like this kind of feeling." . . . It puts you in the ballpark if they can find a piece of music that they kind of like.

Generally, you'll be more successful if you try to find ways to communicate better with the ad people. On the other side of the coin, you don't want to cede so much creative control that you can't do your job well. I once made that mistake while doing a jingle for a large shoe company. When telling the client about the vocal talent that I needed to hire, I foolishly offered to send them some singers' reels so that they could let me know what type of voice they were looking for. Unfortunately, they fell in love with one particular singer who happened to be out of town on the dates I needed to do the vocal session. They insisted that I use this singer, and consequently I had to rearrange my entire production schedule around her availability. As a result, the finishing stages of the job were done in a mad rush and the final product was not what I had hoped it would be. I learned from this that it's good to discuss general concepts with an agency or client, but not to let them have so much control that it interferes with your ability to get the job done. After all, they're hiring you for your expertise, so you've got to convince them that you know what's best for their music.

GETTING FREELANCE COMPOSING WORK FROM MUSIC HOUSES
If you live in or near a major market that has a lot of music production companies, such as New York, Los Angeles, or Chicago,

consider the option of freelancing. It requires much less in the way of start-up capital, and your odds of breaking in are far better than they'd be going direct to agencies—especially if you don't have much previous experience. This is not to say it'll be easy, because it won't. You still have to demonstrate to music houses, through your reel and your attitude, that you have something valuable to offer to them.

Most of the work you get as a freelancer is writing demos, and usually only a small percentage of these will end up on the air as *finals*. The reason for this is that on almost every job you get you're competing against other writers from the music house you're working for, as well as writers from other music houses. It's not uncommon for your demo to be competing against ten or fifteen others. With these kinds of odds, you have to strive to get as many opportunities as you can.

When you do get some finals, they won't be as lucrative as they would be if you got the job directly from an agency, because you'll only get to keep about 30 to 40 percent of the creative fee. For a national spot, your cut will usually end up being between $1,500 to $3,000. Generally, you'll also get a fee of between $150 and $300 for having written and produced the demo (you get this regardless of whether your version wins). In addition, you usually receive four or more *lines* on the American Federation of Musicians contract. For each instrument played, your name goes on one line or slot on the contract (assuming the commercial is not a non-union buyout) and you're paid session fees and residuals for every line that you're on. Push to get at least four lines, if not more—especially if you played all the instruments. You can also sometimes get put on the lines for arranger and copyist. Be aware, however, that even if you did play everything on the spot, music houses use the union contracts as one way to pay their employees. As a result, some of the slots on the contract for your spot may already be spoken for. If there are vocals involved, make sure to get the music house to agree to put you on the SAG or AFTRA vocal contract. Over time, the vocal money can end up being three or four times as much as you're getting for the creative fee. All told, an underscoring spot will net you somewhere between $2,000 and $3,500, and a jingle (assuming you're on the vocal contract) can make you quite a bit more. Although you would earn more doing it direct to an agency, it's still pretty good money for a couple of days' work.

At the risk of sounding like a broken record, the easiest way by far to get hooked in with a music house is to have a contact there. You're much more likely to get through to someone if you can drop a name they know. Rack your brains and your college alumni list to try and find someone you know, if even only vaguely, who works at a music company. The only alternative is to do it the hard way: by cold-calling every music house in town in an attempt to drum up work.

Finding and Contacting the Music Houses

Different music companies are structured in different ways. Some rely strictly on staff writers to handle just about all their work. On the other end of the spectrum are companies that have no staff writers and depend entirely on freelancers. In the middle are houses who have writers on staff, but go outside when they get real busy. The latter two are the kinds of places you need to contact to get freelance composing work.

Get a list of music houses in your area (*The Shoot Directory* is a good source for this information, as is the Internet) and plan to contact each and every one. There are varying opinions as to whether you should call first, or send a letter and a reel first. The advantage to calling is that you can usually get some first-hand information as to whether the company even uses freelancers. It's time-consuming and expensive to send out reels (especially video reels) and you may not want to waste your time and resources sending out tapes to companies you'll never work for anyway.

Assuming that the music houses you approach do use outside writers, you can also find out who the best person to contact is. As when going direct to agencies, you should first try to get an appointment to come in and play your reel. A personal meeting is much more likely to leave a lasting impression because your contact will have a face to go with the reel. In most cases, however, they'll decline your request for a meeting and ask you to simply send in your reel. Make sure to ask for the name of the person to whose attention it should be sent, as well as the name of the person you're speaking with.

Let's say that the person you need to contact is named Mary Smith. The following is a sample letter you might send her to accompany your reel if you've had no previous experience:

Dear Mary,

I spoke with Jennifer from your office and she suggested that I send my reel to your attention. I'm a freelance composer who specializes in techno and sound design. I hope you'll consider me the next time you have an assignment in either of those styles. Thanks for listening.

Best regards,

If you have had previous experience, your letter should go something like this:

Dear Mary,

I spoke with Jennifer from your office and she suggested that I send my reel to your attention. I'm a freelance composer who specializes in techno and sound design. I hope you'll consider me the next time you have an assignment in either of those styles. I've previously worked for H&B Music, Crunchy Productions, and FJL Music. As you'll note from my reel, I've written music for Bell Atlantic, Pizza Hut, and Sunoco. Thanks for listening.

Best regards,

There are a number of lessons to be learned from the above examples. First and foremost, the composer's stylistic strengths (in this case, techno and sound design) should be emphasized to help establish an identity with the music house. Second, previous experience and specific product and music house names should be cited whenever possible. Third, Mary Smith is referred to by her first name because it's considered appropriate in the informal world of the jingle business.

When you send out a reel, make sure to write down the day you mailed it and put a note in your calendar indicating that you need to follow it up with a phone call in about two to three weeks. When you call back, try to speak to the person to whom you sent the reel.

Ask whether he or she received it and has had a chance to listen. If the response is negative, very nicely ask when he or she might be able to get to it. If you're asked to call again in three weeks, then you have your next date to call back. If you're not given a specific date, call again in three to four weeks. You want to be persistent, but you don't want to be a pest. Resist the temptation to call too often.

If your contact has listened to and likes your reel, ask whether there are any upcoming jobs that you might be right for. If, on the other hand, the response is something like, "We'll put it on file," that's often code for, "We didn't like it." Nevertheless, keep calling back every month or so just in case. When you've updated your reel with new material, call to say you've got a new reel and send it on. You can then start the whole procedure over again.

The odds are that most of the music companies you contact aren't going to do much more than ask you to send a reel. Once you've done that, it's usually a dead end. Nevertheless, you've got to keep slogging on and try not to get discouraged, which isn't always so easy. Just trying to reach some of these people at the music houses by phone can be a trying experience. When someone doesn't want to speak to you, regardless of the reason, you're usually told that they're "in session" or "writing." While this is undoubtedly true some of the time, it makes a convenient excuse for avoiding calls. The thing to remember is that if you have talent, persistence, and if you market yourself in a way that showcases your strengths, someone along the way is going to give you a shot. When you get it, make the most of it and you can be on your way.

Music companies get a demo fee from ad agencies, and a cut of that usually gets passed along to the writer who worked on the project. Even so, music houses will sometimes ask writers, especially new ones, to do demos for free. If your version wins, you'll get paid; if it doesn't, it's a freebie. When you're first starting out, it's in your best interest to take whatever jobs you're offered, so it's probably worth your while to do it. It's good experience and you might end up with something for your reel. More importantly, you have a chance to impress the people at the music house, which with luck will lead to paying work. Conversely, while it's okay to do a free job if you're offered it, I wouldn't advertise that you'll do it. Some people, as a way to get in the door, routinely tell music houses that they'll do free demos. By doing this I think you devalue yourself in their eyes and end up looking less than professional.

Things To Remember When You Get an Assignment

It's very important to keep the lines of communication open when you're doing an assignment. Take very good notes when the producer from the music house is describing the assignment to you. In the rush to get the job done (they're almost always one- or two-day turnarounds) you're not going to remember the finer points, so make sure to put them on paper. If you're given creative direction, follow it to the letter. Your contact at the music house has had discussions with the agency and is in a much better position to know what's expected.

Make sure to find out exactly when your deadline is and in what form the mixes are wanted. Your mixes will almost always be on DAT, but sometimes you'll be asked to give them alternate versions of the mix with and without selected elements. You may also be asked for *stripes* or *splits,* which are the individual elements of the mix played alone with a reference click at the top. If you split out all the instruments in a mix, the music house can reconstruct your track if a remix is necessary. This is done by dumping the stripes into a computer-based digital recorder and visually lining up the reference clicks so that the various tracks play in time with each other. It's also helpful to find out at the sample rate at which the DAT should be recorded. Most places will request 44.1k, but occasionally you'll be asked to bring something in at 48k, so it's good to know in advance.

If you don't live in the same town where the music house is located, they'll often overnight you the materials you need, such as the picture or a voice-over. If they're sending you the picture, make sure to specify whether you need 3/4-inch or VHS. If you're sent the wrong format, you'll lose precious hours and you may not have enough time to get a replacement.

It's usually a good idea to keep in touch with the producer as you make progress on the project. Once you've got the spot sussed out and you've put down some rough tracks, call and play it over the phone. It's true that you can lose some creative control this way, but it'll help you from straying too far in the wrong direction. If

Q&A | **MARSHALL GRANTHAM**
CREATIVE DIRECTOR, RUSSO/GRANTHAM PRODUCTIONS

A Music House's Perspective on Freelance Composers

As the creative director for Russo/Grantham Productions, one of New York's busiest music companies, Marshall
Grantham has dealt with numerous freelance composers and has
some definite opinions about what it takes to make it on that scene.

What sorts of reels do you get from composers?
I get the whole range. . . . From a composer's point of view, I get guys
who've scored and want to do stuff. Sometimes it's just a cassette of
some radio stuff they've done. Lots of times it will be a full reel of ten
spots that they've done that are great. Other people who are just
breaking in will send a CD or cassette of their band where they wrote
all the songs, but it's harder to judge that. We do, I'd say, about sev-
enty percent underscoring and thirty percent things with vocals. The
whole thing about underscoring is that it's a completely different art
than writing a jingle. Writing a jingle is like being a songwriter. But
underscoring to picture is a whole different thing. You have to be
able to look at a picture, interpret it, click it out, make hits. So it's
hard for me to ever give someone a shot at underscoring a visual
until I see how they can do that. There are a lot of guys who send me
some good songs, and I say, "Well, alright, I'll give you a shot at something." And I give them a score and they have no idea what to do. It's
just a whole other ball game.

What types of reels do you get from composers with little or no
ad music experience?
It's like any other catch-22: You want to hear a guy's reel, but he has-
n't done anything yet, so what can he give you to break in? Some
people send songs, since that's what most musicians are dealing
with. They'll do things they wrote and send them in, whether they
did them in a full-up studio or a home studio. But actually some people have been kind of clever. They tape stuff [TV spots] off the air
and then they score it. They do about eight spots, make them great,
then make a reel; it's such a great way to break in. It shows great ini-
tiative. . . . We're talking about underscoring rather than jingles, the
difference being that a jingle is generally a thirty- or sixty-second
song and an underscore is more music only—painting moods or

catching hits or doing sound design. . . . It's a great thing to do because again you're really showing your talent with the visual and the sound.

Are you able to listen to everything that comes in?
I genuinely try to listen to the tapes I get. Sometimes I'm backed up for months. But I don't just throw them out; I keep them in a bin and I try to listen to them. Whether it's for a musician, a singer, or especially a composer, because a good composer's a diamond.

Do you get a lot of bad reels?
Yeah, I get a lot of them. First of all, whatever you put in the first three or four minutes is the whole thing. Sometimes I put something on and it's so bad that I say, "Well, if this is first, it isn't gonna go anywhere." Your presentation is definitely important. . . . First of all, I would start with a letter and a tape or a video, or whatever you're going put together. Make sure your presentation is good, and also make sure it's short, because no one is going to sit and listen for twenty minutes.

Should five minutes be the maximum length?
Yeah, if you have eight, ten good things on a reel—assuming you've done stuff—eight, ten things that show what you do. In the letter it pays to describe your strengths. . . . "This is what I do; please listen if you have time and check it out." By letting them know what your strengths are, you prevent a lot of problems. In other words, if I put something in and I hear "orchestral," and the letter says, "Primarily my thing is orchestral; if you have that need I'd like to do some stuff for you," it means more to me than saying, "I can do anything."

So you suggest making initial contact with a music house by sending a letter accompanied by a reel?
I like that better than getting a phone call from someone completely out of the blue. But I'll tell them the same thing: Just send me a tape. . . . It's obviously helpful if you have any contacts in the industry; it's always good to be able to mention a name so you can get someone on the phone.

Do you think freelance composing is a good field to get into?
It's a great thing to do and get good at because you can make really good money and still proceed with other stuff. It's just another good vehicle for making money in music. From a freelance point of view, it's great, but it's a hard thing to be great at. Out of every hundred tapes I listen to, maybe five are great—maybe.

they shoot down a musical idea that you think is really great, you can always submit two versions (assuming you have time): one that reflects the producer's instructions, and one that fleshes out your idea. As long as you cover all the bases they ask you to, no one will object to your submitting an alternate version, which may enhance your chances of winning.

One of the most difficult parts about doing a freelance job is that after you work nonstop for a day or two and put your heart and soul into it, you often have to wait a long time to get any kind of reaction to what you've done, much less find out if you've won. Despite all the rushing and the deadlines that you have to deal with, it sometimes takes a week or more to find out whether your version was chosen. What's even harder is that sometimes you don't get any kind of reaction from the music house after you've handed in the assignment. From their perspective it's not that big a deal, just another freelance assignment handed in, but from your standpoint it's extremely important, and you want to know not only whether you've won, but whether the people who hired you liked your work. There were times when my version actually won and nobody called me. Finally, after not hearing anything for a while, I called the music house; they said, "Oh, didn't we tell you? You won."

FINDING A MUSIC HOUSE STAFF JOB

The most direct, though certainly not the easiest, way to get into the business is to get hired on staff at a music house. These jobs are hard to come by, but if you manage to get one you've got a golden opportunity to permanently establish yourself in the business. Getting hired as a writer is almost impossible for someone without significant experience, however, so often the best strategy is to try to get in as an assistant engineer or production assistant. You'll be starting at the bottom, but you'll have your foot in the door.

Chip Jenkins is a highly successful staff writer at Elias Associates, one of the elite music companies in the country. He got his start when a friend who worked there let him know about an opening for an assistant engineer.

I joined Elias as an assistant engineer, thinking that [would be] my focus. . . . [When] they needed somebody to write something . . . I said I would love to do it. . . . I tried it and really liked it. . . . There [were] . . . more opportunities to write, and it sort of evolved. It wasn't something I was seeking out; it was sort of a left turn.

Jenkins feels that getting on staff is definitely the way to go for new composers. "I would say that if you get a staff position, your odds of making it would be a lot better than if you are just starting out freelancing."

For college students who are in music or engineering programs, there are occasionally opportunities to do internships at music companies. Interns with obvious talent and good attitudes can make valuable contacts that can lead to a job when they finish school.

Those who have finished school and are already in the workforce will have to knock on doors and network in the hope of finding an opening somewhere. You can also keep your eyes on the classifieds (both help wanted and musicians' classifieds), because music house jobs are occasionally advertised that way.

GETTING OTHER COMPOSING WORK

Obtaining other types of commercial composing jobs entails using similar methods to getting advertising work. First and foremost, use any contacts you may have, and after that it's a matter of making calls, sending reels, and following up. Let's look at some of these other areas a little more closely.

Television

Probably your best shot at getting started doing some TV work is to get a freelance assignment from a music company. Unfortunately, unless the company relies entirely on freelancers, most high-level jobs will probably be given to its staff writers. As a result, you'll most likely have to establish yourself with a company first before they'll think about letting you compete for television work. Generally, music houses get jobs doing music for cable networks and local news programming rather than network entertainment shows, which tend to hire well-known, individual composers. Composers on that level often have agents who obtain work for them.

To get television work directly, you need to have established a reputation for yourself and some good, high-level contacts. I got an assignment to write promotional music that aired on a pay-per-view network, based on the fact that I had an old friend who worked there. I still had to send in a reel to demonstrate my abilities, but without that contact it's extremely unlikely I would have even gotten the initial call.

You can try sending reels out, but it's not going to be an easy route in. Los Angeles–based composer Leland Bond had this suggestion for getting television work: "The best approach would be to make contact with the person ultimately responsible for hiring you," he advises. "Be as creative as you're able to be. I'd try to research who that person is, and to send out a reel that is appropriate for that job. As in the agency world, it's most important to give the very best you've got."

Without contacts, you're probably best off trying to establish yourself as a writer of advertising music and hope that the people you meet, and the experience you get, will eventually lead to some TV work as well.

Industrials

Much of the music that is used in industrial videos is taken from stock libraries, though when custom scoring is needed video producers will hire composers. The best place to look for this kind of work is from video production companies, which can also be found in *The Shoot Directory* (see Appendix). There is a huge number of companies listed, so you'll have to do quite a bit of legwork. Expect to get a lukewarm reception at most places you call, but with luck you'll find some places that'll be interested in checking out your reel (a video reel can be helpful but isn't absolutely necessary for getting this kind of work). You also might want to try contacting public relations firms, because they sometimes produce videos for their clients that need to be scored.

It's very likely that if you do get a job scoring an industrial video, the piece will run longer than that for a commercial. Training videos can run ten or fifteen minutes, or even longer. Before you settle on a price, make sure you know how much music you're supposed to write and how much scoring to picture is involved. Find out if you're responsible for sound effects as well. You need to know all this information up front to be able to evaluate whether the job is worth the money that's being offered.

Multimedia

Not surprisingly, you can use the Internet when searching for multimedia producers. In addition, there's a book called *The Multimedia Directory* (see Appendix) which has listings of many new media companies in both alphabetical and geographical groupings. You can contact these in the same manner as you would music companies or agencies. For the sake of appearances, however, you might want to try contacting them via email (get the addresses from their Web sites) rather than calling on the telephone.

Multimedia is such a new field that it's difficult to say precisely how to get the work other than to just get your name and reel out there and start networking. You probably ought to attend as many trade shows and professional conferences on the subject as you can because these are not only good places to gather information, they're also prime networking spots (see "Profile/George 'The Fat Man' Sanger: Multimedia Music Innovator," pages 268–270). Pay particular attention to any information and leads you get concerning music for the World Wide Web, because this area will be booming in the next couple of years.

If doing music for multimedia is where you want to concentrate your career, you might consider trying to get an entry-level job with a new media company and hope that you can work your way into a music-related position from the inside.

If you also have strong programming and computer skills, you might approach music houses for a full-time position from that angle. Many music companies are expanding into new media and someone with a mixture of music ability and cutting-edge computer skills can be very valuable to them. You may also be able to get freelance interactive work from music houses.

Stock Music

Before reviewing how to get work composing stock music, it's helpful to have some background regarding its usage.

Many full-service recording facilities that cater to commercial clients have hundreds of stock CDs from a host of different libraries. When a client needs music for a project they'll specify

GEORGE "THE FAT MAN" SANGER

Multimedia Music Innovator

In the emerging field of music for video games, CD-ROMs, and the World Wide Web, George "The Fat Man" Sanger is by far the most well-known and influential composer. In addition to supervising Team Fat, his Austin, Texas–based team of composers, Sanger has developed many new technologies associated with computer music while producing, composing, and arranging music for such games as "Loom," "Wing Commander," and "The Seventh Guest." Sanger started in the business back in 1983, when music for computer games was looked down on by many composers.

> In those days, I would frequently run into composers who would say, "Of course if I write a good tune I don't give it to the clients for computer games 'cause they're only computer games." There was no concept that computer games should have music. That was where the rubber hit the road for me. I would have to meet people and we would have to share our visions to push that kind of a concept through. We did "Wing Commander" and "Putt Putt Saves the Zoo," which was the first live recording of musicians directly to MIDI for a game soundtrack, and we did "The Seventh Guest," which had the soundtrack as the second disk of the game, which was a first. And it was also the first General MIDI soundtrack for a game by a good long shot. That's just an example. There are others. I've thrown a conference called "Project Bar-B-Cue," here in Texas on three hundred acres of God's country, with thirty-five experts and gourmet chefs—hootin', hollerin', guitar pickin', and hard work. And that was to answer the question of what we wanted to see in hardware and software for music on computers in the next five years.

Because multimedia music is such a new field, Sanger says, there are no routine paths to success, nor are there any standards for payment of composers. "The financial conventions are far from being established, and they have not proven themselves to be viable." Also, he doesn't think that contacting game companies or CD-ROM producers directly is a very promising route to success for those trying to get involved. Instead, he thinks networking is the way to go.

> There is no drugstore at the corner of Hollywood and Vine, no Schwab's where you can hang out and wait to be discovered. I

think that the best bet is to get enough involved in the games so that you start to run into people who are like you—interested in games. You begin to form your own community; you start finding out which of the friends you went to school with is actually making games now, and which is doing a Web site. And you start orchestrating his Web site . . . [to see] if that leads to more people going, "Damn, that's good music; can you do mine?" It's more like building a massage clientele than it is like being discovered and hitting it big.

When asked what skills a composer needs to work in the multimedia field, Sanger said, "I would learn all I could about digital audio: recording it, converting it, sample rates, getting a good sound out of eight-bit, 11k. I would learn about file-naming conventions and archiving. I would learn about playback and editing tools." He also listed some other areas of proficiency:

Digital, MIDI, General MIDI, and whatever the current cutting-edge tools are, such as Thomas Dolby's Headspace Tools and Microsoft's Direct Music. . . . You know what I bet would be real handy thing to have to get an edge on people, at least in the next two years? Java. I bet programming Java will make you desirable.

Technology is only part of what it takes to be a successful multimedia composer, says Sanger.

I keep wanting to emphasize art and heart. When you learn all these tools, your number one mission is to figure out how to express something beautiful through those tools. And everything else that those tools do is just fog on the lens. A tool is not something that you can stand on and get taller and use to prop yourself up and substitute for your being short. A tool is something like a floodgate that opens and lets all the waters of your creativity loose. There has to be waters behind that dam before opening it does any good. A tool's job is to become transparent and disappear, and let you out.

According to The Fat Man, music for the Web is going to provide a lot of work in the future. For the present, though, because there are so many companies vying to establish the standards for delivery of music and audio, it's an uncertain place in which to work. Regarding these companies, Sanger says,

They've got to innovate, they've got to fight politics, they've got to create standards that aren't created yet, and that involves making very difficult decisions. You've got to decide: Do you actually want to get involved in that battle? There are a lot of people moving out west in their covered wagons onto the frontier—the info trail. And they're pushing out there and there's a lot of that. But way, way out ahead there are some scouting parties, and life is rough out there. . . . So what do you have to do? It helps to love what you're doing. It helps to have a mental attitude that's ready to innovate. You have to explore the Web. There's probably a lot of good information to be had just by surfing the Web. You would probably want to go to the Computer Game Developer conference, which happens around April in Santa Clara. [This conference is scheduled to be held in Los Angeles in 1998, and again in Santa Clara in 1999.]

For the immediate future, Sanger feels that most of the Web music work will entail creating music for sites. In the long term, however, he says that creating "interactive environments" will be the hot thing.

At the most clunky level you would create a Web site in which the user's cursor position determines what music is playing and in what way it plays. If he's on the piano [illustration] you might hear the piano playing. And if he's on the button that's going to take him to the list of links you might hear chains rattling. At a less clunky level, you might have a piece of music that plays various lead riffs, depending on how tense a Web game's situation is going. Or you might have something that actually looks like a jam session, where a Web person is pressing on various keys on a piano and one of his friends is somewhere else pressing on keys of another piano, and one of his friends is in Idaho pressing on little pictures of a drum kit. Various riffs are playing at the same time, and they think they're having this great jam session, but you're the guy who played all the riffs the first time. So you become an environment composer rather than a conventional composer.

For more information on The Fat Man, check out his Web site at *http://www.outer.net/fatman/*.

the style they're looking for, and someone who works at the facility will do a *music search,* which is a survey of various libraries of stock music in order to locate CDs in the requested style. The client listens to selected examples from these CDs, then chooses a piece of music for their commercial, industrial, soundtrack, or whatever. The client then pays a fee to the stock library for the usage of the music, depending on what that use is.

Stock music companies fall into two different categories: those that license your music from you in return for a cut of any fees they might generate from it, and those that buyout all rights to it. It's obviously better to go with the former rather than the latter, because when a piece of your music is used by many different clients, you'll get paid each time. Some libraries are also paid *blanket fees* by clients, who then don't have to pay for each individual use. In these situations, a library will often pay each composer a percentage of these blanket fees based on how many compositions they have in the catalog.

Composers are also theoretically due payments from ASCAP or BMI when one of their compositions is aired on TV or radio. These payments come from a huge pool of money that is paid to these performance rights societies by every television and radio station as dictated by federal law. It sounds great in theory, but in practice it's not easy to actually collect any money from ASCAP or BMI because you have to know that your composition was used on the air and be able to document it. The head of a major stock music producer admitted that only a small percentage of the composer's and publisher's payments from the performance rights societies ever gets paid (the company that produces the library is eligible for the publisher's share). Keep this in mind when negotiating with a stock music producer.

As described in "Assembling Reels for Other Composing Work," earlier in this chapter, you'll be most successful with a reel specifically targeted to stock music. Once you have it together, you'll need to find a listing of stock libraries. A partial listing is available on the Internet and is called *The Digital Directory* at *http://www. digitaldirectory.com/muse.html.* You should also look in *The Songwriters Market* (see Appendix), which is available at most large bookstores. Review these listings and contact each company. Send reels and follow up much the same way as you would for advertising work. Be persistent, and don't get discouraged.

COMPOSER'S SURVIVAL GUIDE

• Make sure your reel is tightly edited and that it emphasizes your strongest musical styles.

• Before you accept a job, ascertain exactly what's expected of you and how much you'll get paid for the demo (if there is one) and the final (including the number of contract lines for a union job). Find out when it's due and which format the final mix should be in.

• If you're offered a freelance job from a music house, find out how many other versions they're submitting and if any other houses are involved in the competition.

• Never accept a freelance job from a music house in a style in which you have no expertise. You could blow your credibility and ruin your reputation.

• If you're scoring to a video, make sure to let the music house or agency know whether you need it on 3/4-inch or VHS.

• Make sure to budget your time so that you have enough left to do your mix properly. It's easy to eat up so much time during the composing and recording phases of the project that you end up mixing under the gun in panic mode.

• On an underscoring job, don't let the search for the perfect click override musical concerns. The most important thing is to make it sound good.

• Make sure you're on the same page with the people hiring you when it comes to the style of the piece. If you're working directly with an ad agency, it's helpful to use reference music (temp tracks) to establish a musical dialogue with the creatives. If you're working for a music house, pay careful attention to the instructions and play them your work in progress over the phone.

• Make sure you're always reachable (a beeper would help) so that you don't miss out on any jobs.

• If you have the budget, consider using live musicians and/or a mixing engineer. Bringing in outside talent usually makes the final result better.

• If video is involved and your version goes final, always ask the agency or music house for a copy as soon as the job is over. You'll probably want it for your reel and if you wait, you may never get it.

APPENDIX | SUGGESTED READING AND USEFUL WEB SITES

❖

PLAYING LIVE

Books and Directories
Book Your Own Tour: The Independent Musician's Guide to Cost-Effective Touring and Promotion
Liz Garo, Rockport Publishing, 1995
A good reference if you want to book your band on the road. Aimed primarily at the indie band market, but is useful for any traveling band.

The Musician's Guide to Touring and Promotion
Musician magazine, published annually
(212) 536-5248
http://www.billboard-online.com/musician/
A helpful resource for any band looking to get gigs or get signed. Contains listings of clubs, agents, radio stations, and A & R personnel from all over the country. Also available on disk in Windows and Macintosh formats.

Web Sites
About Nashville Sound
http://www.nashvillesound.com/
A huge listing of Nashville music resources.

Artist Agencies
http://www.soundwave.com/directories/artistagent.html
A listing of booking agencies in the U.S. and Canada.

Austin's List of Music Clubs
http://www.ecpi.com/clubs.html
A list of music and dance clubs in Austin, Texas, one of America's premiere live-music towns.

Club Directory
http://www.bostonphoenix.com:80/alt1/issues/current/music/listings/clubs.html
A listing of Boston-area nightclubs published by the *Boston Phoenix.*

Deterrent DIY Tour Manual
http://www.islandnet.com/~moron/deterrent/tour_gd.html
Helpful listings and links for bands looking to book their own tours.

Directory: Booking Agencies
http://www.smartt.com/worldone.com/Directory/bookingagencies.html
A listing of Canadian booking agencies and musicians. Also features musicians' classifieds.

Grunge Band Name Generator
http://www.planetary.net/robots/grunge.html
An amusing site that generates endless "alternative"-sounding band names.

Jazz Clubs Around the World
http://www.nwu.edu/jazz/lists/clubs.html
Just what the Web site title says.

Jazz Clubs in Canada
http://www.mbnet.mb.ca/~mcgonig
/clubs.html
Canadian jazz venues.

MIDI File Central
http://neburton.simplenet.com
/frame.htm
A great place to download standard
MIDI files of popular songs.

Nashville Music Link
http://www.nashville.net./~troppo
/muslink.htm
Includes listings of Nashville clubs,
agents, and management, as well as a
page of links to musicians' resources.

NJANIGHT: Rock Clubs Directory
http://www.njatnight.com/rock
/club_dir.htm
A selected listing of rock clubs in New
York City and New Jersey, as well as a
few in Pennsylvania.

Open Musical Jam Sessions
http://micro.lib.ox.ac.uk/internet/news
/faq/archive/music.jam-sessions.html
A constantly updated list of jam
sessions arranged by geographical area.

This Is Chicago
http://www.ncsa.uiuc.edu/SDG/IT94
/Venue/NightLife.html#DinnerShow
A listing of Chicago-area nightlife.

Organizations

Hearing Education and Awareness
for Rockers (H.E.A.R.)
50 Oak Street - Suite 101
San Francisco, California 94102
(415) 773-9590
http://www.hearnet.com
This organization is dedicated to
helping raise consciousness regarding
the ever-present problem of noise-
induced hearing loss among musicians.
Check out their excellent Web site.

MUSIC FOR WEDDINGS AND PRIVATE PARTIES

Periodicals
The Wedding Pages
11106 Mockingbird Drive
Omaha, Nebraska 68137-2383
(800) 843-4983
A regionally issued publication in
which bands can advertise.

Web Sites
The Music Company
http://www.musicco.com/
Contains listings of bands from a New
England–based wedding music
company.

Wedding Music Information Source
http://www.nuwebny.com/wedmusic
/index.htm
National and international listings of
wedding bands and musicians.

Wedding Web Los Angeles
http://weddingweb.com/la/la
.music.html
Features listings for wedding music
offices in the Los Angeles area.
Wedding bands can use this regional
publication to advertise for gigs, and
individual musicians can use it to find
out the names of bands.

THEATER MUSIC

Periodicals
Backstage
1515 Broadway - 14th floor
New York, New York 10036
(212) 536-5368
Covers the theater industry (among
other subjects) and publishes summer
stock and regional listings and ads at
certain times during the year.

Web Sites

On Broadway
http://artsnet.heinz.cmu.edu:80
/OnBroadway/pages/MainEnhanced
.html
Theater listings and links.

Stage Manager's Unanimous
Home Page
http://www.theatre.com/theatre.html
More theater links and listings, mostly
focused on the Northeast.

Theatre Central
http://www.theatre-central.com/
All kinds of theater listings nationwide,
including summer stock and regional
theater.

Organizations

Theater Musicians Association
230 Jones Street
San Francisco, California 94102
(415) 775-8118
Affiliated with the San Francisco local
musicians union, this association
publishes *The Pit Bulletin,* a newsletter
containing useful information for
theater musicians. Dues are $28 per
year, which includes a subscription to
the newsletter.

CABARET

Web Sites

The Manhattan Association
of Cabarets & Clubs
http://www.macnyc.com
The homepage of this cabaret
organization. Has club listings as well.

CLASSICAL MUSIC

Books

*How to Get an Orchestra Job—and Keep
It: A Practical Guide Book*
Erica Sharp, Encinitas Press, 1985
A guide to preparing for and taking
orchestra auditions.

*Musical America: International Directory
of the Performing Arts*
Musical America Publications, Inc.,
published annually
A comprehensive listing of contact
information for organizations and
individuals in the performing arts.

Periodicals

*The International Musician: The Journal
of the American Federation of Musicians
of the United States and Canada*
1501 Broadway
New York, New York 10036
(212) 869-1330
Contains listings of orchestra auditions.

Web Sites

Career resources Web page from
The Cleveland Institute of Music
http://www.cwru.edu/CIM/library
/career-resources.html#index
A thorough listing of periodicals, books,
and articles dealing with career
information for classical musicians. A
good place to start your research.

North American Orchestra Auditions
http://idrs.colorado.edu:80/publications
/TWBassoonist/TWB.V5.2/audition
.html
An interesting article on the audition
process that can be downloaded from
the Internet.

STUDIO WORK

Books

The Nashville Number System
Chas Williams, 1991
Available through Corner Music at
(615) 297-9559 and http://www
.nashville.net./~troppo/nns.htm
If you want to do studio work in
Nashville, you've got to know the
Nashville number system for reading
and writing charts. Williams's book is
the most definitive on the subject.

Periodicals

Guitar
P.O. Box 53063
Boulder, Colorado 80328
(303) 678-0349
http://www.guitarmag.com
Check out Carl Verheyen's monthly "Studio City" column for inside stories and information about studio work from a guitarist's point of view.

Organizations

Recording Musicians of America
(800) 762-3444
A subgroup of the American Federation of Musicians, this organization of studio musicians has chapters in some of the larger cities, including New York, Los Angeles, and Nashville. It's primarily involved in the negotiation of contracts, but it could also be helpful to new players from a networking standpoint, as some of the chapters publish directories.

COMPOSING AND MUSIC PRODUCTION

Books and Directories

The Billboard Guide to Home Recording, 2nd Edition
Ray Baragary, Billboard Books, 1997
This recently updated book covers recording techniques as well as equipment issues.

The Contemporary Arranger
Don Sebesky, Alfred Publishing Company, 1984
A classic book on arranging real instruments. Provides ranges, characteristics, and musical examples.

The Film and Television Music Guide
The Music Business Registry, published annually
(800) 377-7411
A directory of names, addresses, and phone numbers of people and companies in the world of film and TV music. It includes composers, music libraries, managers, agents, and many others.

The Guide to MIDI Orchestration
Paul Gilreath, Musicworks
114 Cherry Street - Suite B
Marietta, Georgia 30060
(800) 469-9575
If you're trying to make your MIDI instruments sound like the real thing, Gilreath's book is for you.

Home Recording for Musicians
Craig Anderton, Amsco, 1996
An authoritative book on home studios by a veteran writer on music technology issues.

Modular Digital Multitracks:
The Power User's Guide
George Petersen, Mix Books, 1994
(510) 653-3307
Brimming with useful information on and techniques relating to MDMs.

The Multimedia Directory
The Corranade Group, published annually
(800) 529-3501
http://www.carronade.com
A thorough listing of companies that produce multimedia in the U.S. and Canada. The listings are arranged both geographically and alphabetically.

Shoot Directory for Commercial Production and Post-Production
BPI Communications
1515 Broadway - 12th floor
New York, New York 10036
(212) 764-7300
As is mentioned throughout this book, this directory has extensive listings of ad agencies, video production companies, and music production companies.

The Songwriter's Market
Cindy Laufenberg (ed.), Writers Digest
Books, published annually
Includes listings of companies that
commission original music, such as
production companies and stock music
libraries.

*Synchronization from Reel to Reel, 2nd
Edition*
Jeff Rona, Hal Leonard Publishing, 1994
Gives you the lowdown on
synchronization issues, including
SMPTE time code.

Periodicals

Electronic Musician
(800) 843-4086 (subscriptions)
Another excellent magazine covering
recording and technology issues.

EQ
(212) 378-0400
http://www.eqmag.com
An informative magazine that
concentrates on recording and live
sound issues.

Keyboard Magazine
(800) 289-9919 (subscriptions)
http://www.keyboardmag.com
One of the best music technology
magazines around. You don't have to be
a keyboard player to enjoy this
magazine.

Recording
(619) 738-5571
Yet another good publication that
focuses on the home recording market.

Web Sites

The Digital Directory
http://www.digitaldirectory.com
/music.html
Contains a partial list of stock music
libraries.

Sound Utilities
http://www.wavenet.com/~ axgrindr
/quimby4.html
A great site for downloading useful
music software. Part of the larger
"Partners in Rhyme" site.

The Source-Methenyi
http://www.navgtr.com/sourcetv/index
.html
For a fee, this site can give you access
to lists of creative personnel at many ad
agencies.

The Synth Zone
http://www.synthzone.com
Contains extensive links to synth
manufacturers.

ALL-PURPOSE MUSIC RESOURCES

Books

The Billboard Guide to Music Publicity
Jim Pettigrew, Jr., Billboard Books, 1997
A detailed look at how to generate
publicity in the music business. Helpful
information on putting together press
kits.

*Making a Living in Your Local Music
Market: How to Survive and Prosper*
Dick Weissman and Ronny S. Schiff,
Hal Leonard Publishing, 1990
A valuable guide to employment
prospects in your local market.

*Music Biz Know-How: Do-It-Yourself
Strategies for Independent Music Success*
Peter Spellman, MBS Business Media,
1997
(617) 639-1971
Covers many areas of the business,
including getting college radio airplay,
booking club gigs, music promotion via
the Internet, and multimedia music.

Web Sites

Doing It Yourself: A Guide
to Making Music
http://www.ram.org/music/making
/tips/DiY.html
Provides information on a variety of
topics, including duplicating tapes and
CDs, building a studio, copyrights, and
promotion.

Harmony Central
http://www.harmony-central.com
Great all-around site for musicians that
includes (among other things) industry
news, MIDI information, MIDI files,
equipment and instrument buyer's
guides, and special-interest sections for
guitar, bass, drums, and keyboards.
There's something for everyone here.

IndieCentre
http://www.csd.net/~muji
/indiecentre.html
Billing itself as an "independent label
information site," this Web site has
useful information on a host of topics,
including the recording, mastering,
manufacturing, and printing of CDs and
tapes.

Music Biz Insight
http://www.mbsolutions.com/Info.html
A very informative bimonthly
"infoletter" focusing on music business
career issues.

Webnoize
http://www.webnoize.com/
An online publication that covers music
on the Web.

Periodicals

Musician
(800) 347-6969
In addition to covering technology, this
magazine focuses quite a bit on
information about current and past
performers and recording artists.

UNION INFORMATION

American Federation of Musicians
(AFM)
(800) 762-3444
http://www.afm.org/
Call or visit the Web site to get
information about the union and its
local chapters.

MUSIC BOOK SOURCES

Many of the books listed above can be
ordered through the following vendors:

Amazon.Com
http://www.amazon.com
A very large, general-interest online
bookstore that carries a good selection
of music books. Its best feature: Its
catalog can be searched by author, title,
or subject.

The Mix Bookshelf
(800) 233-9604
http://www.mixbookshelf.com
A huge catalog of books about all facets
of the music business.

Music Books Plus
http://www.vaxxine.com/mbp/
Another good source for ordering music
books online.

LEARN ABOUT THE AUTHOR

To find out more about Mike Levine, visit his Web site at
http://home.earthlink.net/~mwlevine/.

INDEX

❖